REPRESENTATIONS
OF JEWS
THROUGH THE AGES

Proceedings
of the Eighth Annual Symposium
of the Philip M. and Ethel Klutznick
Chair in Jewish Civilization
September 17 & 18, 1995

Studies in Jewish Civilization—8

REPRESENTATIONS
OF JEWS
THROUGH THE AGES

Leonard Jay Greenspoon
Bryan F. Le Beau

Editors

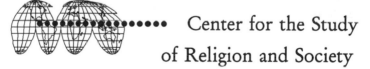 Center for the Study
of Religion and Society

The Klutznick Chair in Jewish Civilization

Creighton University Press
Omaha, Nebraska

© 1996 by Creighton University Press
All rights reserved

No part of this book may be reproduced or transmitted in any form
or by any means, electronic or mechanical, including photocopying,
recording, or any information storage and retrieval system, without
permission in writing from the Publisher, except in the case of brief
quotations embodied in critical articles and reviews.

ISBN: 1-881871-22-3
ISSN: 1070-8510

Editorial:
Creighton University Press
2500 California Plaza
Omaha, Nebraska 68178

Marketing and Distribution:
Fordham University Press
University Box L
Bronx, New York 10458

Printed in the United States of America

In Memory
Ethel Klutznick
1906 — 1996

Contents

Acknowledgments

The papers in this collection were delivered at the Eighth Annual Symposium of the Philip M. and Ethel Klutznick Chair in Jewish Civilization at Creighton University on September 17 and 18, 1995.

We would like to thank the many people involved in the preparation of the symposium. Special thanks to Gloriann Levy, Director of the Jewish Cultural Arts Council, and to its Chair, Seth Bernstein, who were so instrumental in making the Sunday events a success; to Steve Riekes, Chairman of the College of Jewish Learning, a group with a deep commitment to Jewish education; to Howard Bloom, Executive Director of the Jewish Federation of Omaha for his unstinting support; to Caryn Rifkin, for her eighth annual "tour of duty" with the Symposium; to Maryellen Read, for coordinating the event and for her careful preparation of the entire collection of papers; and to Lionel Wolberger for generously giving us the benefit of his vast musical knowledge.

We wish to thank the following for the financial contributions which funded this symposium:

Creighton College of Arts and Sciences
The Jewish Cultural Arts Council
The Henry Monsky Lodge of B'nai B'rith
The Ike and Roz Friedman Foundation

Bryan F. Le Beau, Director
Center for the Study of
Religion and Society
Creighton University
Omaha, Nebraska

Leonard Jay Greeenspoon, Chairholder
Klutznick Chair in Jewish Civilization
Creighton University
Omaha, Nebraska
June, 1996

Preface

The Eighth Annual Klutznick Symposium, held in Omaha on Sunday, September 17 and Monday, September 18, 1995, was something of a first and a last for me. It was the first Klutznick Symposium I attended as Chairholder and successor to Menachem Mor, who had inaugurated the Klutznick Chair in Jewish Civilization at Creighton University and initiated the fruitful interchange that has come to characterize Klutznick Symposia. Since the program had been fully planned by Bryan Le Beau (Director of Creighton's Center for the Study of Religion and Society) and Maryellen Read (assistant to the Chair) before my coming aboard, I was also something of a guest at this Symposium. Undoubtedly, this is the last time I will play so passive a role in an operation that has elicited the active support of so many over the years.

It was a delight for me that the topic for this Symposium was one with broad appeal among both scholars and the general public: "Representations of Jews Through the Ages." When I first saw the list of invited speakers and their topics, I enthusiastically looked forward to each presentation. My enthusiasm was not misplaced.

Leonard Jay Greenspoon, Chairholder
The Klutznick Chair in Jewish Civilization
Creighton University
August, 1996

Editors' Introduction

Among those who study religion as an academic discipline, there are some who emphasize data gathered by observers from outside of a particular religion. Those who are on the inside, these researchers argue, cannot be depended upon to provide objective evaluations or accounts. Other scholars tend to place greater reliance on information gathered from insiders—that is, from those who actually practice a given religion. Only those observations, they assert, get to the very heart, to the experience of religious practice and belief.

Common sense, an oft-neglected component of scholarly analysis, tells us that there is some truth in each of these views, as well as in a third approach that combines insider and outsider perspectives through implicit, if not explicit dialogue. And, as the papers in this volume make clear, this common sense adage is correct: there are some things that are more clearly observed from the outside, some aspects of religion that benefit immensely from an insider perspective, and some elements that we observe through a combination of these vantage points.

In the first section of this volume we have gathered four papers that are primarily intra-Jewish in perspective. The second and largest section brings together six studies that look at Jews and Judaism almost exclusively from the outside. The remaining articles, five in number, encompass a more or less explicit combination of the two viewpoints. It needs only to be added that this is only one possible way of approaching and appreciating the Eighth Annual Klutznick Symposium papers.

The key elements of comparison for Thomas Idinopulos are explicit in his title: "Next Year in Jerusalem: Ritual Memory for Ancient Jews and Modern Israelis." Although Jerusalem was central for both ancient and modern Jews, it did not play identical roles in their respective theologies/ideologies. For Idinopulos, the direction of comparison is clear and crucial: "[T]here is a world of difference between the religious meaning of the Jewish ancestral land . . . and the concrete realization of the land that we find in the modern Zionist movement."

For Marc Singer, study of late nineteenth century editors and readers of *The American Hebrew* brings to light "various divisions, insecurities, and ambivalences that native-born American Jews felt toward other Jews and toward themselves." These major points are clearly visible in the highly evocative title Singer chose for his paper, "JewishIdentity/AmericanIdentity:Self-Representation, Anti-Semitism, and the *American Hebrew.*" Singer concludes:

> More assimilated Jews thus attempted to stress that the objectionable behavior of the newer, more visible Jews was not a genetic trait and could thus be eradicated through good education and proper refinement, as evidenced by their own behavior.

In Kerri Steinberg's view, a series of United Jewish Appeal's photographs from the past two decades is like a "photo album of the extended Jewish family." In developing this simile, she explains that UJA photographs symbolically reunite diverse populations from across the globe. American Jews, she adds, star as the centripetal force within that visual record.

The work of the well-known artist George Segal, and in particular his San Francisco installation *The Holocaust*, is the main focus of Pamela Cohen's paper. In Cohen's analysis, Segal's artistry combines with his Judaism to produce a Holocaust Memorial that is unlike any other. Authenticity, she writes, is important to Segal, and he achieved that authenticity in *The Holocaust* by studying thousands of photographic images of the death camps in the archives of Manhattan's YIVO Institute. To that documentary evidence he added a layer of biblical allusions.

In section two, as in section one, papers generally appear in chronological order. In the first, Gordon Mork summarizes his extensive research on the most famous passion play, that of Oberammergau, Germany, and especially on its changing portrayal of Jews and Christians. In addition to a survey of the play's history and development from 1634-1934, he carefully analyzes successive changes in its two most recent stagings. His comparison of the 1980/84 and 1990 plays demonstrates how the traditional play presented "suffering Christians" and the "wicked Jews," and how by 1990 those images were (or were not) reformed.

As indicated in her title, Regine Rosenthal looks at a number of nineteenth century literary "constructions of the Wandering Jew/ess." Some of the authors she covers (like Eugène Sue and F. Marion Crawford) are largely unknown to today's readers, while others (Nathaniel Hawthorne and Herman Melville) continue to be staples of American literature. Nineteenth century American writers both inherited earlier European traditions about Jews, Rosenthal argues, and creatively reshaped them in the context of American culture. Her paper examines:

> How these writers construct the Jew as cultural Other in their appropriation, modification and/or transformation of the mythical figure of the Wandering Jew and how they conceive of his recurring female counterpart, the beautiful and/or Wandering Jewess.

Greg Zacharias analyzes the "fictional Jew" in the writings of Henry James, in whom, Zacharias points out, there has been a resurgence of interest over the past two decades. In Zacharias' analysis, James' "idea of the Jews rests at the center of his thinking and writing on the individual's relation to culture in general":

> As he rethinks and refashions his idea of his native city and nation and thus refashions his idea of himself and of the American character, he must . . . accept the Jewish contribution to his sense of his national identity, of his personal identity.

"That particular contribution," Zacharias suggests, "may be extended as an idea of how all immigration affects identity itself."

Anti-Semitic caricatures, among them those produced by German-born Hans Schweitzer, were among the most effective methods of Nazi propaganda. In his examination of selected caricatures from Schweitzer's career, Russel Lemmons assesses the crucial role of such cartoonists in the Nazis' rise to power and establishment of the Third Reich. He examines Schweitzer's anti-Semitic cartoons during the Weimar Republic, before the Nazis came to power, and afterwards when the NSDAP persecuted the Jewish people with a cruelty unparalleled in history.

John Calvert focuses on the Egyptian writer, political figure, and radical Islamist Sayyid Qutb (1906-1966). In the following introductory remarks he outlines basic elements in the works of radical Islamists like Qutb that relate to Jews:

Briefly, these writings reduce the policy and behavior of the state of Israel to one residual category—that of its Jewish essence. From the Islamist perspective, Zionism is the inevitable consequence of a duplicity inscribed in the Jewish soul since ancient times. . . . In today's world Jews operate as imperialist spies, agents, and fifth columnists intent upon world conquest.

Richard Levy speaks of the *Protocols of the Elders of Zion* as "the most widely distributed antisemitic work of all time." The *Protocols'* popularity both before World War II and even after the Holocaust, he writes, can be viewed as the result of their combining two distinct motifs: the conspiratorial and the antisemitic. Levy concludes his analysis of the continued and continuing use of the *Protocols* with these sobering words:

> While it is certain that antisemitism in general and the *Protocols of the Elders of Zion* in particular can solve no real problems, they have demonstrated the capacity to poison political life and human relations. Reasonable people have a right to be downhearted about ever conquering such a long-lived, adaptable, and serviceable lie.

Lillian Kremer's discussion of the image of Jews in twentieth century American literature is the first paper of section three. She begins with a survey of non-Jewish writers, but the major portion of her paper deals with Jewish American writers in the post-World War II period. Of them, she writes approvingly:

> At last, a group of American writers brought authentic Jewish characters to national attention in fiction that focused not on the Jew's nose but on the Jew's mind and character, that introduced characters shaped by a distinctive history and culture.

Davida Alperin's paper explicitly contrasts non-Jewish, in this case Black, perceptions of Jews with images of Jews prevalent within the Jewish community itself. In particular, she examines what we might call "talk about cooperation." She explains why:

> When Blacks and Jews try to explain why the two groups have cooperated with each other in the United States, when they discuss reasons Jews and Blacks should or should not cooperate, when they debate the relative value of such cooperative efforts for one group or the other, they often present different images.

Yoram Lubling, along with the author of the following paper, David Porush, was part of a Sunday evening keynote session titled "Representations of Jews in American Film and Television." Lubling's view, as stated in his main title "The Jew as the 'Other,'" is that in the popular visual media of America, Jews have regularly represented "an outside perspective." In other words, "the Jew is authentic only when he/she works from the outside." Lubling is not suggesting that Jews don't work towards the improvement of the human condition, but that they do so from the position of the other.

Porush begins by exploring "the special problem of the Jew" in popular television and film. This discussion establishes the context for his close reading of one episode of *Northern Exposure* titled "Kaddish for Uncle Manny." Porush concludes this reading with the following observations:

> In the very final moments of this final scene, Fleischman stands exposed before America, in the pulpit of the church of the American Religion, in all his naked Jewishness, clothed in a *tallis* and a *yarmulke*. As he recites the *Kaddish* all the congregants embark on their own version of mourning. . . . Fleischman has fulfilled the American dream of the melting pot and finally adopted the American Religion as his own.

Using examples from the Ashkenazic world of Eastern European (especially Russian) Jewry, Izaly Zemtsovsky contrasts outside evaluations of Jewish music with those values uniquely felt within the community. Certain features that claim attention from one perspective may pass almost unnoticed or undervalued when viewed from another vantage point. Touching on a theme found throughout this volume, Zemtsovsky urges us to reflect consciously on the nature of these differences:

> It is natural that the whole world looks at us while we are looking at the whole world. One may say that within human history different musical worlds pulsate by their penetrability/ impenetrability, sometimes coming close to each other and sometimes moving apart. And it is understandable that neither "they" nor "we" think about our mutual vision.

List of Contributors

Davida J. Alperin

Department of Political Science
University of Wisconsin
River Falls, WI 54022-5001

John Calvert

Department of History
Creighton University
Omaha, NE 68178

Pamela A. Cohen

Graduate Program, Art History
Rutgers University
New Brunswick, NJ 08903

Richard I. Cohen

Department of Jewish History
The Hebrew University of Jerusalem
Jerusalem, Israel

Thomas Idinopulos

Department of Religion
Miami University
The Old Manse
Oxford, OH 45056

S. Lillian Kremer

Department of English
Kansas State University
Manhattan, KS 66502

Russel Lemmons

Department of History
Jacksonville State University
700 Pelham Road N.
Jacksonville, AL 36265-9982

Richard S. Levy

Department of History
University of Illinois at Chicago
851 South Morgan, Room 723
Chicago, IL 60607-7049

Yoram Lubling

Department of Philosophy
Elon College
Campus Box 2315
Elon College, NC 27244

Menachem Mor

Department of Jewish History
University of Haifa
Haifa, Israel

Gordon R. Mork

Department of History
Purdue University
1358 University Hall
West Lafayette, IN 47907-1358

David Porush

Department of Language, Literature,
and Communication
School of Humanities and Social
Sciences
Rensselaer Polytechnic Institute
Troy, NY 12180

Regine Rosenthal

Visiting Scholar
Department of German
Carleton University
Ottawa, Ontario, Canada K1S 5B6

Marc Singer

Department of History
Bloomfield College
Bloomfield, NJ 07003

Kerri Steinberg

Graduate Program, Art History
University of California, L.A.
Los Angeles, CA 90024

Greg Zacharias   Department of English
                                  Creighton University
                                  Omha, NE 68178

Izaly Zemtsovsky   Department of Folklore
                                  Russian Institute for History of the
                                  Arts
                                  Isaakievskaia Sq. 5,
                                  190000 St. Petersberg, Russia

Welcome

Kathryn A. Thomas, Associate Vice President for Academic Affairs at Creighton University, made the following remarks at the start of Sunday evening's program:

Good evening and welcome. On behalf of Fr. Michael G. Morrison, President of Creighton University, who unfortunately is out of town this evening, and all the Creighton community, I extend best wishes to all our guests and presenters, many of whom have travelled considerable distance to join us these two days.

As I looked forward to this Eighth Annual Klutznick Symposium, I found myself thinking about the theme, Representation of Jews Through the Ages, and about several of the titles of the individual papers. I also found myself thinking about how the Jewish people have represented themselves, or better, presented themselves here in Omaha, to me a native, over the past half century.

I believe that presentation cuts to the essence, to the heart, of Judaism. To me, the Jews have presented themselves as: a People of the Word; a People of Family and Community; and a People of God.

A People of the Word: A philologist by profession, I value the Jewish community in Omaha as people who have led the city in intellectual pursuits and have encouraged all of us to treasure and study literature, history, philosophy, law, and Scripture.

A People of Family and Community: While this quality may lead to fear and suspicion, I believe that the much more appropriate response to it, in our world of fragmentation, isolation, and deteriorating value systems, is respect and emulation.

A People of God: The Jewish People are a people who recognize that there is a Divine Power above and beyond themselves who gives meaning, who gives grace, who gives hope to our human lives. In my experience, this is the basis for understanding across time and across cultures. This is the common ground for the pursuit of wisdom.

1

Thus have the Jewish People presented themselves in Omaha; and I believe that one of the most significant developments in Omaha history has been the establishment, as a joint effort on the part of the Jewish Community and Creighton University, of the Philip M. and Ethel Klutznick Chair in Jewish Civilization, and the vibrancy of this annual symposium under the leadership first of Menachem Mor and now of Leonard Greenspoon. Through this forum may we continue the dialogue, which increasingly cultivates mutual understanding and friendship.

Next Year in Jerusalem:
Ritual Memory for Ancient Jews and Modern Israelis

Thomas A. Idinopulos

L'Shana Haba Berushalaim. This is a Hebraic expression which means "Next year in Jerusalem." *L'Shana Haba Berushalaim* said at the end of daily prayers, said at the conclusion of family seders on the Passover, said by Jews throughout the world to each other, said by many who have never been in Jerusalem and never will be.

What we have in the expression, "Next Year in Jerusalem," is an expression of ritualized memory. It is an expression repeated whenever one recalls what Jerusalem means in Jewish religious and national history. Jerusalem, the capital of the ancient Davidic monarchy; Jerusalem, the site of the Temple, God's earthly dwelling-place; Jerusalem in Glory, Jerusalem destroyed, lost, rebuilt, reborn. The New Jerusalem of the Messianic Redemption, the new universal city of righteousness prayerfully awaited in the coming days of Yahweh.

Are Jews the only people with such a ritualized memory of a city? Think of the Greeks who to this day, hundreds of years after the loss of Constantinople to the Muslim Turk, will repeat at the close of every baptism, wedding, or supper party, *To Chrono Sti Poli,* "Next Year in Constantinople." Similarly Armenians in exile recall their homeland, and so do the Palestinian children today in the refugee camps of Lebanon, where they are taught to repeat the words, "Haifa" and "Jaffa" with all the nostalgia and idealism that is packed into the phrase, "Next Year in Jerusalem."

What is the purpose of ritualized memory? Answer: to sanctify the past. When memory functions ritualistically, memory functions to raise the past to a level of meaning we associate with the sacred. Ritualized memory is sacred memory.

Jerusalem ritually remembered in scripture, prayer, poetry, and song is such a transcendent and ideal city. Jerusalem ritually remembered is not a city of history, not a city of lost wars, exiled peoples, burned temples. It is not the Jerusalem destroyed by Babylonians and Romans that is recalled in the phrase *L'Shana Haba Berushalaim*. The exact phrase is *L'Shana Haba Berushalaim Habnuya,* "Next Year in Jerusalem Built or Rebuilt." It is the new, rebuilt and redeemed city that the pious will return to by the grace of God.

Similarly the Constantinople remembered by Greeks is not some Near Eastern Turkish capital but rather an original, ideal, prehistorical city in which God, his chosen king Constantine, and his chosen people, the Greek nation, meet to live out their lives in the perfect Christian kingdom on earth. And the Haifa and Jaffa today remembered by Palestinian refugee youth are not the earthly cities of Jews, with their four story-apartment buildings and their Supersol markets but rather perfectly dreamy cities of clean beaches and unspotted hills where the wise holy men of Islam teach their truths to the righteous.

The energy of ritual memory is psychic and healing: to make the disappointments of the past tolerable in the present-day host country so that the future can be lived with more hope and less dread. Next year in Jerusalem or in Constantinople or in Haifa will not be in a city lost and broken but in a new reborn city, empty of one's enemies. Thus the beneficial function of ritualized memory is to keep human experience whole by connecting the past to the present and thereby making a person feel that there is a future worth living for. In a striking way ritual memory is a psychic substitution for concrete reality. He who can repeat the words *L'Shana Haba Berushalaim* or *To Chrono Sti Poli* knows in his heart he cannot regain these cities or win them back as they once were. Thus the need for ritual memory which heals the wound of historical-political reality.

Such psychological fulfillment is not and cannot be physical realization of place. The ritualistic idealization of Jerusalem or Constantinople or Haifa and Jaffa could not be the concrete realization of these places. Quite the opposite. Ritualized memory performs its function very well because there is no intention, no real plan to regain the lost city or country. And it is precisely because there is no concrete plan to regain territory that the ritualized expression of that territory serves such an important, even necessary psychological role. For lost territory is the lost past and the past which remains lost injures the body of experience. To heal the body of experience the past is recovered through ritual idealization. A city remembered is a city idealized and a city to which no one can return.

Now there is a world of difference between the religious meaning of the Jewish ancestral land, which we find expressed in the phrase *L'Shana Haba Berushalaim Habnuya,* and the concrete realization of the land that we find in the modern Zionist movement of immigration and settlement in late nineteenth and early twentieth century Palestine. That difference is crucial. What impresses me about the evidence of Zionist commitment was how decidedly non-ritualistic it was.

The modern Zionists would not have remade Palestine into a modern Jewish nation-state had they submitted to the psychology of ritual memory; it was precisely because the energies feeding Zionism were secular, activist, and political, that Zionism succeeded as it well as it did. By the same token we immigrant Greeks would not have educated ourselves and prospered in America had we stayed in the Greek language and immersed ourselves in ritual celebrations of Constantinople or with the mother country, Greece.

There is a tension between Jewish ritual memory of Jerusalem, Zion, and the biblical land of Israel on the one side, and on the other side the concrete realization of a newly remade land and capital which would become the place of the modern Jewish state. But this is not a new tension introduced by Zionism. That tension has always been there in Jewish history. In the remainder of this essay I should like to discuss two examples of this tension between ritual memory of place and concrete realization of place in Jewish history.

The first example is drawn from the time of the ancient Persian King Cyrus in his dealing with Israel in the late sixth century BCE and the oracles of the biblical writer we know as Second Isaiah.

Fifty years after the destruction of Jerusalem and its Temple, Cyrus decreed that all Jews who wished could return to the ancestral homeland. While the exaggerated figure of 40,360 is given in the Book of Ezra (2:64), it is doubtful that more that a few hundred accepted his invitation. The question is why so few. That question has plagued historians for centuries. There is no satisfactory answer. Had the decree of restoration come to the first generation living in exile, one imagines that the overwhelming majority of Jews would have gathered up their belongings and started toward home. But the decree came to the second generation, fifty years after the expulsion. None of them had memories of the homeland; whatever they knew of Judea they learned from their parents. It made eminent sense to them to heed Jeremiah's advice to "seek the welfare of the city where I have sent you into exile" (29:4-7). They married, had children, built homes, planted gardens, and lived with security and prosperity under a set of fairly benign Persian rulers. Undoubtedly they thought of Jerusalem as the national capital, the site of the destroyed Temple. But everyone knew this city as an earthly place that had fallen on evil times. No one was willing to make of the city an idolatrous altar of self-sacrifice. Jerusalem was not the Covenant law. And everyone understood that the nation could lead its life through the Covenant law outside the capital and without the Temple.

So Jerusalem would not be forgotten. Jerusalem would be remembered. The messianic prayer of deliverance was recited daily in the hope that by Yahweh's grace, more than by Cyrus' generosity, the whole nation of Israel would by restored to Jerusalem and the land. Remembering Jerusalem would become a sacred obligation expressed through prayer. The Psalmist articulated the feeling:

> By the waters of Babylon—
> where we sat and wept
> when we remembered Zion. . . .
> How shall we sing the Lord's song in a foreign land?
> If I forget you, O Jerusalem,
> let my right hand wither!
> Let my tongue cleave to the roof of my mouth,
> if I do not remember you,
> if I do not set Jerusalem above my highest joy.
>
> Psalms 137: 1, 4-6

When we consider the hardships involved, the remarkable fact is not the refusal of the exiled community to pack its belongings and set off as one man for the ancestral land, but that a few small groups actually did so. There were a sufficient number of "Zionists" who were willing to leave comfortable homes and secure jobs to make a dangerous journey of six hundred miles, and then to undertake the arduous life of the pioneer.

The second example is drawn form the Middle Ages, at the time of the messianic movements, the most noteworthy of which was the movement led by the messianic pretender, Shabbtai Zvi. This Jerusalem teacher of Cabbalistic mysticism organized a mass migration of Jews to the Holy Land to await the redemption expected in 1666. Zvi and other preachers of the redemption claimed the title of "Messiah" or had it attributed to them. They were able to uproot whole groups of Jews form their villages and towns, convince them to sell their goods, and set out by foot, wagon, and ship in the direction of Jerusalem, a journey which almost always ended in disaster. Many died in travel; a few were fortunate to reach the Holy Land. So many deprivations were suffered that some returned to their original countries.

The messianic movements proved so disruptive of diaspora Jewish communities that rabbinical leaders of those communities often pronounced anathemas against anyone joining them—even when that meant sacrificing the chance to live in the Holy Land.

Here then are two examples of Jews not returning to Zion but rather ritually expressing the memory of Zion to console themselves for the necessary and wise decision not to return to Zion. For ritualized remembering heals the wound of the lost past, but does not regain what is lost; particularly so when what is lost cannot realistically be regained.

But what then of the modern Zionists who not only remembered Zion, but returned to Zion, and founded a whole new commonwealth in Zion? Did ritual memory play a role with the earliest Zionist philosophers and pioneers? The answer is very little. In fact for such early Zionist philosophers as Herzl, Pinsker, and Nordau, the struggle to immigrate, settle, upbuild, defend and secure the land was so great that there was little time and patience for ritual memory or any other kind of ritual. The anticipated struggle of remaking Palestine into a Jewish homeland was so demanding, so unceasing that the spiritual Jerusalem in the phrase, "If I forget you, O Jerusalem," seemed quaint and irrelevant. Palestine and Jerusalem in the late nineteenth and early twentieth centuries were rude and dangerous places, not dreamy idealizations and fond memories of distant kingdoms and temples. But it was precisely these rude places that the Zionists chose to make a new Zion, not of palaces and temples but of boulevards and apartment blocks. Exactly those things which Jews needed to break the chains of the past and to be politically and nationally free for the first time in two millennia.

The key words in understanding the Zionist relationship to the diaspora past are "newness" and "freedom." In his speech to the First

Zionist congress of 1897, Max Nordau proclaimed: "Emancipation has totally changed the nature of the Jew and made him into another being." Nordau saw emancipation as the first stage of the freeing of the Jew legally, by the granting of civil rights, in western society. But the last, culminating stage of emancipation could only come with the establishment of an independent Jewish state. For only with statehood could the new Jewish human being come to fulfillment.

This new Jewish self-fulfillment, not tempted to ritually idealize the past, but rather expressing itself through a political independence that breaks with the confining ghetto past, shines through these remarkable works which Theodor Herzl wrote in his monograph, *Die Judenstaat* (The Jewish State), which appeared in February, 1896:

> The Jews have dreamed this princely dream [the Jewish state] throughout the long night of their history. "Next year in Jerusalem" is our age-old motto. It is now a matter of showing that the vague dream can be transformed into a clear and glowing idea.
>
> For this, our minds must first be thoroughly cleansed of many old, outward, muddled, and shortsighted notions. The unthinking might, for example, imagine that this exodus would have to take its way from civilization into the desert. That is not so! It will be carried out entirely in the framework of civilization. We shall not revert to a lower stage; we shall rise to a higher one. We shall not dwell in mud huts; we shall build new, more beautiful, and more modern houses, and possess them in safety.

For the Zionists the expression "Next Year in Jerusalem" could only become a slogan for a brand new Jerusalem for a brand new people in a brand new land. The Zionists were not romantics. They did not see or really want any continuity between their New Jerusalem and the Jewish communities of old Europe and the medieval Arab world. These latter places were sooner forgotten if the task of building the new Jewish world of Palestine was to be accomplished. They did not have to say "Next Year in Jerusalem" because they were energetically building a new city in a new state that bore little relationship to anything that went before them.

"Loud in Talk, Flashy in Dress, Offensive in Display of Jewelry": *The American Hebrew* and Distinctions among American Jews

Marc Singer

The *American Hebrew*, a Jewish weekly newspaper, began publication November 21, 1879. Although not the first Jewish publication in the United States, it quickly became one of the most influential and widely-read, with a circulation that peaked at over 20,000 in the early years of the twentieth century.[1] Although this number is small, especially when considered next to the vast numbers of Jewish immigrants to the United States in the late nineteenth and early twentieth centuries, it nonetheless has significance because the *American Hebrew's* readership was largely drawn from the American Jewish elite of the period: assimilated, for the most part financially successful urban Jews of German, Spanish, or Portuguese extraction who had immigrated generations earlier. The editorial board of the *American Hebrew* reflected its readers' backgrounds and, based on the fact that circulation remained constant, their values as well.[2]

The *American Hebrew* communicated the concerns, the fears, and the aspirations of its readers. While such concerns were voiced in numerous ways throughout every issue of the *American Hebrew*, one special issue, entitled "Prejudice Against the Jews: Its Nature, Its Causes and Remedies," epitomizes and summarizes the various divisions, insecurities, and ambivalences that native-born American Jews felt toward other Jews and toward themselves. In "Prejudice Against the Jews," the *American Hebrew's* editors' attempt to discover the root causes of anti-Semitism among Christians unwittingly revealed their own prejudices about the new Eastern European immigrants and the newly rich. Ultimately, their representations of the new arrivals bespoke a widening cleavage in the American Jewish community, going a long way toward eroding the definition of Jews as a race in favor of the more flexible, less determinative identification of Jewishness as a religion. More assimilated Jews thus attempted to stress that the objectionable behavior of the newer, more visible Jews was not a genetic trait and could thus be eradicated through good education and proper refinement, as evidenced by their own behavior.

In the decades before the massive immigration of Jews from Russia and Eastern Europe to the United States, the influence of native-born Jews on American society in industry, in arts and letters, and in political life was considerable. This was due, no doubt, to their prosperity, their educational and skill attainments, and to their desire to assimilate, to blend in with other Americans, but the potential for still greater achievement seemed limited. These Jewish Americans perceived what must have been a forerunner of the modern-day "glass ceiling," which allowed them to attain only so much and then no more. No doubt they began to feel this even more acutely during the period 1880-1910, during which hundreds of thousands of Eastern European and Russian Jews emigrated as America's industrial growth brought fortune to Americans of nearly all backgrounds.

In the intertwined business and social worlds of their home cities, upwardly mobile American Jews found themselves confronted with widespread, frequently overt, discrimination by Christians, if not actual legal exclusion and segregation, which would manifest itself even more markedly in later decades.[3] One example was the use of restrictive covenants in the sale of real estate, which in some areas carried legal weight, while in others were enforced through a "gentleman's agreement." While there had always been anti-Jewish sentiment in some American quarters, by the late nineteenth century it was particularly stinging because there were increasing numbers of well-to-do Jews, many of whom, no doubt, were readers of the *American Hebrew*, who had begun to aspire to move in polite society with well-to-do Christians.

The response of the native-born Jewish community to this form of American anti-Semitism was complex, a mixture of finger-pointing, fence-mending, and circling the wagons. Many of the more established communities, in order to assimilate and blend in more easily, had gone a long way in distancing themselves from their former Old World customs and practices; other communities had assimilated into European Christian society even before emigrating. For some Jews, the only way to be accepted as equal was to cast off anything that made them stand out. Their response reflected ambivalence over the issue of their separateness, not only from other Americans, but also from the "greenhorns," as the newer Jewish immigrants from Russia and Eastern Europe were called. Their poverty and ignorance of "American" ways were embarrassing and often perceived as threatening to the more established Jewish community. This is not to say that everyone agreed that all recognizable marks of Jewishness were to be discarded: for the *American Hebrew*'s editors, some Jews had gone too far in distancing themselves from Old World customs to win acceptance. One rather sarcastic editorial provides an example:

> The approach of the Passover Holidays, when the Jewish housewife is naturally interested in all pertaining to her duties on those days, causes the various Jewish newspapers to devote more or less space to that subject. This it is, we presume, that occasions the publication in our unique contemporary, the *Hebrew Leader*, of an article on "The Effect of Liquor On Pigs." Interesting to Jews at all times, this topic is of course peculiarly apropos at present.[4]

Undoubtedly the pressure to assimilate (and, linked to this, to succeed in the new country) made such articles as the one in the *Hebrew Leader* of interest to at least some people in the Jewish community, if only for use in conversation with pig farmers. Other notices warning the unsuspecting against the threat of trichinosis from undercooked pork are another indication of such assimilatory pressures. For such readers, there was, at best, to be an uneasy coexistence between Jewish tradition and American lifestyle.[5]

Perhaps the most important indicator of this uneasy fit was the split of the Jewish community into Reform, Conservative, and Orthodox movements, each interpreting the need to reconcile Jews and Jewish life to their new homeland in a radically different manner. The *American Hebrew*, after attempting for some years to straddle the debate, ultimately threw itself behind Conservative Judaism, rejecting Orthodoxy as "fossilized Judaism, repugnant to cultured Jews," but rejecting what it saw as the excesses of the Reform movement, especially after the Hebrew Union College *trefa* banquet in 1883, at which shrimp was served.[6]

Continuing debates on an endless number of issues, as reflected for decades in the *American Hebrew*, focused on subjects such as whether the American Thanksgiving was to be celebrated, whether any of Reform Judaism's modifications of the dietary laws were acceptable for Jews, and, of course, the extent of American Jewish responsibility to new immigrants and to those still remaining in Eastern Europe. This ambivalence was reflected in various ways: for instance, editorials which admonished and chastised Christian ministers for attempting to convert or Christianize Jewish children might appear on the same page as advertisements for sheet music for Christmas songs or "A Christmas Holiday tour to Washington, D.C., under Pennsylvania Railroad Company's Personally-Conducted System."[7] The music columnist praised Wagner's *Tannhauser*. Jokes published every week further muddy the waters, as very few of them relate to Jewish culture or concerns. Some, in fact, are clearly identifiable as Christian in origin:

> TOM: "I say, Bob, are you superstitious about dining with thirteen at the table?"
> BOB: "That depends."
> TOM: "Depends upon what?"
> BOB: "The dinner."
>
> PAUL: "Mightn't I have a donkey, Papa?"
> PAPA (THE NEW VICAR) [!]: "I'm afraid not, my boy. There would be nobody to look after it, you know."
> PAUL: "Oh, the curate could do that!"[8]

Evidently, these were provided to the weekly by a syndication service of some kind. Nonetheless, the editors must have agreed to print them, indicating either that their readers were familiar with Christian ideas and mores, or that such humor might provide readers useful insight (or merely cocktail party smalltalk) into American Christian society.

There is a general sense, in fact, throughout the *American Hebrew* that its editors and, by extension, its readers looked for validation from the Christian community. Not only in the content of the paper, but in its tone as well, the weekly paper seemed to have an eye on portraying the Jewish community on its best behavior. This is not to say that every news article was a puff-piece; on the contrary, the habits and behavior of lower class and *nouveau riche* Jews were often under attack. This was, perhaps, a way of anticipating and deflecting outside criticism. Philip Cowen, the publisher of *American Hebrew*, admitted some years later that the paper's main goal was "an adequate representation of the Jewish community to the world outside. . . . We wanted our paper to be sought by the best classes of non-Jews."[9] Publication of Henry Ward Beecher's sermons to his Congregationalist church on "German intolerance" and "the debt civilization owes the Jews" exemplifies both the paper's hope to appeal to non-Jews and its readers' need to see Judaism praised by American Christian leaders.[10] On the other hand, the editors condemned instances of this need for Christian approval when they felt them to be in conflict with their own conception of the Jewish religion as separate and distinct from Christianity. A Peoria synagogue, for example, was criticized for having a Christian minister deliver a prayer at its consecration, and its rabbi's competence was called into question: "How does he translate the Fourth Commandment, to keep the Sabbath holy?" asked the editors.[11]

The best example of the *American Hebrew*'s need for external validation of Jewish status was its "Special Passover Number" of April 4, 1890, which was devoted in large part to the theme "Prejudice Against the Jews: Its Nature, Its Causes and Remedies. A Consensus of Opinion by Non-Jews." Simply enough, the goal of the editors of the paper was that "we might know what is the true character of this prejudice, and to dispel it if possible."[12] The prejudice to which they referred was of a particular type; drawing prejudicial distinctions was not a bad thing in and of itself, especially in a society obsessed with social proprieties and class distinction, in which these Jews actively participated. No: the kind of prejudice they wished to combat was that which tarred established, native-born Jews with the same brush as newly-arrived Eastern European Jews and *arrivistes*.

> The fact is recognized that there are offensive and vulgar and ill-behaved Jews. The correlative fact is, however, also recognized that the Jews do not monopolize that phase of humanity. The very natural conclusion is, therefore, drawn that offensive persons should be excluded from good society because they are offensive, and not because they are affiliated with any religion or race.[13]

American Hebrew readers would have agreed. After all, the *American Hebrew* was not a paper for all Jews: the mass of working-class Jews and new immigrants had the Yiddish-language *Jewish Daily Forward* and other publications catering to their interests, as well as encouraging their acculturation and assimilation. As a leading Anglo-Jewish weekly, the *American Hebrew* would support the rights of immigrants and encourage their rapid assimilation and adoption of Americanized standards, but it did not speak directly to those immigrants. Rather, it was oriented to, and most concerned with, the point of view of its own clientele, who looked upon these "co-religionists" with what often amounted to distaste and horror. The majority of assimilated, "cultured" Jews would distance themselves from the new arrivals if they could.[14]

Except to the extent that they themselves could eventually be affected, native-born Jews had little problem with discrimination against the new immigrants or the Jewish *nouveaux riches* who were so embarrassingly visible in society. In fact, such discrimination seems to have been viewed by upper-class Jews as a beneficial thing, a means of forcefully encouraging Jews to "modernize" and cast off their ways of the Old World, of poverty. Prejudice against the poor of all ethnicities went hand-in-hand with the reform impulses of the Progressive era; many native-born Jewish women, reacting to the "otherness" of the immigrants, lent their energies to the reform and domestication of those who, nonetheless, remained fellow Jews.[15]

The *American Hebrew*'s Special Passover Number reveals all of this prejudice and condescension the native-born Jews felt toward the newer immigrants. The issue consists of the responses to a question-naire, designed by the editors, of sixty well-known Christians, who ranged, as more than one commentator would note, over "all shades of religious belief and unbelief...from Cardinal Gibbons to Mr. Robert Ingersoll."[16] No matter their religious orientation, each man (all but two participants, were men)[17] was posed the same four questions, notably:

> Can you, of your own personal experience find any justification whatever for the entertainment of prejudice towards individuals solely because they are Jews?

> Have you observed in the social or business life of the Jew, so far as your personal experience has gone, any different standard of conduct than prevails among Christians of the same social status?

> Can you suggest what should be done to dispel the existing prejudice?

The other question asked whether the Church's teachings that the Jews killed Jesus could help account for anti-Semitism among Christians.[18]

Not only the way the questions were phrased, but also that they were directed at a particular group of Christians—generally educated men in positions of influence, well-schooled in civility—all but guaranteed a response favorable to the editors and readers of the *American Hebrew*. In his response to the questionnaire, the Rt. Rev. H.C. Potter, Episcopalian Bishop of New York, made mention of this: "As your questions are cast, there is . . . hardly room for any other than one answer to them." The intention of his statement was to say that no true Christian would condone prejudice or injustice against any group, especially Jews, but he also acknowledged that the way the question was framed left him little room to state his opinion without causing offense and compromising his position as a religious leader in a diverse community. In a response to the special issue reprinted by the *American Hebrew* the following week, the *Commercial Advertiser* likewise commented:

> These letters we must say, are rather shadowy contributions to the solution of the question. They are, for the most part, civil replies to civil interrogatories, and, taken together, leave the impression of a certain lack of rugged frankness.[19]

The editorial writer for the *Commercial Advertiser* astutely summed it up: by posing the problem of anti-Semitism as a question of the incivility of one group toward another which, apart from the fact that it celebrated the Sabbath on the wrong day, would otherwise be their equal in values, taste, and sensibility, the editors of the *American Hebrew* received, for the most part, an acknowledgment and validation of their position. Prejudice against the Jews, it was to be agreed by all parties, was "as un-Christian as it is un-American," as the *AH* had put it, especially insofar as it:

> Manifests itself in the refusal to admit Jews to summer resorts, in the exclusion of Jewish children from various private schools—all at the demand of Christian patrons—in the black balling at clubs of proposed Jewish members; and in various other forms.[20]

The editors of the *American Hebrew* thus attempted to speak to two communities at once—in fact, to thereby bring the two together. For their Jewish readership, the prejudice they had heretofore encountered would be confirmed as a by-product of the publicly displayed poor manners and general vulgarity of the new immigrants and the *nouveaux riches,* which by no means should reflect upon them, the natural elite of American Jewry. For "the best classes of non-Jews," that audience coveted by publisher Philip Cowen, the special issue would tell them two things: first, that well-regarded Christians condemned blanket anti-Semitism (although it would still be acceptable to continue to look down upon certain classes of Jews), and second, that there were some Jews with whom it should be acceptable to associate as equals.

This is not to say that all of the *American Hebrew*'s respondents answered in the same way, with the same message. On the contrary, especially on the question of whether the Church's teachings were somehow responsible for prejudice against the Jews, there were reactions ranging from defensive to apologetic to flatly disclaiming. A few, for example, notably the Rev. Alvah S. Hobart of Yonkers, attempted to both deny and justify such teachings:

> The prejudice is not, I think, at all due to the teaching of the church and Sunday-school that the Jews crucified Jesus. Shakespeare's Shylock has done more than Sunday-schools. But Americans do not act on an old affair like that. Whatever cause there is, is to be found in some prevailing, persistent, present conduct on the part of the Jews; or in some deficiency in them which unfits them to be good companions for the unalloyed rest and enjoyment of a summer vacation.

The Rev. Hobart went on to say that the Jews and Christians were not fitted in their deepest sympathies and that "it is to me as much a wonder that the Jew has a desire for Christian company, as that the Christian has little for the Jew." He likened the wish on the part of some Christians to exclude Jews from their resorts to "the dislike which some have to boarding with many children. . . . Quiet sober men do not go to noisy drunken hotels. Circus men are not wanted at many of the best hotels."[21]

Even this sort of negative response was useful to the *American Hebrew* readership, however. The Rev. Hobart, in fact, provided a suggestion for overcoming such prejudice as Jews might encounter at resorts:

It can only be dispelled by making the Jews more in sympathy with Christian ways and the Christian Sabbath; or by making the Christians more Jewish. Perhaps as time goes on something may be gained by both which will give them more common ground, and more fellowship will result.[22]

Hobart's comments, while often contradictory (he swings between justifying anti-Semitism on the grounds that Christians prefer to be with their own kind and denying that it exists among true Christians), purport to provide insights into the situation, but, more than that, confirm *AH's* own precariously balanced, sometimes contradictory view: Jews are permanently different from Christians but, *within the same social class,* ultimately the same under the surface.

What develops in the pages of the special issue, then, is an ambiguous definition of Judaism, both by Christians and by Jews. Jews are not quite a race, yet they are clearly more than a religious group. That the *American Hebrew's* editors themselves had experienced prejudice implies a perception, at least in those who would discriminate against Jews, that Jews had some physical or mental traits in common, although, as enunciated by the respondents to the questionnaire, these traits did not necessarily have anything to do with the religious tenets of Judaism.

It is this idea that religion gives way to social (or unsocial) commonalities that the editors were attempting to combat. At the very least, Jews were to be divided into two groups: upper-class, refined Jews, and everyone else. Each of these groups, it seemed, had traits inherent to its members and not present in the other. For the *American Hebrew,* whose readers belonged to the former group, it was more fruitful and more flattering to their sense of themselves to focus on the common origins of Christians and Jews, to identify themselves as Americans of a certain social standing, or better, simply as members of the upper classes which exist in any Western culture:

We admit that Jews, like all human beings, have their ignoble as well as noble types, but this difference is as between members of the human family, and is not due to their faith, a faith to which, it will be admitted, all the dominant sects owe their origin.[23]

A letter by a Jewish reader the week following the Special Passover Number went even further in making this link between Jews and other Americans: "It seems almost incredible," wrote J.C. Levi, "that we should find here and there in these letters the erroneous idea that 'Jew' and 'American' are opposite and inconsistent terms. . . . The whole trouble . . . is that they cannot entirely disabuse their minds of the vulgar error that 'Jew' and 'Hebrew' are national or geographical, and not exclusively religious terms." Mr. Levi went on to relate the story of a "fellow student" who would not believe he was a Jew because, said the student, "'you don't look and speak like a Jew.'" According to Levi, such ignorance obscured the fact that "the words 'Jew' and 'American' bear the same co-relation as the words 'Protestant' and 'German,' or 'Catholic' and 'Spanish' . . . we American Jews have precisely and identically the same dislike of and distaste for un-American tastes and habits as the American Christians have—not one whit more or less."[24]

The suitability of this identification with America and American Christians was confirmed by *AH's* Christian contributors. Mr. Henry T. Finck, for instance, who identified himself as an agnostic, wrote that "the most refined Jews, as a rule, do not betray themselves by a marked Hebrew physiognomy." This he regarded as unfortunate, but in a way that might have been most flattering to J.C. Levi: it was the main reason why "the vices and vulgar manners of the common Jews are accepted as typical" of all Jews.[25] If refined Jews did not blend in so well with others of their class, in other words, it would be plain to see how capable of appropriate behavior well-bred Jews could be. According to Robert Ingersoll, "Good Jews are precisely the same as good Christians, and bad Christians are wonderfully like bad Jews."[26] And Rev. Washington Gladden went even further. He attributed negative perceptions of Jews to the fact that more Jews were involved in commercial pursuits than other Americans were, and thus were more likely to possess the commercial spirit: "like the average American, only more so."

In keeping with this idea, Jews were praised by some for their achievements as much as they were criticized by others for their shortcomings: H.E. Krehbiel, of the Metropolitan Opera, praised Jews for their "artistic interest and love" of music and drama, in doing so inadvertently pointing out the extreme extent to which Jews had turned their backs on religion in pursuit of acceptance. "Jewish patronage . . . has been most generously bestowed on the Wagnerian list; yet, you remember, it was Wagner who wrote the pamphlet on 'Judaism in Music,' which stirred up a polemical tempest in Germany forty years ago."[27]

As noted above, however, there were numerous accusations and justifications for anti-Semitic actions hurled at the *American Hebrew*. W.M. Thornton, president of the University of Virginia, expressed his belief that there were in fact racial differences between the Jews and Christians. Further, Jews' values were different:

> They certainly care less for what is embraced in the term culture than Christians who are equally well off. They are immersed in business and money-getting. . . . We have never had in my day a really scholarly man among [Jewish students at the university] . . . they are almost always in Professional Schools.

Rev. J.R. Day, in his contribution, stated that "my observation has been that the Jews as a class are somewhat 'loud' in talk, 'flashy' in dress and offensive in display of jewelry, etc. . . . In business the name has become an odious synonym because of the practice of the small shop-keeper who seeks the dollar without regard to the quality of goods. . . . To 'Jew' is to cheat in a petty and shrewd way." Day, however, ascribed such practices to the Jews' historic ostracism "which emphasized the necessity of sharp personal contest for existence." It was this which had made the Jews themselves, and not Christians, exclusive, both religiously and socially. The distinctions between Jews and Christians could be fixed, however: "The remedy is to discourage everything exclusively Jewish, except your worship and sacred days. . . there must be a merging of national peculiarities and an abandonment of marked personal difference of habit and taste."[28]

While the *American Hebrew* in its following issue rejected Day's assertions of Jewish exclusivity, which had been seconded by a few other respondents, as beside the point,[29] it handled those criticisms epitomized by President Thornton's remarks somewhat differently. Yes, it agreed, there were such people whose lives were devoted to business, and who possessed, as another magazine characterized them, "a lack of sensibility and tact, and an aggressiveness which is unmistakably disagreeable to the majority of their fellow men."[30] These people, however, were not to be taken to be representative of all Jews; those who mistakenly did so had likely not had much contact with Jews, as indeed many of the respondents to the questionnaire professed. "There is no hesitation," wrote the editors, "to allude to certain traits of *some Jews* [emphasis added], which must naturally be offensive to refined people, whether Jews or Christians." In an attempt to explain how such traits could be thought indigenous to all Jews, they added, "Persons who have never come much in contact with Jews regard them very much as the average Englishman regards the American—as a sort of half-savage."[31]

As far as the paper's effort to find a religious basis for anti-Semitism was concerned, no consensus was achieved. Only a few respondents acknowledged the possibility that the Church's teachings—specifically, that the Jews caused the death of Christ—were responsible for prejudice against the Jews. Most, however, did not. Their statements reveal how slippery was the issue of defining Jewish identity. The Rev Chas. H. Eaton attributed prejudice against the Jews to a flaw in Christian society: "Analyze the feeling of antagonism, and it is found to consist, not in any intellectual denial of the worth and rights of the Hebrew race, but in social custom and class distinctions which exist in relation to other nationalities, and various classes without regard to race."[32] Many others saw it differently: "It is a prejudice against the race and not against the faith, and its grounds are racial and social and not religious," wrote Anna Laurens Dawes. John Boyle O'Reilly, editor of *The Pilot*, agreed that anti-Semitism was "not at all religious"; rather, it was "wholly racial and commercial." E.N. Capen, President of Tufts, explained it more fully. "While the Jews differ in religion, they maintain their race peculiarities. They do not assimilate like other aliens; they are always Hebrews . . . it renders them separate. They can never be Americans, pure and simple."[33]

As discouraging and as permanent as these leading lights made prejudice against the Jews out to be, this perspective actually was more suited to the goals of those Jews who saw anti-Semitism as having only a social basis. Having received reassurance that prejudice was not based on religion per se, the *American Hebrew*'s readers could now focus on eradicating the so-called race peculiarities from their own social personae without having to worry about their religion being an impediment to acceptance.[34] The negative traits associated by the writers with Jews in general could be displaced by *AH* readers, Jewish and Gentile alike, from the well-born Jews onto the lower classes, the recent arrivals, and the newly rich, just as they could among Christians of the same ilk. Without a prejudice based on religion, refined Jews had no obstacle to block a social alliance between themselves and refined Christians. The *American Hebrew* was proud of what it saw as its accomplishment, printing commentary and reviews from other publications on this special issue, discussing it for months, and publishing editions of the issue in book form as late as 1927. "Prejudice Against Jews" was a document created by Jews and Christians together, and its conclusions were encouraging to striving Jews.

Thus, the ambivalence of native-born Jews toward Eastern European and Russian Jews temporarily found a means of expression. Through its representation of these newcomers as "the other," and of its readers as Jewish Americans rather than as American Jews, the *American Hebrew* could relieve its anxiety without committing itself to an ever-broadening definition of Jewishness in America. Of course, within a few years the numbers of newcomers would dwarf the more established Jewish communities, and with this demographic shift would come a shift in the balance of power in the Jewish community. The *American Hebrew* ultimately would also lose its influential position, becoming a small anachronistic voice from an earlier time, much as its many Christian counterparts would. For many Judaism would shift once again. Having first been identified as a race, then as religion, it would ultimately come to view itself as a nation.

NOTES

1. Yehezkel Wyszkowski, "The *American Hebrew*: An Exercise in Ambivalence," *American Jewish History* 76 (March 1987): 342.

2. The editorial board of the *American Hebrew* pledged itself to anonymity in order to stress Jewish unity over division—its members' identities were eventually revealed years later.

3. Actually, legal restrictions on Jewish faith and practices, such as Sunday blue laws, did exist in the late nineteenth century, but if these were more than a minor inconvenience, the *American Hebrew* did not take note. Legal restrictions on Jewish immigration, for example, did not exist until after World War I. What is most important here is Jewish perception of the problem of anti-Semitism during this period.

4. *American Hebrew*, 1 April 1881, 73.

5. Ibid., 10 December 1880, 37. A recent death, editorialized the paper, "should be of no special interest to us. But in our time when the so-called enlightenment and culture have learned that the Mosaic Dietary Laws are not binding upon us, our co-religionists who have thrown aside all these

regulations as being intended only for a particular time and climate, will do well to look to their healths."

6. Ibid., 4 August 1882, 138, quoted in Wyszkowski, 349.

7. Ibid., 14 November 1890, 35; Ibid., 28 November 1890, 78.

8. Ibid., 7 November 1890, 8; Ibid., 14 November 1890, 38. One other *AH* joke that does, indirectly, comment on the question of Jewish identity in the New World: "I beg your pardon, sir, but is your name Smythe?" Second Gentleman—"No sir; my name is Smith. You have undoubtedly mistaken me for my son."

9. Wyszkowski, 341.

10. *American Hebrew,* 31 December 1880, 74.

11. Ibid., 24 December 1880, 61.

12. Ibid., 4 April 1890, 165.

13. Ibid., 164.

14. In contrast to the *American Hebrew*'s peak circulation of about 20,000, the *Forward* reached up to 500,000 across the United States. See Gerald Sorin, "Tradition and Change: American Jewish Socialists as Agents of Acculturation," *American Jewish History* 79, no. 1 (Autumn 1989): 42-43.

15. Jenna Weissman Joselit, "'A Set Table': Jewish Domestic Culture in the New World, 1880-1950," in Susan L. Braunstein and J.W. Joselit, eds., *Getting Comfortable in New York: The American Jewish Home, 1880-1950* (New York: The Jewish Museum, 1990), 21-34; see also Charlotte Baum, Paula Hyman, and Sonya Michel, *The Jewish Woman in America* (New York: Plume/New American Library, 1975), esp. chapter 6.

16. *The Examiner* (date unknown), quoted in *American Hebrew,* 18 April 1890, 239. Cardinal Gibbons was the nominal head of the Catholic Church in America, of Baltimore; Robert G. Ingersoll has been described as a free-speech advocate, a humanist and civil libertarian, well-known in his day as "The Great Agnostic," among other things. Philip Mass, "Robert Green Ingersoll: A Tribute to One of America's Foremost Humanists," *Humanist* 48, no. 6 (November 1988): 29.

17. In addition was George Eliot, who was posthumously represented by an 1876 letter to Harriet Beecher Stow, under the title "An Answer from the Grave."

18. *American Hebrew,* 4 April 1890, 165.

19. Ibid.; *Commercial Advertiser* (date unknown), quoted in Ibid., 11 April 1890, 215.

20. *American Hebrew,* 4 April 1890, 165.

21. Ibid., 170.

22. Ibid., 171.

23. Ibid., 165.

24. Ibid., 11 April 1890, 217.

25. Ibid., 4 April 1890, 195.

26. Ibid., 196.

27. Ibid., 195.

28. Ibid., 191, 172.

29. Ibid., 11 April 1890, 214. "If we cannot get into non-Jewish society, shall we abjure Jewish society as well? Let the managers of the Harmonie, Freundschaft, and Progress clubs be asked how many applications they have received from non-Jews to join these magnificently-appointed organizations". A few of the respondents to the questionnaire implicated Jewish dietary restrictions as responsible for promoting exclusivity.

30. *Commercial Advertiser* (date unknown), quoted in *American Hebrew*, 11 April 1890, 215.

31. *American Hebrew*, 4 April 1890, 164; 11 April 1890, 213.

32. Ibid., 4 April 1890, 172.

33. Ibid., 192, 194.

34. In fact, this attitude would prove in later decades to have been rather optimistic.

From Stereotype to Archetype: Demystifying American Jewish Identity in the Photographic Campaigns of the United Jewish Appeal

Kerri Steinberg

World War Two and the atrocities of the Holocaust mark an abyss in the history of the twentieth century that Jews continue to negotiate as we prepare for the twenty-first century. While Jewish history abounds with examples of discrimination, persecution, and exile, it is this insidious time period that most immediately recalls the plight of European Jews as utterly passive and helpless victims in the face of the Nazi extermination machine. The loss of six million Jewish lives during the Holocaust invokes an image at once tragic, heroic, and rootless. The haunting images of Jewish corpses at the Nazi death camps and of excruciatingly degenerated Jewish survivors in the immediate aftermath of the Holocaust reverberate today as painfully striking, yet stereotypical images of Jewish powerlessness.

As the negative stereotypes of weakness and victimization weave their way throughout the history of the Jews, the very longevity of Jewish existence attests to a positive resilience that has equally characterized Jewish life. In this essay[1] I will explore the complementary paradigm of the negative stereotype and the positive archetype. While the stereotype emphasizes the tragedy and passivity of Jewish existence, the archetype focuses on the vibrancy and triumph characterizing Jewish life, especially in the wake of disaster. These complementary positions will be reconstructed by first equating the United Jewish appeal with the archetype, and then examining the effects of its relief programs which ultimately transform the recipient's life from the stereotype into the archetype.

25

On January 10, 1939, the Joint Distribution Committee (JDC) merged with the United Palestine Appeal (UPA) and the National Coordinating Committee for Refugees to establish the United Jewish Appeal (UJA). As the most extensive collective response to the persecution of Jews in modern Jewish history, the UJA represented an affirmative position of American activism in the face of Jewish degradation abroad.[2] The newly constituted UJA emerged as the single American Jewish fundraising organization for the work of relief and rehabilitation in Europe, for immigration and settlement in Palestine, and for refugee aid in the United States.[3] Since the deportation of European Jews had ruptured Jewish nuclear families, the new alliance of Jewish organizations responded with the paradigm of an extended Jewish family. The UJA sounded the slogan "We are one!" as both a literal and symbolic assertion of Jewish solidarity. Such a declaration of solidarity, intended to embrace Jewish people throughout the world, implied a singularity of purpose, a sense of mutual responsibility, and a homogeneity uniting Jewish people.

The powerful assertion of unity embodied in "We are one!" might further be understood as a defensive response to a "malaise" affecting the identity of the Jewish people since the beginning of modernity, which emerged with particular vengeance in the twentieth century. As early as 1928, Salo Baron addressed this condition in the now classic article, "Ghetto and Emancipation: Shall We Revise the Traditional View?"[4] Baron questioned what emancipation really meant to Jews. His compelling argument claimed that if the status of the Jews during the Middle Ages were not as low as had been generally assumed, then the miracle of emancipation may not have been as great as was customary to suppose.

In the twentieth century tradition of self-examination, Arthur Hertzberg contemplated the prospects of American Jewish survival in his 1963 article, "The Present Casts a Dark Shadow." He declared a "crisis of faith," and attributed the erosion of Jewish group vitality to a loosening of family ties.[5] Hertzberg's proclamation was echoed by Alain Finkielkraut in *The Imaginary Jew* (1980), in which he interpreted the "family-centrism" of the Jews as a counterweight to assimilation.[6] During the 1970s, major Jewish intellectuals like Jacob Katz and Hannah Arendt also considered the dissolution of the traditional Jewish community. While Katz theorized how such a phenomenon paved the way for Jewish emancipation, Arendt speculated on how it might have begun the process of Jewish entrapment, culminating with the atrocities of the Holocaust.[7]

With one eye cast towards the future and the other towards the past, these scholars look back to the more insular and traditional way of life associated with Jewish existence prior to the modern era, and observe a more cohesive and resilient Jewish Identity. To the extent that a desire for acceptance and the weakening of tradition have resulted in a modern crisis of identity, especially for many American Jews, this essay locates the ambivalent American Jewish identity specifically within a selection of photographs sponsored by the United Jewish Appeal between 1984-1994. The photographic campaigns of American Jewish philanthropies such as the UJA present a new medium through which we can examine the ongoing emotional and physical struggles of Jewish life. To this end, I will analyze a selection of photographs from Operations Exodus, Moses, and Solomon (American Jewish relief and rehabilitation campaigns for their Soviet and Ethiopian brethren). At the center of this study is the conflicted identity of many American Jews who remain invisible even as they provide the funds necessary for successful campaigns. In an era of secularism, for a particular constituency of American Jews, does philanthropic involvement substitute for ritual observance? This essay will demonstrate how the photographs under analysis appropriate the "malaise" of "other"[8] Jewish populations in need of rescue and relief, in order to confirm a sense of purpose and to rehabilitate the troubled American Jewish identity.

I. THE MULTIFARIOUS AMERICAN JEWISH IDENTITY

In 1990 the Council of Jewish Federations conducted a National Jewish Population Survey to study the social, demographic and religious structure of the American Jewish community. It concluded that each successive generation of American Jews in the United States was further removed from traditional Judaism.[9] A random sampling of 2,500 families which contained at least one person identified as currently or previously Jewish was used to represent approximately 3.2 million American households nationally. The results of the survey, which sent shock waves throughout the organized American Jewish Community, pointed to a pattern of assimilation, conversion, and secularism. While an estimated 16% of the total American Jewish population regarded itself as secular, another 50% who were born

Jewish were currently married to non-Jewish spouses. Moreover, since 1985 twice as many mixed couples had been formed compared to Jewish couples. Even more alarming, only 50% of the children surveyed were being raised Jewish. Clearly, the study indicated a trend away from traditional Judaism. Whereas 42% of Jews identified themselves as Reform, only 7% identified themselves as Orthodox. The National Jewish Population Survey documented a crisis in Jewish continuity which completely contradicted the notion of a monolithic entity suggested by the UJA's "We are one!"

In light of the movement away from traditional Judaism, we must ask what comprises the substance of "Jewishness" or Jewish identity in America today? How do philanthropic American Jews (with the exception of Jews who identify themselves as Orthodox) exercise their religious objectives? And how might the *spiritual absence* of the faltering American Jewish identity be offset by a substantial *material presence*? In the 1991 publication, *Contemporary Jewish Philanthropy in America*, Mordechai Rimor and Gary Tobin examine the relationship between Jewish identity and philanthropy. They propose that Jewish identity and philanthropic behavior are closely associated. The Jewish community, they argue, is bound together by an organizational and institutional structure in which fundraising campaigns play a central role in the survival of both the community and the philanthropic organization.[10] Furthermore, they observe that while the philanthropic Jew may be active in the organized Jewish community, he/she is not necessarily religiously active.[11] Rimor and Tobin's study highlights the correlation between unobservant or secular Jews and those involved in general Jewish organizations.

This suggestion is further developed by Marc Lee Raphael and Arnold Gurin in *Understanding American Jewish Philanthropy*. According to Raphael, while Jewish philanthropy has been a prominent feature of Jewish society and religious life throughout the ages, it has become the primary expression of Jewishness today.[12] Prior to the onset of modernity, the autonomous Jewish community (*kehillah*) regulated Jewish religious and cultural life, but during the course of the nineteenth century, events such as the migration of Eastern European Jews, emancipation, and the Enlightenment shattered the older model of the Jewish community.[13] Gurin proposes that following the migration of Eastern European Jews to America, the purpose of Jewish institutions was to assist the acculturation process. In America the vital *kehillah* shrank to a mere congregation. In the twentieth century, its previously pivotal role was assumed by local Federations, community organizations working with the voluntary sector to enhance the social welfare of the Jewish community.[14]

This association between an autonomous Jewish community and the Federation as its twentieth century rendition assumes a cohesive American Jewish community. In *Jewish Polemics,* Arthur Hertzberg calls attention to the multiple cultural, political, and religious perspectives within the so-called American Jewish community.[15] Hertzberg specifically invokes the rallying call of the UJA, "We are one!" to highlight real tensions arising from the allocation of funds, which are divided between causes in Israel and causes at home in America.[16] The only homogeneity characterizing Jewish philanthropists, according to Gurin, is their elite socio-economic status, not typical of the general Jewish population.[17]

Such an assessment underscores the correlation between social mobility and Jewish identification. To the extent that board members occupy positions of leadership and are expected to solicit funds for their causes from the population at large, their own financial contributions must generally be exemplary. The tension between upper middle-class status and Jewish identification is documented by Steven Cohen in "Dollars and Diplomas: The Impact of High Social Status upon Jewish Identification." Cohen suggests that high social status fosters a participation in religious institutions, while eroding traditional ritual practice.[18] His argument is based upon the assumption that many upwardly mobile American Jews have an advanced education which often imparts values such as cultural relativism, toleration, and individualism—values at odds with traditional Judaism. According to this argument, such Jews may then turn to Jewish institutional life as a means of satisfying their religious desires.

Samuel Heilman documents a reversal of this trend with respect to Orthodox Jewish communities. Heilman defines Orthodox Jews as those who follow the codified Jewish law (*halakha*).[19] The Orthodox community more closely resembles the traditional *kehillah* because many Orthodox Jews choose to live within close proximity to the synagogue, the center of activity.[20] Heilman suggests that communal proximity is very important to the Orthodox Jews, since they frequently constitute a minority in the Jewish community as a whole.[21] Therefore, giving to the synagogue or to another cause with which the community has associated itself represents a way for individuals to demonstrate their loyalty to the community, and by extension, for the Orthodox community to evidence its vitality.

Significantly, Orthodox Jews tend to support their own Orthodox Jewish causes rather than more general Jewish agencies like the local Federations. According to Heilman, the Orthodox communities believe that if they do not assume primary support for their own charities, no one else will.[22] Gurin's research on the characteristics of Federation Board members shows that only 2% of the Board Members declared Orthodox affiliation, while the balance was divided among Reform and Conservative members.[23] While philanthropic commitment underscores the Jewish tenet of mutual assistance, the involvement in specific charitable causes can be correlated with religious affiliation.

Israel figures centrally when American Jews, especially non-Orthodox, are identified with Jewish philanthropy. Sociologist Nathan Glazer once stated that Israel has become the religion of those whose affiliation with Judaism has drifted away from ritual observance.[24] Alain Finkielkraut suggests this passion for Israel is the indication of a "malaise" in Jewish identity:

> This unconditional support for every Israeli policy is the symptom of a malaise. The Diaspora, prey to a vague sense of guilt, compensates with vehement loyalty. Absence makes the heart grow fonder, and Jews in exile exorcise their historical situation by sticking to the official Zionist line, indeed by taking it one step farther. There's also something more serious than their material comforts to be atoned for: the pleasure they take in watching Israel exist in the face of every peril and risk it can handle. . . .
>
> Of the many anxious pleasures they enjoy, the crown jewel for Diaspora Jewry is the lucky stroke of having charged Israel, that country on the globe that *always makes the front page*, with the task of defining and representing them. Such audiovisual permanence allows the Diaspora to serve its own cultural extenuation.[25]

Finkielkraut observes two categories of practicing Jews: "the devout who attend synagogue, and the much more numerous who produce a running commentary on the situation in the Middle East as their form of observance."[26] This bifurcation of religious identity confirms his notion of a Jewish identity in crisis, particularly with respect to those "empty Jews" whose understanding of judaism or the Jewish past represents only the vacant space of a *tabula rasa*—a blank slate.[27] Yet, Finkielkraut defends the attachment to Israel, maintaining that in the wake of the devastation caused by the Holocaust, every aspect of Israel offers a bit of dignity returned to the Jews. Furthermore, by invoking an image that is at once ordinary and heroic, and mixing the roles of the victim and hero into one, Israel provides Jewish existence with a welcome balance. And thanks to Israel, the Jews of the Diaspora possess the courage to flex their strength and to speak out loud.[28] Knowing that a Jewish homeland exists, Jews thriving in Diaspora nations can assert their independence with relative peace of mind.

Accordingly, Israel Katz asserts that the role of Diaspora Jews has been to raise as much money as they can both to "help" Israel, and to insure their own safety.[29] Katz's identification of Diaspora Jews, namely Americans, as the financiers of Israel implies a paternalistic pattern. To the extent that American dollars demonstrate support for Israel, at least for a particular contingent of American Jews as Katz suggests, the paternalistic paradigm casts Israel as the matriarch of the world's Jews. Thus, American Jews might be likened to an absentee father who subsidizes the mother (and children) in order to ensure the continued survival of the family. Such an analogy reinforces the notion of a symbiotic relationship between American Jews and Israel, in a sense, arguing for both Israel and America as the substance of Jewish existence whose union is expressed in the UJA's "We are one!"

II. FROM STEREOTYPE TO ARCHETYPE

The recurring tension between absence and presence in American Jewish identity is also a central theme in the photographic record of UJA campaigns. Whereas the *spiritual absence* of the faltering American Jewish identity is offset by a substantial *material presence*, in the UJA's photographs, the visual *absence* of American Jews is offset by their strong *presence* in the corresponding written captions. When we equate passive models of Jewish existence with stereotypical conceptions of persecution and degradation, and active models of existence with self-empowerment and triumph, a division emerges between the American Jews as rescuers and the "others" whom they rescue. American Jews, as founders and supporters of the UJA, can be likened to the *archetype*—a positive ideal—activists on behalf of Jewish survival. In celebration of its fiftieth anniversary in 1989, the UJA published a pictorial history entitled *Keeping the Promise: The First Fifty Years at the United Jewish Appeal.* This retrospective reviews the heroic achievements of the UJA during its first half century, marking 1939 as the year that witnessed the birth of American Jewish activism.[30] The notion of American Jewish activism is perpetuated by Abba Eban's contribution to this jubilee publication, in which he characterizes the UJA as "not just a fund," but rather, a "movement." Clearly, the idea of an activist movement, which "embodies the idea of union that draws Jews everywhere into a single chain of creativity," underscores the role of American Jews as positive archetypes—movers and shakers "in the service of higher human ends."[31]

Such a concept of Jewish solidarity reinforces the noble sense of mutual responsibility articulated in "We are one!" as well as the idea of an extended Jewish family. Moreover, it implies that the extended Jewish family is sustained through the efforts of the American Jews participating in the UJA. Stanley Horowitz, Chief Professional Officer of the UJA when *Keeping the Promise* was published, declared that the story of the UJA was not only about the Holocaust and Israel, but also about the coming of age of American Jews.[32] To equate the coming of age of American Jews with events such as the Holocaust and the establishment of the state of Israel argues for the centrality of American Jews to modern Jewish existence. Conceivably, the absence of American Jews from the Jewish homeland provokes an activist defense of their residency in America, where the opportunities for providing the lifeline of Jewish continuity are made possible. To this end, their invisibility in the photographs, compared to their commanding presence in the written text, suggests an omnipotence or an archetypal, exemplary existence.

Take, for example, the original caption of the first photograph (Figure 1): "I'm going home! This child is one of 133 immigrants who took the 'flight of dreams' out of Uzbekistan and into Israel. The immigrants were joined on their flight by forty American Jewish leaders who were visiting the Moslem Republics of the former Soviet Union as part of the United Jewish Appeal Operation Exodus mission. Operation Exodus is a special UJA/Federation campaign to raise money for the immigration of Soviet Jews to Israel." Although the "American Jewish leaders" do not physically appear in the photograph, the text establishes their presence and notes that they accompanied the immigrants out of Uzbekistan and into Israel on their "flight of dreams." The caption portrays the Americans as positive role models, fulfilling their Jewish obligation of mutual assistance. Moreover, it flatters the Americans, who, through their relief and rehabilitation efforts, transform the immigrants' dreams into reality. The visual absence of the forty Americans evokes a sense of omnipotence—the notion that their physical and emotional strength and their deep connection with their brethren abroad allows them to heal from afar through their fundraising efforts. American Jews as agents of the UJA, though usually not in the photographs, are nevertheless presented through the captions as a healthy, resourceful constituency of the Jewish population, as are those Jews now dwelling in Israel, thanks to American dollars.

In contrast, the *other*, non-Western or Eastern European Jews, shown in the midst of crises, are locked out of these two centers and define the stereotype of the passive and unsettled wandering Jew. In his 1938 *Social and Religious History of the Jews*, Salo Baron refers to negative perceptions of Jewish history as "lachrymose" or "mournful." He associates these images with the Christian characterization of the "wandering Jew" who "could not find rest in his perpetual migrations," as Cain was condemned to be a fugitive and vagabond.[33] The stereotype is characterized by those Jews who are caught in an impossible web of uncertainty, helplessness, and humility (Figure 1). When the UJA's photographs of rescue and rehabilitation campaigns are viewed within a context that begins with tragedy and culminates in triumph, a more decisive pattern charting the progression from stereotype to archetype emerges.

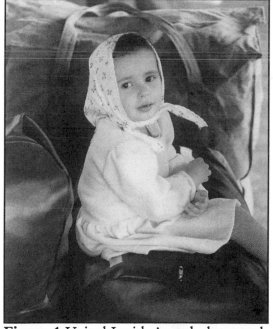

Figure 1 United Jewish Appeal photograph

III. A CALL TO RESCUE

It is the act of rescue that has helped define the United Jewish Appeal.[34] As Stanley Horowitz recounts in *Keeping the Promise*, "Wherever there are Jews in need, the UJA, through the Joint Distribution Committee (JDC), funds a steady lifeline to ensure Jewish survival and Jewish hope."[35] The UJA's photographic documentation of the unfavorable conditions of Jewish life in Diaspora countries (other than America) epitomizes Baron's term, "lachrymose." These photographs play with the viewer's sensibilities in an effort to strengthen bonds of faith irrespective of whether this faith is motivated by ritualistic or materialistic concerns.

The tiny girl in transit between Uzbekistan and Israel (Figure 1) offers the quintessence of a wandering Jew. Overshadowed by the luggage, she obediently sits atop her bundles. Through a rather hazy composition—perhaps prompting associations with the viewer's own ancestral past—this image features the young girl close-up and all alone, wearing the traditional babushka of Russian women. It evokes a parental urge to help and implores the assistance of Jewish American dollars. Presumably such assistance will provide for the physical and emotional relief of this child. This kind of image is clearly intended to arouse the viewer's sympathy, triggering his/her Jewish instinct for self-help.

Although the photograph appears as if it were lifted from "reality," in fact, staging and cropping enhance its naturalness and drive home the contrast between the stereotypical passive, helpless Jew and her heroic, archetypal rescuers. The photograph is cropped around the edges so that the bundles appear to overwhelm her. We interpret this as an indication of her helplessness and uncertainty. Certainly, the artifices of staging and cropping would seem to contradict the ostensible objectivity supposedly inherent within the documentary mode of photography. In this case, however, the image makes a powerful visual and verbal impact precisely because it embodies the contrast between the stereotype of a young, vulnerable girl, who must be looked after, and the completely self-sufficient, (presumably) male American archetypes who come to her rescue. The visual image of vulnerability and helplessness is ultimately transcended by the written message of American strength, determination, and triumph.

Quoting former Israeli President Chaim Weizmann, Horowitz writes that because of the UJA:

We can assure the newcomers freedom from fear. We can assure them that they will be safe and secure in our midst, once the Jews of the United States will help to insure them from want.[36]

Thus, by freeing the immigrants from lives of degeneration in their indigenous countries and bringing them to safety in Israel, American Jews not only fulfill the responsibility to act as their brother's keepers, but they also establish their identity as central to Jewish existence.

IV. PHOTOGRAPHING THE PASSAGE

The regeneration of immigrants rescued by American funds begins with the passage from the indigenous country to the new country. The camera, documenting the passage between two worlds, functions as the purveyor of modernity. These photographs typically show the immigrant boarding or leaving an airplane. The image of an Ethiopian girl brought to Israel through Operation Solomon (the weekend airlift of nearly 15,000 Ethiopian Jews to Israel in May 1991) (Figure 2) is an example of this category. In the photograph, the ramp functions as a symbolic bridge between the child's life in Ethiopia and her future in Israel. The photograph's cropped edges highlight the angle of the ramp and bring the child closer to the viewer, so that we are sure to notice her hesitancy and trepidation. Moreover, they draw attention to the child's self-conscious awareness of her many cultural differences as she prepares to take the first steps in her new homeland. The notion of difference or

Figure 2 UJA photograph

otherness is further reinforced by the number pressed to her forehead, in stark contrast to her dark skin. While the number fulfills a practical function, recalling the organized efforts of American Jews together with Israelis in completing this mission, it might also imply the ordering of black Jews, calling attention to their sense of otherness and difference.

In *Keeping the Promise,* Stanley Horowitz recounts that the coming of age of American Jews coincided with the emergence of America as a major world power. As the United States assumed a more influential role in international affairs, so too were American Jews assuming greater leadership in Jewish life across the globe.[37] Horowitz's connection between the preeminence of America as a nation and the preeminence of American Jews not only underscores the beneficence of American Jews involved in philanthropic work, but also might be further interpreted as an American Jewish expansionist enterprise. It is as if by spreading the American Jewish sphere of influence, American Jews not only secure the survival of their co-religionists abroad, but also safeguard their own harmonious lives in America.

V. TRIUMPH MODERNIZED

Photographs of regeneration suggest the rejuvenation and ultimate triumph of immigrants, both young and old, upon their resettlement in Israel (Figure 3). The weathered, close-up physiognomy of the former Soviet woman conveys that it is never too late for renewal in Israel. Similar to the caption corresponding to the photograph of the young girl in transit to Israel (Figure 1), the caption in Figure 3 also pays respect to American Jews, by thanking them for the funds raised through the Operation Exodus campaign. Here too, the reverence paid to the Americans establishes their ubiquitous presence as the overseers of Jewish welfare, despite the fact that they do not appear in the photograph.

The ideology of rejuvenation in Israel is consistent with Zionist rhetoric which perceives Israel as the organic center of Judaism. In fact, Theodor Herzl believed that the rehabilitation of world Jewry would begin with the cultivation of the soil in the national homeland.[38] Thus, images of agriculture express the Zionist ideal by celebrating the dynamism and vibrancy of Jewish life (Figure 4). Moreover, these images illustrate how UJA funds assist Israel in overcoming famine, joblessness, and lack of housing.[39] As the immigrants (*olim*) cultivate their new homeland, they also participate in their own self-cultivation or modernization. This suggests that sufficient funds allow the immigrants to integrate into Israeli society. However, notice how the Soviets in Figure 5 are "helping to build the country," implying that their presence and skills will serve Israel in the future, while the Ethiopian in Figure 4 is "tilling the soil," reinforcing his "primitive" origins and agricultural roots. Clearly, the objective of the photographs is to position Israel as the utopian *telos*, where *olim* from different parts of the world come together and where cultural barriers are lifted. Nevertheless, an Eastern/Western distinction is subtly presented.

Figure 3 UJA photograph

Figure 4 UJA photograph

This split in the division of labor underscores Ella Shohat's and Robert Stam's assertion in *Unthinking Eurocentrism* that science and technology are frequently considered "Western" properties, corresponding to the notion that all theory is "Western." According to this Eurocentric ideology, the West is projected as "mind" and theoretical refinement, while the non-West is projected as "body" and unrefined raw material.[40] In this respect, it is significant that the caption describes the Ethiopian as "tilling the soil," despite the fact that he is mounted upon a tractor, a sign of modern technology. The caption recasts the message that is implied by the visual image. It corroborates an Orientalist ideology which seeks to hold the non-West fixed in time, while hailing the advances of the West. Thus, while the Ethiopians from Operation Solomon continue their manual labor of "tilling the soil" in timeless fashion, Operation Exodus, nicknamed the "brain-drain" of the Soviet Union, constructs a profile of the former Soviets as highly educated and civilized.

Such Eurocentric ideology continues in photographs depicting the *olim* in their ultimate triumph of having transcended the life of laborers, now participating in a Western lifestyle replete with its emphasis on recreation and stardom (Figures 6-7). Having been rejuvenated by the Jewish American package of enlightenment, civilization, and financial assistance, the Soviet children who receive tennis lessons (courtesy of the UJA) have now been transfigured into products of American success. These photographs present a dynamic and modernized existence, implicitly negating the previous lives of the immigrants. The triumphalist images project the American success story onto the immigrants; the prevailing tone is one of victory. One need only compare the young Ethiopian girl rescued in Operation Solomon (Figure 2) to the photograph of the Ethiopian super-star model rescued seven years earlier in the Operation Moses campaign (Figure 7) to see how the progression from stereotype to archetype unfolds. Compared to the stereotype of poverty and helplessness, the photograph of the Ethiopian beauty represents a positive Western image. Even so, we must recognize that the reclining female corresponds to a different Western stereotype, that of the female nude as a sumptuous object to be adored by men. Sometimes even the archetype associated with determination, strength, and perfection represents just another formulation of the stereotype.

The photographic journey from stereotype to archetype not only illustrates the transformation of refugees into productive Israeli citizens,

Figure 5 UJA photograph

Figure 6 UJA photograph

but also establishes the Americans (whose presence almost always is implied) as the arbiters of success and triumph. The rescue and rehabilitation of *other* immigrants confirms a sense of purpose and affords a reconstitution of American Jewish identity, which, in spite of the UJA slogan, is not "one" but is splintered into numerous fragments. Inasmuch as "We are one!" represents an American fabrication circulated by American Jewish philanthropists, it extols American Jews as the force behind the wheel of Jewish continuity.

While affirming the Jewish tenet of mutual responsibility, "We are one!" glosses over the differences inherent in modern Jewish existence in order to promote the idea of one extended family whose patriarchs are American Jewish fundraisers. However, the Eurocentric and Orientalist implications in the photographs render the notion of an extended Jewish family problematic. For example, in the photograph of a newly arrived Ethiopian family being welcomed by an Israeli family (Figure 8), the Israeli family is represented in a much more commanding position, with the Israeli adults' arms extending across two-thirds of the picture. The juxtaposition of the inhibited Ethiopian family compared to the dominant Israeli family reinforces typical Orientalist perspectives.

Figure 7 UJA photograph

VI. DEMYSTIFYING THE PHOTOGRAPHIC "DOCUMENT": DOCUMENTING JEWISH AMERICAN SUCCESS

While purporting to document the inferior conditions of Jewish brethren abroad, the UJA photographs also confirm the prosperity and importance of American Jews in the relief efforts, and the instrumentality of American Jewish dollars in effecting their rejuvenation. This tension between the subjects depicted and the agency behind the photographic campaign is characteristic of documentary photography. The documentary mode is inherently problematic. While it claims to objectively record the conditions of the subjects, the image can never be entirely separated from the interests of the sponsors. When we accept that there are ideological effects inherent within documentary practice, we realize that the photograph is a subjective "document." Although photo historians and critics have pointed out the ideology intrinsic to the documentary tradition, its effects of naturalness and transparency make it difficult to identify its ideology for it is constructed within the image itself.[41] Abigail Solomon-Godeau notes that, in contrast to hand-made images (e.g., paintings, drawings, etc.) in which the image lies on the surface of the paper or canvas, the photographic image appears to be contained within the paper. By effacing the conditions of its production, the image seems to have produced itself. This "naturalizes" the image and underscores photography's mythic value of transparency.[42]

Figure 8 UJA photograph

It is specifically the presumed objectivity and transparency of the photographic "document" which renders it most effective in philanthropic campaigns such as the UJA's. Although American Jewish philanthropists do not appear in the photographs, their commitment to Judaism, which takes the form of philanthropic involvement, is clearly acknowledged. To this end, the photographs are just as much about American Jewish philanthropists confirming their sense of purpose as Jews as they are about the depicted refugees. The

photographic journey from stereotype to archetype—the transformation of tragedy into triumph—conceals the identity crisis of
American Jews by celebrating their contributions as Jewish
humanitarians.

According to Stanley Horowitz, American Jews have thrived as
philanthropists because of the "unparalleled opportunities of the
American economic system" resulting in "sums unequalled in
philanthropic history."[43] From an economic perspective, Jews are
acknowledged to be the most successful group in American society.[44]
In "A Unique People in an Exceptional Country," Seymour Martin
Lipset compares the experience of American Jews to that of their co-
religionists abroad. The Jews of America, by and large, faced
significantly less discrimination. They were accepted as fully equal
citizens in America earlier than anywhere else. Although they
constitute under five percent of the national population, they have
been given thirty-three percent of the religious representation. As a
group, Jews are among the wealthiest in America, and are
disproportionately present among various sectors of the elite.[45] Lipset
suggests that the ability of Jews to prosper in America may be related
to an emphasis on education; an urban background which prepared
individuals to succeed, especially in business; and a historical
rootlessness which stimulated an ability to form relationships in new
environments.[46] Lipset's insights underscore the high level of success
and comfort attained by many Jews in America. The conflicted
identity of many American Jews is resolved through philanthropy,
which allows them to demonstrate their devotion to less fortunate co-
religionists, while demonstrating the necessity of their residency in
America. However, as Steven Cohen concludes, there is an additional
price often paid for this success; namely, a high rate of assimilation
and, by extension, a loss of Jewish affiliation.

Since the formation of the state of Israel, Lipset maintains that the
nature of American Jewry has been determined by concerns about, and
links to, Israel.[47] As the photographic narrative reveals, the UJA, with
American dollars, has worked to fashion Israel into an exemplary
society, rather in its own likeness. While this might easily be read as
narcissism, or interpreted as an indication of a malaise in Jewish
identity as Finkielkraut suggests, it may alternatively be interpreted as
a healthy strategy of self-preservation. In an age where secularism and
assimilation are rampant, the *Haskalah* slogan, "be a man on the street
and a Jew at home," has been inverted to reveal that, although

Jewishness may be flaunted on the outside, inside there is an absence of Jewish traditions. Thus, the UJA's insistence on Jewish solidarity represents a last ditch effort to save that which is threatened—Jewish belonging and affiliation.

VII. THE PHOTO ALBUM OF THE EXTENDED JEWISH FAMILY

Photographs as mnemonic devices are an ideal medium in situations where the preservation of either individual or group identity is at stake. As mnemonic devices, UJA photographs of the 1980s and 1990s, when the crisis of Jewish identity in America reached a climax (as documented by the National Jewish Population Survey), reference how some American Jews, through philanthropic involvement assisting "others," attempt to rehabilitate their own transgressive Jewish identities. The triumph of Judaism for some Americans is thus achieved through financial support and cultivation of Jewish populations abroad and the Israeli state.

The photographs featured in this essay, representing a narrow sampling of the UJA's extensive collection, function as publicity for specific campaigns responsible for assisting hundreds of thousands of Jews in their immigration and resettlement within Israel. As expensive campaign materials, these photographs are not widely disseminated, but are seen by a select audience targeted for substantial contributions. Typically, these photographs are viewed in the context of fundraising events, ranging from intimate gatherings in the living room of a home to formal affairs featuring renowned speakers or performers. Both the success of the campaigns and the success of the elite group of viewers as a life-saving and life-giving source confirm the photographs' value as "documents."

Given the facts that the photographs play upon the fiction of performing a documentary function, that they are not intended for a wide viewing audience, and that their role is self-affirming, they could be likened to a "photo album of the extended Jewish family." A family photo album may feature numerous images, but it is most often compiled for the viewing pleasure of immediate family members. Moreover, it functions to preserve for posterity the lives of the family members, thereby ensuring a connection between the past and the present, and perpetuating the survival of the family.

In contrast to the fragmentation and rupture of current Jewish existence, this UJA photo album embraces all Jews, and stirs a sense of belonging. It fulfills a symbolic role in the work towards Jewish rejuvenation. When the UJA's photographic record is likened to the "photo album of the extended Jewish family," the diverse populations across the globe are symbolically reunited, and American Jews star as the centripetal force behind Jewish continuity. This album constitutes a visual record of American Jewish accomplishment, illustrating how underprivileged Jews are provided for and "Westernized" under the auspices of American Jews. Ultimately, the "photo album of the extended Jewish family" documents a transformation that is twofold: while it first records the journey from the stereotype into the archetype taken by the recipients of the UJA's funds, it simultaneously confers a renewed identity and sense of purpose for American Jews as powerful agents of rescue and relief.

NOTES

1. This essay is part of my larger dissertation project which examines how American Jewish identity is constructed within the photographic sponsorship of Jewish American philanthropies. I wish to thank Penny Buccafuri at the United Jewish Appeal in New York for her invaluable assistance in making the UJA's photographic collection accessible. I would also like to express my gratitude to Eric Nooter at the Joint Distribution Committee in New York for his assistance with the JDC's extensive photographic collection. Special thanks to my advisors Al Boime and David Myers for having read and commented on earlier versions of this essay, and for their steadfast encouragement of my work. My gratitude finally to Ruth E. Iskin whose keen insights have helped to guide this project from its inception.

2. Admittedly, a designation such as *modern Jewish history* is somewhat arbitrary. For a historiographic overview regarding various periods of "modern" Jewish history see Michael Meyer, "Where does the Modern Period of Jewish History Begin?" *Judaism* 24 (Summer 1975).

3. Marc Lee Raphael, *A Short History of the United Jewish Appeal 1939-1982* (Brown University: Scholars Press, 1982),1.

4. Salo Baron, "Ghetto and Emancipation: Shall We Revise the Traditional View?" *The Menorah Journal* 14 (June 1928).

5. Arthur Hertzberg, "The Present Casts a Dark Shadow," in *Being Jewish in America* (New York: Schocken Books, 1979), 82-84; "Current Issues in Jewish Life in America and their Meaning for the Jewish Community Center," in *Being Jewish in America*, 127-132.

6. Alain Finkielkraut, *The Imaginary Jew* (Lincoln and London: University of Nebraska Press, 1994), 104-108. Originally published *Le Juif Imaginaire* (Editions du Seuil, 1980).

7. Hannah Arendt, *Origins of Totalitarianism* (New York: Harcourt Brace Jovanovich, 1973); Jacob Katz, *Out of the Ghetto* (Cambridge, Massachusetts: Harvard University Press, 1973).

8. In his 1978 book, Edward Said defines orientalism as the ensemble of discourses through which the West has perceived and defined for itself the essential characteristics of Islamic civilizations; these have included literary and artistic representations in addition to more scholarly treatments. Ultimately, Said sees Orientalism as a way of distinguishing the Western and European "self" from the foreign, and oriental inferior "other." Edward W. Said, *Orientalism* (New York: Pantheon Books, 1978).

9. The Council of Jewish Federations (CJF) refers to the continental association of 189 Jewish Federations. For the results of the 1990 National Jewish Population Survey see Barry A. Kosmin et al., *Highlights of the CJF 1990 National Jewish Population Survey* (New York: The Council of Jewish Federations, 1991).

10. Mordechai Rimor and Gary Tobin, "The Relationship Between Jewish Identity and Philanthropy," in *Contemporary Jewish Philanthropy in America*, ed. Barry A. Kosmin and Paul Ritterband (Savage, Maryland: Rowman and Littlefield Publishers, Inc., 1991), 34-51.

11. Ibid, 49.

12. Marc Lee Raphael, *Understanding American Jewish Philanthropy* (New York: Ktav Publishing House, Inc., 1979), 4.

13. Kosmin and Ritterband, vi.

14. Arnold Gurin, "What We Say vs. What We Do," in *Understanding American Jewish Philanthropy*, 70; Raphael, *Understanding American Jewish Philanthropy*, viii.

15. Arthur Hertzberg, *Jewish Polemics* (New York: Columbia University Press, 1992), 178.

16. Ibid., 177.

17. Arnold Gurin, "The Characteristics of Federation Board Members," in *Understanding American Jewish Philanthropy*, 33-35.

18. Steven Cohen, "Dollars and Diplomas: the Impact of High Social Status upon Jewish Identification," in *American Modernity and Jewish Identity* (New York and London: Tavistock Publications, 1983), 80.

19. Samuel Heilman, "Tzedakah: Orthodox Jews and Charitable Giving," in *Contemporary Jewish Philanthropy in America*, 133.

20. Ibid., 138.

21. Ibid.

22. Ibid., 142.

23. Gurin, "The Characteristics of Federation Board Members," 37.

24. Quote by Nathan Glazer in Seymour Martin Lipset, "A Unique People in an Exceptional Country," *Society* 28 (November/December 1990): 11.

25. Finkielkraut, 131.

26. Ibid., 132.

27. Ibid., 145. Finkielkraut's implication of a bifurcation in religious identity between those who are observant of the Jewish rituals and those who substitute philanthropy or loyalty to Israel for religious traditions and beliefs corroborates the findings of sociologists Steven Cohen, Arnold Gurin, and Samuel Heilman reviewed earlier.

28. Ibid., 125-139.

29. Israel Katz, "Israeli Society and Diaspora Philanthropy: How Well Does the Gift Perform?" in *Contemporary Jewish Philanthropy in America*, 232.

30. Abba Eban, "The Toil and the Harvest: 50 Years of the UJA," in *Keeping the Promise: The First Fifty Years at the United Jewish Appeal*, ed. Donna Lee Goldberg (New York: United Jewish Appeal, 1989), 8.

31. Ibid., 9.

32. Stanley Horowitz, "Keeping the Promise: Yesterday, Today and Tomorrow," in *Keeping the Promise: The First Fifty Years*, 12-13.

33. Salo Baron, *A Social and Religious History of the Jews* (New York: Columbia University Press, 1938), 31-32.

34. Goldberg, ed., *Keeping the Promise*, 18.

35. Horowitz, 14.

36. Ibid., 12.

37. Horowitz, 12-13.

38. See Theodor Herzl, *The Jewish State* (London: Rita Searl, 1946).

39. Horowitz, 12.

40. Ella Shohat and Robert Stam, *Unthinking Eurocentrism* (London and New York: Routledge, 1994), 14.

41. For a critical perspective on the documentary tradition of photography, see Abigail Solomon-Godeau, "Who is Speaking Thus? Some Questions about Documentary Photography," in *Photography at the Dock: Essays on Photographic History, Institutions, and Practices* (Minneapolis: University of Minnesota Press, 1991). Also see Roland Barthe, "The Rhetoric of the Image," in *Classic Essays on Photography*, ed. Alan Trachtenberg (New Haven: Leete's Island Books, 1980); Allan Sekula, "Dismantling Modernism: Reinventing Photography" in *Photography Against the Grain: Essays and Photo Works* (Halifax, NS., Canada: Press of the Nova Scotia College of Art and Design, 1984); Victor Burgin, "Photography, Phantasy, Function," in *Thinking Photography* (London: Macmillan Education, Ltd., 1982); and John Tagg, *The Burden of Representation* (Amherst: The University of Massachusetts Press, 1988). All four writers are concerned with how documentary practice has become institutionalized, disseminating the ideological agendas of their institutional sponsors.

42. Solomon-Godeau, 180.

43. Horowitz, 14.

44. Barry Kosmin, "The Dimensions of Contemporary American Jewish Philanthropy," in *Contemporary Jewish Philanthropy in America*, 21. According to Kosmin, the economic success of many American Jews derives from their advanced educations, which results in more lucrative occupations.

45. Lipset, 4. Lipset notes the distinguished presence of Jews as Nobel Peace Prize winners, professors at leading universities, partners in leading law firms, high level civil servants, reporters, editors, writers, executives of major print and broadcast media, and producers of the fifty top grossing motion pictures between 1965 and 1982.

46. Ibid., 9.

47. Ibid., 11.

George Segal's Holocaust Memorial

Pamela A. Cohen

George Segal's *The Holocaust* (1984) (Figure 1)[1], installed in San Francisco's Lincoln Park, is an arrangement of eleven figures cast in bronze with a white patina. A lone death camp survivor stands behind a barbed wire fence. Behind him lies a pile of ten corpses. The scene is familiar to anyone who has seen photographs of the death camps taken upon their liberation. In this we might assume that Segal has taken a strictly documentary approach to his subject. Yet this seemingly random pile of corpses is more ordered than a quick glance indicates; three biblical references are buried among the dead. The biblical stories represented span both the Hebrew Bible and the Gospels, and include the Expulsion, the Binding of Isaac, and the Crucifixion. Segal has drawn upon the Hebrew Bible in other works,[2] but this is the only occasion in which he uses the Gospels as well. The documentary veneer, when coupled with these biblical references, allows the memorial to function on both literal and metaphorical levels. By placing biblical history in a modern context Segal emphasizes historical continuity, demonstrating the Bible's relevance in the late twentieth century.

Authenticity is always important to Segal when he works; this is especially true in the case of *The Holocaust*. Segal's primary visual source was the photographic archives at Manhattan's YIVO Institute, where he poured over thousands of images of the death camps. Segal then enriched this documentary evidence with a layer of biblical allusions. Both are common approaches to Holocaust art. Turning to the photographs was common among artists in the aftermath of the Holocaust. In her study of Holocaust imagery, Ziva Amishai-Maisels explains: "Non-witnesses, confronted only by photographs and

49

films . . . were preoccupied with the aesthetic problem of turning the documentary photographs into meaningful, expressive works of art."[3] The use of biblical allusions to commemorate the Holocaust appealed strongly to Jewish artists who had been brought up on the concept of the identification between past and present expressed in the Passover *Haggadah*: "'In every generation in turn, they [Israel's enemies] rise against us to destroy us' and 'In every generation a man must view himself as though he himself had come forth from Egypt.'"[4] While there is considerable precedent for both approaches, Segal's memorial is unique in its combination of sources, thus straddling two traditions of Holocaust representation.

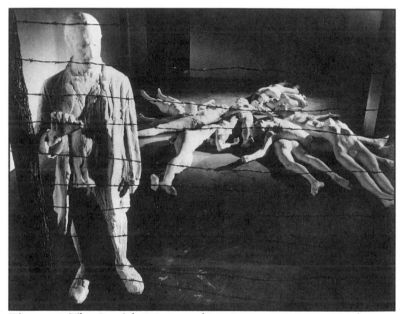

Figure 1 The Jewish Museum/Art Resource, New York

Initially Segal was not interested in this commission. Although he had been asked to submit a model for a proposed Holocaust memorial in San Francisco by Mayor Diane Feinstein's Committee for A Memorial to the Six Million Victims of the Holocaust, he hesitated, "because I knew I would have to saturate myself in death."[5] At the request of the steering committee he agreed to stop in San Francisco to see the site on his way home from a trip to Japan. Shortly before leaving Tokyo, he and his wife Helen heard of Israel's invasion of

Lebanon, but as neither spoke Japanese, they could not get any details. Anxious for news, the Segals immediately turned on the television upon arriving in their hotel in San Francisco. The American news coverage convinced Segal he must submit his model: "For the first time in my life I heard anti-Semitic noise coming out of the American tube. I had been born and raised in America, and in light of the enormity of the Holocaust, this was inconceivable. I decided then and there to make the piece."[6] Segal reacted strongly to American reporters' irritation with the Israeli military censorship, and the reporters' naive repetition of PLO claims.

> I had been to that part of the world, and I knew how small the cities were. Yet they were reporting casualties in Sidon and other Lebanese cities that were larger than the entire population. Something was out of kilter. I retain an innocent faith in ideas of American freedom and democracy, and my family has lived freely expressing Jewishness all these years. I was shocked.[7]

Segal's work is grounded in the literal. A specific event usually provides the catalyst. Although Segal lost relatives during the Holocaust, they were people he'd never met. He himself is not a Holocaust survivor, nor is he the child of survivors. For someone whose art is so strongly motivated by his reactions to personal experiences, his relationship to the Holocaust alone was not sufficient to inspire him to create a Holocaust memorial. In the absence of that very specific and personal catalyst, it was a contemporary event, Segal's reaction to the anti-Semitic news coverage of the Israeli invasion of Lebanon, which provided this catalyst. While Segal was too far removed from the Holocaust itself, an anti-Semitic act reminded him of history's cyclical nature. Once he felt compelled to act a flood of more intimately linked memories was evoked, further justifying his decision.

Having experienced the Holocaust second-hand, Segal drew upon two sources of his own memories of the Holocaust as an American Jew: the news coverage and stories told within his local Jewish community. Segal vividly recalls one story in particular, told to him by German neighbors: "They were fragile people with bad hearts who told me in mild, benign voices of all the awful things that happened—of police dogs trained to leap, to tear a baby out of its mother's arms, to murder the child savagely."[8]

The media provided a visceral visual source: "My greatest memory of the Holocaust was my horror at the photographs in *Life* magazine that appeared at the time of the uncovering of the camps."[9] Thus Segal further expanded the Holocaust's impact on him from a current event to communal horror, eventually distilling his immediate reactions to encompass America's collective horror. What most horrified Segal about the photographs of the camps was the blatant disregard for the dead:

> The one visual hook I uncovered was the arrogant contempt displayed by the Germans in their chaotic heaping of corpses. In any culture, if a human being dies, there's an elaborate, orderly ritual that accompanies the burial. The body is laid out in a straight line. Hands are crossed. There's a burial case and a prescribed, almost immovable succession of events that involve the expression of grief of the family, the expression of love, the expression of the religious beliefs in whatever civilization. It's a prescribed order, and if a modern state turns that order topsy-turvy and introduces this kind of chaos, it is an unthinkable obscenity. I determined that I would have to make a heap of bodies that was expressive of this arrogance and disorder.[10]

In these photographs, the corpses are piled in one of two ways: like cordwood, with the head of one body resting on the feet of another, or they are randomly heaped. The latter resonated more strongly with him, and it is on this image which he built his memorial. Such an arrangement lent itself to richer expressive possibilities. As Segal was not limited to simply stacking his figures head to foot, he could position his models with infinite variety. This enabled Segal to introduce his biblical subtext:

> Once I decided to use live models I also decided to work on my hidden agenda, since . . . they were intelligent people, thoughtful and sensitive. I plotted to have them be aware that they were playing dead, but also acting out a collapsed version of ancient Hebrew Bible stories.[11]

This provided him with an opportunity to deal with his horror over the Nazis' lack of respect for the dead. Thus Segal could utilize the artistic process to reorder chaos.

The effect of looking at so many photographs of corpses is dehumanizing. Segal's casting process provided him with a way to counteract this. Authenticity is of the utmost importance to Segal, and when his doctor offered to get him access to the morgue at a local hospital he seriously considered using corpses.[12] Segal ultimately rejected this possibility, most obviously because of the excessive morbidity. Segal had hesitated to consider this commission because he did not want to be so close to death. "It's physically just as possible to make a stomach wrenching image, as any other kind, and I made the choice not to do that."[13] Using corpses would have been a pointless exercise, reiterating tragedy rather than healing it.

Moreover, working with corpses would have been antithetical to Segal's method of working. He has always enlisted live models and seldom employs professional models. Rather, he asks his friends to pose. To be asked to pose by Segal implies a certain intimacy with the artist. Yet not any friend is right for any particular job. Segal carefully chooses among his friends, and the dialogue between artist and model is crucial. This is especially true of the Holocaust Memorial, where Segal's process lent itself to rejecting the specter of death and the anonymity of genocide. He did his best to animate the hollow casts by choosing models with strong personalities, and solicited their opinions as to how they should pose. The result was a group of models who collaborated with him during the casting sessions, rather than passively posed for him.

The sculptor Isaac Witkin posed for the figure of Abraham. Segal explained to Witkin that he would be collapsed with a young boy at his side. "I said, 'How would you pose if you're playing Abraham and the boy is your son Isaac?' [Witkin] instantly said to me, 'I would cover his eyes!' And that's precisely how we did it."[14] Segal's friend Danny Berger posed for the only figure who is fully naked. Segal recalls that it was Berger's idea to pose this way. "Danny insisted on that, saying, all those Jews, the victims, who were naked corpses, and everything on them had been stolen. He thought it was a stronger point to reveal their nakedness," and Segal conceded.[15] For the figures of Adam and Eve he had friends who were a couple pose; such intimacy was important to him. The same is true of Segal's friend Martin Weyl, Director of the Israel Museum, who was cast as the survivor. Segal felt this was most appropriate, as Weyl himself was a camp survivor. Segal relayed that, "[Martin] told me that he went through an intense memory of his experience in the camp and he kept shrinking and shrinking, and his shoulders kept getting more stooped."[16] Although this casting session was difficult for both men, it was essential that Segal's model had personally experienced the Holocaust in order for him to get the correct emotional pitch.

In the resulting image, the pile of dead bodies pulsates with life. Despite having examined countless photographs of concentration camp corpses in preparing *The Holocaust*, Segal consciously chose to animate his figures. Ziva Amishai-Maisels explains that Segal's "need to express survival also helps to explain the 'living' quality of the dead: they are not the camp corpses who visually proclaim the idea of death and destruction, but vibrant people, several of whom seem to be asleep rather than dead."[17] Segal acknowledged that a monument which so pervasively reeks of death must ultimately be mitigated by life, "It's almost incredibly difficult to begin to deal with the fact of the Holocaust unless there is some celebration of life or some strong statement of the value of continuing life."[18] For this reason he felt it was essential:

> To make some kind of reference to the mental life of these people . . . who had been strongly connected with a compli-cated history—a history of spiritual invention—transcendent thought. This poverty stricken mass of dirt that was dead had this connection with an incredible amount of spiritual energy. This connection is what I was after. . . . It was quite important that this whole other aura take place . . . an intensely felt spiritual life.[19]

This duality between vitality and death is encompassed by the very nature of Segal's casting process, in which he effectively mummifies his models. Death is evoked, but ultimately life prevails.

The biblical allusions buried among the bodies enhance this life affirming message. The three stories illustrated include the *Akedah*, the Expulsion and the Crucifixion. The *Akedah* is depicted by an older man covering the eyes of a young boy who lies next to him with his hands bound behind his back. A naked woman lying on her back holding an apple is Eve; Adam lies next to her. More than one figure has his arms splayed, crucifix style. The meaning of *The Holocaust* does not depend on these biblical references; they are subtle and can be easily missed. Only with prolonged study of the work do they become apparent. Once recognized, they add a rich layer of metaphor.

Reference to the *Akedah* in a Holocaust work is a natural association for Jewish writers and artists.[20] Elie Wiesel has noted that Isaac is the original holocaust because in Hebrew the word sacrifice is associated with the word holocaust. Thus Isaac's near sacrifice is considered a paradigm of Jewish martyrdom.[21]

Inclusion can also be linked to Isaac. In Christian iconography, Isaac is considered a type for Jesus.[22] There are several similarities between Isaac's near sacrifice and Christ's death at Golgotha. Both were their father's only sons, and both were bound and led to death. Jesus carried the cross as Isaac carried the wood to his sacrifice altar. Both were to be sacrificed by their father, and both went willingly. For Christians, Isaac's near sacrifice, "was an instance of faith rewarded, a proof that souls trusting in divine mercy should have renewed and continued life, and an assurance that the course of safety lay in placing themselves in the hands of God."[23] In this context we are also reminded of Jesus' Jewish origins. More broadly, Segal's inclusion of both Isaac and Jesus reminds us that the Holocaust is not simply a Jewish tragedy, thus putting it in a universal perspective.

In *The Holocaust* Segal conflates life and death. Isaac, Eve and Christ are all examples of resurrection. According to certain Midrashim, Isaac was sacrificed and reborn. In Hebrew, Eve is *Chaya*, which means life. Jesus' own resurrection completes this triumvirate. Yet in *The Holocaust*, all are dead. Although Isaac was ultimately saved on Mount Moriah, here both father and son have perished. The same could be said of Jesus; here Segal has dashed any Messianic hopes. By losing their immortality Adam and Eve were given a second chance, yet here God has not been so merciful. This ambiguity between life and death enriches the meaning of *The Holocaust*, which embodies the circle of life. While death cannot be avoided, the figures evoke it without dwelling solely on it. When the figures are examined together in the context of the biblical allusions they comprise, they ultimately present a life affirming message.

NOTES

1. Jewish Museum/Art Resource, NY, U.S.A.; George Segal, The Holocaust, 1982. Plaster.

2. Segal's biblical scenes include The Expulsion, The Binding of Isaac, Lot and his Daughters, The Parting of Abraham and Ishmael and Jacob's Dream.

3. Ziva Amishai-Maisels, *Depiction and Interpretation. The Influence of the Holocaust on the Visual Arts* (Oxford: Pergamon Press, 1993), 57.

4. Ibid., 155.

5. George Segal, "George Segal," interview by Stephen Lewis, *Art out of Agony* (Montreal: Canadian Broadcasting, 1984), 111. For similar remarks see Segal, "Segal's Holocaust Memorial," interview by Matthew Baigell (South Brunswick, 18 March 1983), *Art in America* 71 (Summer 1983): 134.

6. Ibid., 112.

7. Ibid.

8. Segal in Baigell, 134.

9. Ibid., 136.

10. Ibid.

11. George Segal. Interview by author, 12 May 1995, South Brunswick, New Jersey, tape recording.

12. Ibid. See also Michael Brenson, "Why Segal Is Doing Holocaust Memorial," *New York Times*, 8 April 1983, C 16; Baigell, 136; and Lewis, 113-14.

13. George Segal. Interview by author, 12 May 1995.

14. Ibid.

15. Ibid.

16. Ibid.

17. See Amishai-Maisels, 90.

18. Doug Adams, "George Segal's *The Holocaust*: Biblical Subject Matter and God as Center," chap. in *Transcendence with the Human Body in Art* (New York: Crossroad, 1991), 38.

19. Ibid., 34.

20. See Amishai-Maisels.

21. "Then one day God decided once more to test [Abraham]. . . . Take your son and bring him to Me as an offering. The term used is *ola*, which means an offering that has been totally consumed, a holocaust." Elie Wiesel, *Messengers of God. Biblical Portraits and Legends* (New York: Random House, 1976), 71.

22. Jewish exegesis does not accept this notion of prefiguration.

23. Alison Moore Smith, "The Iconography of the Sacrifice of Isaac in Christian Art," *American Journal of Archaeology* 26 (1922): 159. The earliest surviving textual prefigurations are found in Galatians 3:16 and 4:21-31, as well as in Hebrews 11:17-19. See also Isabel Spejart van Woerden, "The Iconography of the Sacrifice of Abraham," *Vigilae Christianae* 15 (1961): 214-255.

(Re)Imagining Jews in Twentieth-Century American Literature

S. Lillian Kremer

Literary portraits of Jews in twentieth-century American literature exhibit radically divergent characteristics, largely dependent upon whether they issue from the pens of Gentiles or Jews. Christian writers often create Jewish characters based on anti-Semitic paradigms inherited from British literature. Physicality and greed are accentuated in shallow stereotypes, one dimensional figures void of Jewish historic memory, religious and cultural background. These characterizations attest to the authors' ignorance of Jewish life and bear little relationship to reality. In contrast, portraits rendered by Jewish writers evidence fully rounded characters reflecting a widely divergent Jewish history and multifaceted culture, protagonists who have escaped Russian pogroms and survived the Holocaust, the religious and the secular, capitalist and socialist, millionaire and pauper, sweatshop worker and university professor, intellectuals, professionals, laborers and businessmen, men and women assimilated in American society, yet responsive, either positively or negatively, to their Jewish identity,

I

Since the Diaspora, Jews have been negatively defined by others and, while it is painful, it is no surprise to find those images in Western literature, including our own and in our time, in canonical works by respected American writers. How does the negative image of the Jew find respectability in our literary culture? Our literary anti-Semites have adapted and transplanted the archetypes of British models—

Geoffrey Chaucer, William Shakespeare, and Charles Dickens. The triumvirate helped foster dominant Christian libels of the Jewish male as usurer and mutilator, and of the Jewish woman as seductive other, or in flattering portrayals, as apostate and betrayer of her own people.

Chaucer's Prioress tells of a little boy who so angered the Jews by singing the praises of the Virgin Mary that their community hired a killer, who cut the child's throat. Shakespeare continues and elaborates the myth of the knife-wielding usurious Jew. The title character of *The Merchant of Venice*, the vengeful Shylock, is a vulgar caricature of the Talmudic mind attracted to legalism rather than the spirit of law. The formulaic literary pattern requires that the Jew be dehumanized prior to his punishment. The Snake enters the hearts of Jews in Chaucer, and Shylock is not merely compared to, but is a dog. Chaucer's Jews are tortured and then killed; Shakespeare's proud Jew is thoroughly humbled and demeaned before suffering conversion to Christianity at peril to his life, while his treacherous daughter, Jessica, is presented favorably because she conspires with Christians against her father. In the nineteenth century, Dickens reinforced the Medieval and Renaissance anti-Semitic models of the money-loving Jew in the persona of Fagin and added the notion of the Jew as corrupter of children whom he educates into thievery to satisfy his greed.

Despite a growing Jewish population in America, one that doubled in the 1880s and again in the 1890s, the image of the Jew in our national literature remained the province of non-Jews. Writers ignorant of Jewish life, history, and civilization furthered the European defamation of Jew as usurer, avenger, and evil incarnate. While isolated affirmative portrayals appear in fiction by non-Jews, principally the biblical Israelite of nineteenth-century American writing, and contemporary Jews in the work of Hutchins Hapgood and Sinclair Lewis, the spirit of malevolence toward Jews continued to dominate. When Jews appeared in this fiction, they were presented in a manner that would cheer the hearts of a Streicher or Goebbels. Physically repulsive and morally unscrupulous, the characters were rapacious, social pariahs and cultural polluters. Consider the dehumanized portrait of a Polish Jew in Frank Norris's naturalistic novel, *McTeague*, which appeared in the last year of the nineteenth-century. Reminiscent of *Oliver Twist's* Fagin, Zerkow is the hideous incarnation of Jewish greed:

> He had the thin, eager, cat-like lips of the covetous; eyes that
> had grown keen as those of a lynx from long searching amidst

muck and debris; and claw-like prehensible fingers—fingers of a man who accumulates but never disburses. It is impossible to look at Zerkow and not know instantly that greed—inordinate, insatiable greed—was the dominant passion of the man. He was the Man with the Rake, groping hourly in the muckheap of the city for gold, for gold, for gold. It was his dream, his passion; at every instant he seemed to feel the generous solid weight of the crude fat metal in his palms. The glint of it was constantly in his eyes; the jangle of it sang forever in his ears as the jangling of cymbals.[1]

The early years of the twentieth-century and even the decades of the twenties and thirties are no better for the literary image of the Jew. The art dealer whom Adam Verver and Charlotte Stant visit in *The Golden Bowl* is "remarkably genial, a positively lustrous young man," but when they meet his family, Henry James offers readers the genteel version of the Jewish stereotype as oriental and exotic. Charlotte's impression of his eleven children is one of indistinguishable "little brown clear faces, yet with such impersonal old eyes astride of such impersonal old noses." She perceives the adult family members as "fat ear-ringed aunts, and the glossy, cockneyfied, familiar uncles." The unnamed Jewish shopowner—referred to contemptuously as "the little swindling Jew"—knows that the bowl is flawed but would have sold it to Charlotte and the prince had not the prince detected the crack. He later sells the golden bowl at an exorbitant price to the unsuspecting Maggie Verver. When he goes to Maggie's home to set matters right, James explains, "the vendor of the golden bowl had acted on a scruple rare enough in vendors of any class, and almost unprecedented in the thrifty children of Israel."[2] Louis Harap cogently argued that "the symbolic function of the golden bowl as representing flawed human behavior is mediated by a Jew, thus rendering him an agency for dubious moral relations. He is subtly implicated in the commission of evil."[3]

With the advent of modern banking in America that included the system of borrowing for interest, the usury theme of Christian anti-Semitic literature generally gave way (aside from a few diehards like Ezra Pound) to characterizing Jews as practitioners of dubious business methods; personal unattractiveness demonstrated by repulsive physical appearance and social gaucherie; and, in a chilling herald of Nazi rhetoric, as cultural polluters. Scott Fitzgerald's Anthony Patch in *The*

Beautiful and Damned describes Jewish businessmen as having "intent eyes—eyes gleaming with suspicion, with pride, with clarity, with cupidity, with comprehension." He is upset by the "upward creep of this people—the little stores growing, expanding, consolidating, moving, watched over with hawk's eyes. . . ."[4] His rival is a Jew, whose nostrils are "overwide," who is "overdressed," and who speaks in an apparently undeserved assured manner. Edith Wharton adored Meyer Wolfsheim of *The Great Gatsby* as that "perfect Jew."[5] Her own pushy little Jew, Rosedale in *The House of Mirth*, is another anti-Semitic caricature of the social upstart. He is introduced as "a small, flat-nosed Jew [who] raised his large head and regarded me with two fine growths of hair which luxuriated in either nostril," "covered Gatsby with his expressive nose," "flashed" his nose "indignantly," and "turned his nostrils . . . to me in an interested way." Similarly, his speech is ridiculed with references to Oxford University as "Oggsford College" and to his interest in forming a "business gonnegtion."[6] Among other Gentile jabs at Jewish noses are Willa Cather's Louis Marcellus of *The Professor's House* whose face betrayed nothing Semitic, except his nose "that took the lead. . . . It grew out of his face . . . like a vigorous oak tree growing out of a hillside."[7] Dos Passos's Harry Goldweiser, the curve of whose nose "merges directly into the curve of his bald forehead," and his Mr. Goldstein who is described as "a larvashaped man with a hooked nose a little crooked in a gray face, behind which pink attentive ears stood out unexpectedly." The grotesque portrait is completed with reference to his "suspicious screwedup eyes." Both Jews are further stereotyped by the common "gold" prefix in their names. Dos Passos's presentation of other Jewish characters includes mockery of their immigrant accents and broken English. Uncle Jeff takes the occasion of a dinner party in *Manhattan Transfer* to denounce the impact of the newcomers: "New York is no longer what it used to be. . . . City's overrun with kikes. . . . In ten years a Christian won't be able to make a living."[8]

More fully developed than the odd beggar or gangster is Hemingway's anti-Semitic portrait of Robert Cohn in *The Sun Also Rises*. He is socially unattractive because he is a Jew, hardly a man in Hemingway's macho universe since he is bored by bull-fighting. Cohen is condemned by the novel's protagonist, Jake Barnes, for his "hard, Jewish, stubborn streak," his "air of superior knowledge" so "superior and Jewish."[9] A far cry from the vulgar infiltrators of Edith Wharton's world, Cohn, son of a wealthy assimilated family with elite Princeton credentials, is nevertheless unwelcome in the company of less well educated and financially privileged old-stock Americans and Britons who treat him as an intruder and finally reject him. Fellow novelist Thomas Wolfe writes contemptuously, in *The Web and the Rock* and in *You Can't Go Home Again*, of self-assured Jewish women, of bejeweled women with melon breasts; of hawk-beaked Jewish men manipulating the world of wealth and power from behind the scenes.

Ezra Pound returns to the medieval calumny of the Jew as usurer and the chief image of the enemy, "the Yid . . . the essential evil of all social life."[10] His "poetic" descriptors of Jews as "rats," "bedbugs," "vermin," "worms," and "parasites" is contemporary, however, in its mimicry of Nazi racist rhetoric. In accord with his mentor, T.S. Eliot, whom generations of American students have been taught to venerate in literature classes, he railed, in his book *After Strange Gods*, against "excessive tolerance" warning that "reasons of race and religion combine to make a large number of free-thinking Jews undesirable" in the ideal Christian commonwealth.[11] Is it any wonder that when the Jew appears in Eliot's poetry, it is in a low animal context: "The rats are underneath the piles./ The jew is underneath the lot. . . ." [12]Is it any wonder that Eliot portrays the Jew as the corrupter of Christian culture? Cultural pollution of a similar ilk is expressed by Katherine Anne Porter in an assault in a *Harper's* article accusing writers of whom she disapproves, "with headquarters in New York," of "a deadly mixture of academic, guttersnipe, gangster, fake-Yiddish, and dull old wornout dirty words—an appalling bankruptcy in language, as if they hate English and are trying to destroy it along with all other living things they touch."[13] For these writers, the Jew is drawn not only in the Shylock/Fagin mode, but as Louis Harap observes, as "the symbol of modern social disintegration."[14]

Even in later decades, in the post-Holocaust period and into the nineties, it is difficult to find admirable and/or culturally credible Jewish characters fashioned by gentile writers. John Updike's Jewish American novelist, Henry Beck, while not an anti-Semitic caricature from the Eliot-Pound mold, is void of historic memory and is, in Cynthia Ozick's words, "theologically hollow." For Ozick, "Beck-as-Jew has no existence."[15] Beck's Jewish nose and Jewish hair are not attached to a Jewish head. Rather, he is Updike's version of the New York Jewish Intellectual shaped by literary modernism and *The Partisan Review*, alienated from the main currents of American society and no longer at ease in Jewish society; Updike's vehicle for announcing the end of the heyday of Jewish American writing.[16] More recent entries into the ranks of literary anti-Semites, and among the most visceral, are African-American writers. In their fictions, the Jew is not the NAACP lawyer or civil rights activist who championed and contributed more than any other white group to improving the lot of African Americans, but is presented as exploiter and oppressor. Representative of this "black rage," is Imamu Amiri Baraka (LeRoi Jones) who writes in "On Black Art":

> We want poems
> like fists beating niggers out of Jocks
> or dagger poems in the slimmy bellies
> of the owner-jews. . . .

In "For Tom Postell, Dead Black Poet," he presents his version of Hitler's Final Solution and a threat of more violence against Jews:

> Smile, jew. Dance, jew. . . . I got something for you, . . . this thing goes pulsating through black everything universal meaning. I got the extermination blues, jewboys. I got the hitler syndrome figured. . . . So come for the rent, jewboys, . . . or sit in the courts handing down yr judgments, still I got something for you, gonna give it to my brothers, so they'll know what your whole story is, then one day, jewboys, we all, even my wig-wearing mother gonna put it on you all at once.[17]

II

Leslie Fiedler notes in "The Jew in the American Novel," "one of the problems of the practicing Jewish American novelist arises from his need to create his protagonists not only out of the life he knows, but *against* the literature on which he, and his readers, have been nurtured."[18] This two-fold obligation has been addressed admirably by a significant number of Jewish American authors writing after World War II. At last, a group of American writers brought authentic Jewish characters to national attention in fiction that focused not on the Jew's nose but on the Jew's mind and character, that introduced characters shaped by a distinctive history and culture. These novels and short stories evidenced the particularity of Jewish languages, history, religious philosophy and traditions. Immigration, assimilation/acculturation, and rediscovery of Judaism and Jewish community are among the recurrent contextual frames privileged in American Jewish fiction.

An important precursor of themes and characters in postwar Jewish American fiction that fully contextualized Jewish characters was Abraham Cahan's classic immigration novel, *The Rise of David Levinsky*[19] (1917). Lauded by Isaac Rosenfeld as "one of the best fictional studies of the Jewish character in English,"[20] Cahan's novel recounts the transformation of the protagonist from poor Russian Talmud student to American capitalist. It is an engaging saga of a character shaped by the historic and economic forces Jewish American immigrants encountered. Unlike the one-dimensional Zerkows and Cohns, Levinsky's life and sensibility are related to experiences common to many Jewish immigrants and are politically, religiously, and economically contextualized. A member of a detested minority, Levinsky is the victim of pogroms in Czarist Russia; he is the naive immigrant at the mercy of exploitative American and immigrant businessmen and the beneficiary of charitable Jews. Celebrated in his own community for his Talmudic intellect, Levinsky applies himself to learning English and business as means for assimilating into American society. In the land of opportunity, Levinsky moves from bewildered peddler to millionaire, from exploited employee to exploitative employer, from socialist sympathizer to union antagonist.

A committed socialist, Cahan was critical of the capitalist, but his portrait of Levinsky is free of anti-Semitism. In the anti-Semitic caricature of Zerkow as the incarnation of greed, Norris presented his readers with a repulsive one-dimensional figure. Although Cahan, disapproves of his protagonist's business practices, he depicts a complex figure who engages readers on several levels and whose psycho/social motivation he explores painstakingly. Readers attend with interest as they follow Levinsky wrenching himself from Old World traditions and values to accommodate American practices, subjugating all questions of ideals and ethics to the ethos of success, becoming a cynic when he discovers the discrepancy between the American ideals taught in night school and the American reality learned in ward politics, in railroad dinning cars, and in garment industry sweatshops.

More significant than Levinsky's economic transformation is his religious and intellectual metamorphosis from Talmudist to Spencerian Darwinist. Cahan traces David's development from bright *cheder*

(Hebrew school) and pious Talmud student, to secret admirer of Russian literature, to temporary apostate harboring a nostalgic yearning for piety, to avid reader of British classics and Spencer's social Darwinism, and finally, in an ironic turnabout, to disaffected business tycoon and secret admirer of religious orthodoxy. He craves a more spiritually satisfying life and envies his distinguished compatriots in science, music, and literature. Through David Levinsky's character, Cahan captured the duality of the Jewish American immigrant experience. He introduced the theme that would dominate later Jewish American fiction: the tension between the sacred and the profane, between Jewish morality and American materialism.

Further evidence of historically contextualized portraits in fiction by Jewish Americans are Holocaust survivors, immigrants of a vastly different sort from those in Cahan's world, who are frequent centers of consciousness in postwar fiction. Unlike earlier immigrants who arrived in this country full of hope, eager to assimilate to American life, joyous despite their poverty, Edward Lewis Wallant's Sol Nazerman,[21] Saul Bellow's Arthur Sammler,[22] I. B. Singer's Herman Broder,[23] Susan Fromberg Schaeffer's Anya Savikin,[24] and Cynthia Ozick's Rosa Lublin[25] are deeply wounded, suffering the aftereffects of physical and psychological battering in ghettos and concentration camps, the anxiety associated with being fugitives in Nazi-occupied Europe, and adjusting to postwar life bereft of family and friends. The economic ambition of pre-Holocaust immigrants is often absent in these Holocaust survivors who are disinterested in the material beyond mere sustenance. The desire to assimilate into American society, so typical of earlier immigrants, is supplanted by the tendency to remain apart, to live in survivor enclaves where others will understand the hell they have experienced. The fiction focuses emphatically on survivors plagued by Holocaust events still intruding into their lives; survivors reliving wartime horrors in daytime memories and nighttime dreams; experiencing guilt, disturbances of self-image, professional and educational limitations, and social alienation. Sol Nazerman hides in his pawnbroker's cage unsuccessfully trying to repress memories of Holocaust atrocities suffered by his family and anesthetize himself against feeling; Anya Savikin and Rosa Lublin inhabit a small apartment and hotel room respectively and work in neighborhood antique shops, Anya hearing the voices of her beloved parents beckoning her, and Rosa imagining lives for her infant daughter who was hurled against an electrified concentration camp fence. Well-educated and members of the professions before the war, their careers have been truncated. These Jews bring to the reader's attention, not the anti-Semitic literary stereotype of the Jew as mythic slasher or Christ-killer, but the reality of Jew as victim of Christians, and the historic reality of Christians as assassins of Jews.

Unlike the psychiatric literature which is devoted to survivors who remain traumatized by their Holocaust experiences, Jewish American Holocaust fiction includes a more balanced view of survivorship. The characters include those who are well-adjusted to contemporary life and are dedicated to bearing witness and preserving Judaism and the Jewish people. Illustrative of this pattern are Chaim Potok's rabbis and yeshiva teachers[26] and Cynthia Ozick's Buchenwald survivor rabbi in "Bloodshed," who counters the nihilism of an apostate by making him the subject of a Hasidic exemplum revealing the theological and human implications of the Holocaust;[27] her *midrash*-designing logician and her advocate of a dual Western and Hebraic school curriculum in *The Cannibal Galaxy.*[28] These figures resist full assimilation, not because they are broken, but because they are engaged in a mission to preserve Jewish traditions, language, history, and morality. Other survivors in this literature are cast as moral mentors to lapsed American Jews as are Bellow's Arthur Sammler, Bernard Malamud's comic mentor, Suskind, and Philip Roth's yeshiva head in "Eli, The Fanatic."[29] Arthur Cohen's survivors of In the Days of Simon Stern,[30] are dramatized, as are I. B. Singer's, Cynthia Ozick's, and Elie Wiesel's, posing theological and ethical questions, issuing moral commentary, and evidencing commitment to a collective Jewish future. Cohen's survivors are rescued by an American Jew who envisions and builds a fortress to safeguard a Holocaust remnant from assimilation and anti-Semitism. Affirming the restorative and regenerative approaches to Holocaust tragedy espoused by theologian Emil Fackenheim, Cohen's Jews, like Ozick's rabbis and Chaim Potok's survivor-scholars, respond to Holocaust loss by undertaking a major project of repair to strengthen Judaism and Jewry. Similarly, Marge Piercy's Jacqueline Levy-Monot is transmogrified by the Holocaust from ardent supporter of France to committed Zionist.[31]

The fictional American-born Jew is also transformed by the Holocaust. George Steiner observed:

> The idea that Jews everywhere have been maimed by the
> European catastrophe, that the massacre has left all who

survived (even if they were nowhere near the actual scene) off balance, as does the tearing of a limb, is one which American Jews can understand in an intellectual sense.[32]

Ozick's Enoch Vand, an American recorder of Holocaust history, the moral register in her magnificent first novel, *Trust*, adopts the Lurianic Hasidic belief in man's restorative task in history. Beyond his compulsion to bear witness to the Holocaust, Vand seeks to reinvigorate the Jewish people and to rebuild Judaism, and he commits himself to prayer and study. Guided by a Holocaust survivor, he learns Hebrew; studies the Bible, the Talmud, and *Ethics of the Fathers*.[33] The wives of Holocaust survivors in Norma Rosen's fiction share their husbands' pain, try to protect their children from the trauma associated with second generation suffering, occasionally reject God and religion, and confront Germans in imagined and real encounters.[34] Potok's yeshiva student, Reuven Malter, helps prepare guns for transport to the nascent Jewish state attacked by five Arab nations,and his blocked artist Asher Lev resumes successful work only after he begins to paint Holocaust themes.[35] Bellow's American victim of anti-Semitism, Asa Leventhal, reacts to a series of anti-Semitic insults with a reference to the enormity of Holocaust losses;[36] his historian, Moses Herzog, repeatedly visits the Warsaw Ghetto, "the stones still smelling of war-time murders;"[37] and his Billy Rose plays a central role in an elaborate plot to smuggle Jews out of Europe during the Holocaust.[38] In the course of imagining Anne Frank, Roth's young Nathan Zuckerman considers her Holocaust history in *The Ghost Writer*[39] and listens, as a mature writer in *Operation Shylock*, to the Holocaust testimony of Aharon Appelfeld and another survivor.[40]

Between the poles of the early twentieth-century immigrant and the mid-century Holocaust survivor, the fictional Jew is most frequently portrayed as an assimilated, acculturated American with Jewish sensibilities variously intact. Michael Gold's proletarian novel, *Jews Without Money*, captures the ambiance of Jewish socialists and secular utopians, a significant segment of Jewish society, albeit one distanced from traditional Jewish life. Gold focuses on growing up amid the poverty and blighted conditions of New York's Lower East Side to chronicle the passage of a man from Judaism to Communism. The pattern, followed by other Jewish leftists, is to characterize "Jewish nationalism" and Judaism as reactionary, while transferring traditional Jewish Messianic longing to secular messianism in the form of Marxism and demonstrating that the economic hardships of lower class Jews was inextricably linked to the fate of all exploited workers in capitalist societies.[41] Similar religiously estranged yet culturally aligned Jews appear in Tillie Olsen's widely anthologized story, "Tell Me a Riddle." The elderly couple of this tale is shaped by Yiddish socialism, seeking justice, an end to discrimination and oppression on a universal rather than a national scale.[42] Olsen conceived of Eva and David as "a celebration of fervent Jewish revolutionaries during the early years of the century and of a time of boundless hopes and richly humanist fervor."[43] The characters' Yiddish-inflected speech, their interest in Russian and Yiddish writers, and their workers' community all suggest the experience of Jewish socialists. Further removed from Jewish values than the socialists are the Jewish self-haters, characters who have responded to a history of persecution and anti-Semitism by distancing themselves from Judaism and Jewish community, characters such as Malamud's ironic self-invented Freeman in "Lady of the Lake,"[44] who travels to Europe to learn something about history while steadfastly denying his own; Roth's self-denying Woodenton suburbanites in "Eli, the Fanatic"; and Portnoy lusting after *shiksas*.[45]

More prominent in fiction than the self-haters and socialists are assimilated characters who remain comfortable with their ethnic identities. Bellow's cerebral picaro, Augie March, is as much at home in Chicago as Huck Finn was on the banks of the Mississippi, yet he is attuned to religious tradition when he encounters it.[46] Moses Herzog, intellectual *schlemiel*, historian of ideas, is at home in the great books and intellectual controversies of the modern era, yet, he recites Hebrew prayer and is nostalgic for the ethnic family life of his immigrant forebears as is his scientific counterpart, Dr. Samuel Braun of "The Old System."[47] Philip Roth's thoroughly American young novelist, Nathan Zuckerman, is attracted to the work of an elder Jewish writer both for its stylistic perfection and heroes who "seemed to say something new and wrenching to Gentiles about Jews, and to Jews about themselves" because of "the feelings of kinship that his stories had revived . . . for our own largely Americanized clan, moneyless immigrant shopkeepers to begin with, who carried on a shtetl life ten minutes walk from the pillared banks and gargoyled cathedrals of downtown Newark; . . . for our pious, unknown ancestors, . . . [and] the sense given by such little stories of saying so much."[48] While the mid and late century literature contains multivaried Jewish figures, most prominent in the second half of the twentieth century are Malamud's Jew as suffering Everyman in conjunction with his use of Jewishness as a metaphor of the central drama of the human condition; Bellow's dangling man, prototype of the alienated modern and his alterity, the righteous Jew, moral guide to his neighbors, exemplified in Bellow's holy sinners; Roth's literature professors and writers, inheritors of the Western literary tradition; and Ozick's Judaically literate Jews.

With the exhaustion of the immigrant and assimilationist themes, a growing number of writers secularized and modernized stock characters from the rich repertoire of Yiddish fiction, drama, and folklore, incorporated legendary and historic Jewish figures, and broadened the Jewish context of the narrative to include protagonists in European and Israeli contexts as well as American Jews grappling with theological questions. Representative of the fictionalized versions of historic figures playing a role in twentieth-century traumatic Jewish experience are Malamud's fixer and Leslie Epstein's enigmatic Lodz ghetto leader. Malamud's title character of *The Fixer*, Yakov Bok, brutalized in Czarist Russian jails on trumped up ritual murder charges is based on Mendel Beleis, accused of ritual murder, tried and eventually acquitted after being subjected to horrendous prison conditions.[49] Leslie Epstein created a pastiche from documentary evidence and invention to delineate the tragic career of Chaim Rumkowski for his controversial Holocaust novel, *King of the Jews*.[50] Alternatively, Curt Leviant and Melvin Bukiet revive eastern European shtetl life. In an enchanting metafiction in the *midrashic* mode, Leviant invents stories for Nachman of Bratslav, a Hasidic *tzaddik* and grandson of the founder of Hasidism, who believes that God has chosen him for messianic assumption.[51] Melvin Bukiet's splendid stories of childhood in a pre-Holocaust Polish shtetl, *Stories of an Imaginary Childhood*,[52] are reminiscent of the world of Scholom Aleichem in their re-creation of the lost world of European Jewry and the life that might have been Bukiet's had his parents remained in Europe.

Influential and dazzling mythic counterpoints to fictional characters who are historically and sociologically rooted, are culturally rooted direct descendants of stock types in Yiddish literature and folklore, readily recognizable *schlemiels, schnorrers, schadchans,* and *tzaddikim*. Malamud's rendition of Pinye Salzman in "The Magic Barrel" is a straightforward and masterful appropriation of the *schadchan* figure and a less obvious, but nonetheless brilliant, borrowing of the *lamed vov tzaddik*, the hidden saint, for the spiritual facilitator of a modern religious allegory cast as love story.[53] Saul Bellow's *Seize the Day*, is a highly allusive spiritual allegory set in the *Yom Kippur* season, a *tour de force* incorporating transmogrified composite Yiddish character constructs. The tale's deceptively simple plot encompasses a day in the life of Tommy Wilhelm, an ordinary middle aged man, who visits his father seeking emotional and financial assistance in coping with a series of personal and business failures. Rebuffed, he turns to Dr. Tamkin, who willingly assumes the roles of emotional healer and financial consultant. As a traditional *schlemiel*, Tommy, is an awkward bungler, behaving in a foolhardy manner, accumulating mishaps as he drifts through life. College dropout, failed actor, unemployed salesman, separated from his wife and children, estranged from his mistress, Tommy's life has epitomized the *schlemiel* character as he repeatedly sabotages his chances for success and happiness. Dr. Tamkin, the enigmatic holy conman, is an amalgam of secular and contradictory ethnic roles. Consistent with the contemporary American setting, Bellow secularizes Tamkin as psychologist and financial advisor. However, the key to his character lies in Bellow's exquisite overlay of folkloric *schnorrer* with multiple versions of the *tzaddik*, including the *lamed vov tzaddik* allowing Tamkin to hide behind a mask of boorishness to prepare his candidate for spiritual recovery. Claiming to be "a radical in the [psychiatric] profession,"[54] Tamkin posits the views of the Hasidic *tzaddik*, asserting that he belongs to humanity, that he shares the wounds and suffering of his patients, and that charitable behavior toward others is its own reward. He instructs via parable and anecdote rather than modern psychiatric clinical method and evidences more concern for his client's ethical conduct than do psychologists, advising Tommy to live a holy life. Complicating Tamkin's role even further is Bellow's superb additional union of historic rivals in Tamkin's character. More compelling than the adaptation of the *schnorrer* is Bellow's fusion of the Hasidic venerated saint with the incompetent fraud of opposing orthodox and progressive hermeneutics, the corrupt wonder-working charlatan of anti-Hasidic *maskil* satire, borrowed from Joseph Perl's *Megillah Temirim*, (*Revealer of Secrets*). This adroit blending of Yiddish character types and personas complicates Tamkin's portrait, accounts for his comedic villainy and his detractors' arguments regarding his professional credentials and ethics.[55]

Concomitant with the introduction of Yiddish character constructs is the Americanization of *dos kleine menshele*, the common man of Yiddish literature, and elevation of the intellectual as literary hero. As a result of centuries of dispersion, persecution, and powerlessness, Yiddish culture and literature tended to devalue the heroic figure of Western literature, who was often given to cruelty as well as courage. Instead, Jewish writing validates the ordinary person, struggling with the pressures of daily life. In opposition to the western ideal of physical heroism, exemplified by the knight given to brutality as well as bravery, the dragon-slayer, and the bull-fighter, the respected figures of Jewish writing are the common man, the intellectual, the moral advocate, any person committed to the code of *menshlichkayt*, which Irving Howe defined as "a readiness to live for ideals beyond the clamor of self, a sense of plebeian fraternity, an ability to forge a community of moral order even while remaining subject to a society of social disorder, and a persuasion that human existence is a deeply serious matter for which all of us are finally accountable."[56]

Complementing the preference for the ordinary over the heroic is the preference for the thinking man to the man of action who wins approval in American literature. Reflective of the high value placed on reason and intellect that pervades Judaism, Jewish American literature is populated to a large degree by smart and wrong-headed intellectuals. Beginning with David Levinsky, who mourns his lost formal education, yet studies independently, the literature is rich with thinkers: Wallant's pawnbroker is a former philosophy professor; Potok's protagonists are students, teachers, and Bible scholars; Ozick's are lawyers, mathematicians, teachers, scholars; Roth's are professors of literature and creative writers, and Bellow's fictional universe is dominated by intellectuals. Representative is the historian of ideas, Moses Herzog, a portrait of man thinking about the conditions of modernity. He is a letter-writer to the living and the dead, seeker of an intellectual position responsive to the complexity of the reality he perceives, acutely aware by novel's end of the value and limits of the intellect. Aside from Wallant's pawnbroker, these Jews are fully assimilated Americans, teaching in our universities, writing books, interpreting American ideas, but doing so from the special vantage point of an older cultural heritage and a recent post-Holocaust consciousness, thinkers fully cognizant of the horrors of modernity, yet rejecting wasteland nihilism to privilege a Judaic affirmative stance.

Just as dense historic/cultural components distinguish Jewish characters of Jewish and gentile writers, so does the degree to which religion is identified as a component of the character's sensibility. As Jewish American writers have become accepted in the American literary establishment, and as they have less frequently, as Ruth Wisse observes, had to "defend themselves from real or imagined charges of parochialism," they have introduced religious themes embodied in characters whose lives culminate in spiritual return following a lapsed period and characters who are Jewishly educated and religiously observant throughout their lives. Jewish penitents and spiritual questers have, in recent years, succeeded immigrant and de-Judaized Jews as privileged fictional characters. Central to the development of these characters is the Jewish principle of t'shuvah, the idea of turning to God for redemption that underlies the longing for messianic salvation transmitted as moral and spiritual restoration in the literature. Illustrative are Malamud's tales of moral turning such as Leo Finkle of "The Magic Barrel" who realizes, through the machinations of an unlikely spiritual guide, that except for his parents, he has never loved anyone; that he has even come to God, not because he loved Him, but because he did not. After terrible suffering following his recognition, he seeks the marriage broker he earlier scorned and selects the least likely prospect to woo, precisely because he sees suffering in her eyes and wants to be of service, "to convert her to goodness, himself to God."[57] Cynthia Ozick's Puttermesser stories resonate with repair and redemptive themes and exemplify an organic integration of Jewish principles of tikkun (repair) and t'shuvah (redemption) to enhance the portrait of contemporary moral questers.

Among characters fashioned in the penitent mold (baal t'shuvah) are Anne Roiphe's young woman in Lovingkindness,[58] daughter of a disapproving assimilated feminist, who emigrates to Israel where she joins a fundamentalist settlement and undertakes a religiously disciplined life in flight from self-indulgence and self-destruction of her American existence, just as Nathan Zuckerman's brother in The Counterlife abandons sexual dissipation and adultery to embrace redemptive piety and political commitment in Israel.[59] Bleilip, the lapsed Jew of Cynthia Ozick's "Bloodshed," arrives at a Hasidic colony in scorn, but realizes that he had unconsciously come "for a glimpse of the effect of the rebbe [the Hasidic spiritual leader]" and senses that "the day . . . felt full of miracles." The suicidal skeptic is actually metamorphosed into the identity he had earlier misappropriated when he identified himself to the believers as "a Jew. Like yourselves. One of you."[60] Two among I.B. Singer's Holocaust survivors, Herman

Broder of *Enemies, A Love Story* and Joseph Shapiro of *The Penitent*,[61] the first at the early stages of contrition and spiritual return and the second who attains restoration by asserting his Jewish identity and returning to Torah Judaism, are vivid examples of the *baal t'shuvah* in American fiction.

Another manifestation of Jewish American writers' confidence is an affirmative stance toward ethnicity in contrast to the immigrant generation writers' promotion of total assimilation. Roth's characters illustrate this phenomenon effectively. In contrast to Portnoy's repudiation of ethnic values and community is return to community by the mature Zuckerman at the end of *The Counterlife* and by Philip in the self-reflexive *Deception*. Armed with new comprehension of Jewish community following his Israeli sojourn and his exposure to genteel British anti-Semitism, Zuckerman insists at the conclusion of *The Counterlife* that his son, by a Christian wife, will be circumcised "because there is an us."[62] Similarly, Roth's next writer-protagonist, Philip, of *Deception*, flees England to return to New York in order to live among unabashed Jews, exhibiting a revitalized connection to Jewish community.[63] These Jewish American writers appear to be drawing their literary energies from a rediscovery of ethnic sources which situates them comfortably in the larger national interest in ethnicity.

Just as vibrant Jewish American literature emerged from the immigration and assimilationist experiences in the fictions of Bellow, Malamud, and Roth, so too has a strong new trend emerged based on characters' discovery of or return to Jewish life. Led and influenced by Cynthia Ozick, this movement also claims Chaim Potok, Hugh Nissenson, Arthur Cohn and, more recently, able younger writers such as Nessa Rapoport and Allegra Goodman. For these authors Yiddishkeit and Jewish education is the donée of their characters. They feel no need to introduce the pious as exotics or penitents traumatically motivated to religiosity. In contrast to immigrant Jewish American writers like Abraham Cahan and Anzia Yezierska, whose protagonists' goals were assimilation at any cost, the religiously committed characters of these assimilated authors lead distinctively Jewish lives. They assert the worth of life lived according to Jewish values and religious law, even when that means a measure of separation from the larger society. A departure from sociologically textured fictional Jews, these characters are products of Judaically educated, confident writers. The Jewishly illiterate characters of Bellow, Malamud, and Roth have

been succeeded by characters steeped in Jewish learning, characters who
regularly quote Torah and Talmud in the original languages and opine
on the sages' commentaries and *midrashim*. Representative of
religiously oriented and educated characters are Chaim Potok's young
rabbinic students dramatized analyzing Talmud and studying cabbalah;
Ozick's Puttermesser, whose passion for Judaic ethics is derived from
classic Jewish texts from which she discerns a civilization, a value
system, a distinctive culture, and forges her link to the history of the
Jews;[64] Hester Lilt, who fashions her lectures on the Akiva model,
and Joseph Brill, fabricator of a dual western and Judaic school
curriculum, both of *The Cannibal Galaxy*; and Enoch Vand of *Trust*,
who begins to study sacred texts in his maturity.

Younger writers educated in Jewish orthodoxy from childhood,
Allegra Goodman, Rebecca Goldstein, and Nessa Rapoport, writers
who are critical insiders rather than alienated outsiders, confidently
present Jewish culture as the focus of their characters' lives, allude to
classic Jewish texts and infuse them into their American fictions. Like
Ozick's characters, who are equally at ease in Western and Hebraic
culture, Allegra Goodman's universe is totally immersed in Jewish
sensibility, acculturation and Orthodoxy. A case in point is the pious,
ritually observant Shavian scholar, Cecil Birnbaum, equally adept as a
scholar of British literature and as a *baal koreh*, reader of the Torah
service. Indicative of the change in Jewish American literature is the
contrast between Malamud's Yiddish speakers, designated by inverted
sentence structure, and Allegra Goodman's Hawaiian Jews who speak
mamaloshen, whose English sentences are unapologetically peppered by
transliterated Yiddish and Hebrew as well as Hawaiian terms; her
women who keep kosher kitchens; young parents who send their
children to orthodox day schools; intellectuals who debate *halakhah*
(religious law); poets who write in Hebrew and English; Judaic scholars
in conference settings; rabbis and congregants in synagogue politics;
traditional women content to worship behind the *mechitzah* (the
partition separating men's and women's sections in an Orthodox
synagogue) and feminists demanding an equal role in the conduct of
religious services.

Increased attention to Jewish tradition and liturgy has emerged as
a dominant theme in the work of Jewish feminists who are composing
new texts as they claim a place in what had been exclusive male
territory. Cathy Davidson lauds E.M. Broner for "finding new forms
for fiction . . . [that] encompass a radical feminist reordering of social

and fictional hierarchies, . . . [for] the way in which she employs an inheritance of Yiddish and Hebrew themes and tones in an experimental fictional mode that celebrates the female hero."[65] Echoing the rebellious voice of Anzia Yezierska, for whom the patriarchal hierarchy was oppressive and exclusive, but reaching beyond Yezierska to constructive and creative confrontation and engagement, Broner refashions Judaism in a feminist mode, writing novels which move from secular feminism to feminist Judaism. Illustrative is *A Weave of Women* chronicling a feminist vision of a utopia in Israel, women creating their own feminist liturgy with attendant ceremonial literature and myth. Broner offers a Jewish feminist declaration of independence from the constraints of Jewish patriarchy. Her women live communally in Israel and create feminist Jewish ritual, voice and action where there had been silence and passivity. Their rituals parallel, but are distinguished from traditional rituals in order to demonstrate women's Jewish cultural identity and authenticity. The new liturgy is a celebration of women's lives and a contribution to a dynamic, vibrant Judaism.[66]

III

A more startling transformation than that of the Jewish male in twentieth-century American fiction has been the representation of the Jewish woman. While Jewish men have been presented in the variety and fullness of their lives, Jewish women have received short shrift by Jewish men. Like Jewish men in fiction by Gentiles, Jewish women in fiction by Jewish American men are often little more than caricatures. Unlike the admiration evident in traditional Yiddish literature for forceful, assertive, highly verbal, clever Jewish women who conducted the family business and thereby freed men to devote themselves to study and worship, Jewish American literature written by the sons of assertive women often compared them unfavorably with restrained, docile, polite, 'real' American, gentile women. The Jewish mother is often transformed from Yiddish literature's self-sacrificial enabler to American literature's selfish, domineering, guilt-inducing castrator of the men and boys in her family. In Henry Roth's atypical masterpiece, *Call It Sleep*,[67] Genya Schearl is the beloved *yiddishe mama* in the tradition of Yiddish literature, an immigrant woman with great reserves of strength, providing love and security for her sensitive, intelligent, terrified son and psychotic husband. More often, American men caricature Jewish mothers as pathologically dominating, infantalizing and emasculating their husbands and sons. Philip Roth's Sophie Portnoy, the apotheosis of the "smothering mother," is obsessed with controlling every aspect of her son's life, from the food he imbibes to the matter that he eliminates. Similarly subject to the barb of male invective is the daughter of the Jewish mother who has come to be known as the "Jewish American Princess." She is satirized as materialistic and manipulative, a resurgence of the old anti-Semitic stereotype of the Jew in love with money, overlaid with misogyny. Philip Roth comes to mind once more as the writer perfecting the type in the self-centered Brenda Patimkin of *Goodbye, Columbus*.

Far more arresting as literary characters and human beings than Shakespeare's Jessica paradigm and caricatures of the domineering, guilt-inducing Jewish mother and her "Jewish American Princess" daughter, shopper extraodinaire and sexually frigid tease, popularized by Philip Roth, Thomas Wolfe, and William Styron, are the female protagonists crafted by Jewish feminists. With the publication of Jewish feminists, portraits of Jewish American women change radically. Intelligent, assertive women are the protagonists in short stories and novels celebrating the enormous changes achieved in recent decades in American women's lives. Reversing the movement by male precursors toward assimilation, many Jewish feminists fashion protagonists who either return to or re-evaluate traditional Judaism and seek entree into spiritual practices that had been exclusive male domains. In dramatic contrast to Roth's knife-wielding Mrs. Portnoy, shrill nudge, Mrs. Patimkin, or Bellow's raucous Aunt Rose and his sweet-tempered *mavens* of sponge cake and chopped liver, Jewish feminists delineate women who are generally mute on shopping and cooking, but vocal about religious ambivalence and spiritual seeking; intelligent, Jewishly and secularly educated, at ease with Judaica and Western high culture. These women battle the limited position of women in Orthodox society that frequently relegates women to marginal positions as well as misogynist stereotypes found in high and popular culture. These protagonists generally struggle to liberate orthodox women from behind the *mechitzah* into the main sanctuary where they may read the Torah from the *bimah* (the synagogue dais). While Anne Roiphe's redeemed American Jewish woman is content with patriarchal orthodoxy—despite her liberal feminist mother's objections—as she finds, in tradition, a valued sense of order, meaning, and sanctity of life, most protagonists of contemporary Jewish feminists resist the traditional orthodox role for women and strive for gender equality in ritual observance. In a creative alliance between feminism and Judaism, the new female protagonist knowledgeably addresses Jewish texts, liturgy, and history; and some, like Broner's women, explore alternative and non-traditional possibilities for women's spirituality while still others, like Nessa Rapoport's Judith Raphel, seek to encourage change from within orthodoxy.

A precursor of contemporary Jewish feminists, Anzia Yezierska celebrated the positive image of the assertive Jewish woman. She relates the hardships of immigrant woman and the forces which impede their opportunities for happiness. In a 1925 novel, *Breadgivers*, a work acclaimed by feminists despite its limited literary value, she foresees the critique Jewish women will register against Jewish patriarchy in later decades. Sara Smolinsky turns against her father, "a tyrant from the old country where only men were people,"[68] but she is not modeled on the apostate, Jessica. She is escaping patriarchal dominance and a constraining view of women's place, to seek autonomy and a better life, not a Christian husband. As the novel's subtitle, *The struggle of a father of the Old World and a daughter of the New*, makes evident, she is engaged in a generational and gender conflict. She rejects the Torah-scholar's conviction that every woman should be a self-sacrificial nurturer of men and children. Yezierska's women typically struggle to leave the physical and spiritual ghettos of their childhood, to pursue dreams of assimilation and acculturation with energy and determination. They confront old world patriarchs who would narrowly circumscribe their dreams, and they defy patronizing New World WASPS who would similarly restrict them, albeit for different reasons.

Illustrative of contemporary religious feminists is Nessa Rapoport's Judith Raphel, a young Orthodox woman who chooses allegiance to orthodoxy despite dissatisfaction with its patriarchal dominance and marginalization of women. *Preparing for Sabbath*[69] scrutinizes the life from childhood to adolescence and beyond of this descendant of a long rabbinical line. Judith's spiritual quest is influenced by women, by her devout and intellectually gifted grandmother, by a great-aunt she is said to resemble, who introduces her to a sympathetic Israeli poet with whom she studies, and finally, by a young woman leading her to a Hasidic *shul* where she finds spiritual fulfillment. Faithful to her ancestral links, even as she forges new directions, Judith Raphel is representative of the new Jewish woman of American fiction. Judith thinks through her social/sexual/spiritual positions and values with reference to Jewish ideals. She argues for political commitment because "Judaism says we're supposed to seek justice, it's our responsibility to guard and keep the earth, which means not abusing anything with life in it."[70] She withdraws from a romantic relationship with a non-Jew because he is outside the realm of her religious and cultural experience. She is empowered by her Jewish education to fight the battle for women's equality within Judaism and posits a learned critique against the exclusion of Jewish women from religious practice.

A generation of Jewish American writers has emerged in the last quarter of the century, that is far more free than Saul Bellow and Bernard Malamud were to explore the particularity of Jewish life. This is a self-emancipated generation, expressing its artistic visions in Jewish terms; diverging from the early masters of Jewish American literature, whether they were practitioners of the immigration/assimilation/acculturation school, or the Roth academy of social satire. These writers have and are continuing to re-imagine Jews in diverse contexts, authentic Jews far removed from both Christian anti-Semitic paradigms that stained American literature and from the immigrant figures and ambivalent Jews of postwar Jewish American novelists. The grandchildren of Jewish immigrants and children of acculturated American Jews are rediscovering Judaica and Jewish community as viable literary subjects. We and American literature are the beneficiaries.

NOTES

1. Frank Norris, *McTeague* (San Francisco: Rinehart Press, 1950), 31-32.

2. Henry James, *The Golden Bowl* (New York: Charles Scribner's Sons, 1914), 1:215, 216; 2:228.

3. Louis Harap, *The Image of the Jew in American Literature: From Early Republic to Mass Immigration* (Philadelphia: Jewish Publication Society, 1974), 374.

4. F. Scott Fitzgerald, *The Beautiful and Damned* (New York: Charles Scribner's Sons, 1922), 283, 283.

5. Qtd. by Barry Gross, "Yours Sincerely, Sinclair Levy," *Commentary* 80 (December 1985): 56.

6. F. Scott Fitzgerald, *The Great Gatsby* (New York: Bantam Books, 1925), 77-80.

7. Willa Cather, *The Professor's House* (New York: Alfred A. Knopf, 1925), 43.

8. John Dos Passos, *Manhattan Transfer* (Boston: Houghton Mifflin Company, 1925), 182, 182, 366, 101.

9. Ernest Hemingway, *The Sun Also Rises* (New York: Charles Scribner's Sons, 1926), 10, 95, 96.

10. Quoted by Leslie A. Fiedler, "What Can We Do About Fagin?: The Jew Villain in Western Tradition," *Commentary* 7 (May 1949): 414.

11. T.S. Eliot, *After Strange Gods: A Primer of Modern Heresy* (London: Faber and Faber Limited, 1934), 20.

12. T.S. Eliot, "Burbank With a Baedeker: Bleistein With A Cigar," *The Complete Poems and Plays 1909-1935* (New York: Harcourt, Brace and Company, 1952), 23-24.

13. Katherine Anne Porter, "A Country and Some People I Love," *Harper's* 231 (Sept. 1965): 68.

14. Louis Harap, *The Jew in American Literature*, 154.

15. Cynthia Ozick, "Cultural Impersonation: Beck Passing," *Art & Ardor* (New York: Alfred A. Knopf, 1983), 113-115.

16. John Updike, *Beck: A Book* (New York: Alfred A. Knopf, 1970).

17. Le Roi Jones, *Black Magic: Collected Poetry, 1961-1967* (Indianapolis: The Bobbs-Merrill Company, 1969), 116-117, 154.

18. Leslie Fiedler, "Zion as Eros," *The Jew in the American Novel* (New York: Herzl Institute Pamphlet No. 10, 1959), 8.

19. Abraham Cahan, *The Rise of David Levinsky* (New York: Harper and Row, 1960).

20. Isaac Rosenfeld, "David Levinsky: The Jew as American Millionaire," *Commentary* (August 1952) rpt. in *An Age of Enormity: Life and Writing in the Forties and Fifties* (Cleveland: The World Publishing Company, 1962).

21. Edward Lewis Wallant, *The Pawnbroker* (New York: Harcourt Brace Jovanovich, 1961).

22. Saul Bellow. *Mr. Sammler's Planet* (Greenwich, Ct.: Fawcett Publications, 1970).

23. Isaac Bashevis Singer, *Enemies, A Love Story* (New York: Farrar, Straus, Giroux, 1972).

24. Susan Fromberg Schaeffer, *Anya* (New York: Macmillan Publishing Co. Inc., 1974).

25. Cynthia Ozick, *The Shawl* (New York: Alfred A. Knopf, 1989).

26. See Chaim Potok, *The Promise* (New York: Alfred A. Knopf, 1969); *In the Beginning* (New York: Alfred A. Knopf, 1975); *The Book of Lights* (New York: Alfred A. Knopf, 1981).

27. Cynthia Ozick, "Bloodshed," *Bloodshed and Three Novellas* (New York: Alfred A. Knopf, 1976).

28. Cynthia Ozick, *The Cannibal Galaxy* (New York: Alfred A. Knopf, 1983).

29. See Bernard Malamud, "The Last Mohican," *The Magic Barrel* (New York: Farrar, Straus, and Cudahy, 1958); and Philip Roth, "Eli, the Fanatic," *Goodbye, Columbus* (Boston: Houghton Mifflin, 1959).

30. Arthur Cohen, *In the Days of Simon Stern* (New York: Random House, 1972).

31. Marge Piercy, *Gone to Soldiers* (New York: Summit Books, 1987).

32. George Steiner, "A Kind of Survivor," *Language and Silence: Essays on Language and Literature and the Inhuman* (New York: Antheneum, 1977), 143-144.

33. Cynthia Ozick, *Trust* (New York: New American Library, 1966).

34. Norma Rosen "Fences," *Orim: A Jewish Journal at Yale* 1 (Spring, 1986): 75-83; "The Cheek of the Trout," *Testimony: Contemporary Writers Make the Holocaust Personal,* ed. David Rosenberg (New York: Times Books, 1989), 398-411; "The Inner Light and the Fire," *Forthcoming: Jewish Imaginative Writing* 1:3/4 (Fall 1983): 4-9.

35. Chaim Potok, *The Gift of Asher Lev* (New York: Alfred A. Knopf, 1990).

36. Saul Bellow, *The Victim* (New York: Vanguard, 1947).

37. Saul Bellow, *Herzog* (New York: Viking, 1964), 37.

38. Saul Bellow, *The Bellarosa Connection* (New York: Viking Penguin, 1989).

39. Philip Roth, *The Ghost Writer* (New York: Farrar, Straus, Giroux, 1979).

40. Philip Roth, *Operation Shylock: A Confession* (New York: Simon and Schuster, 1993).

41. Michael Gold, *Jews Without Money* (New York: Liveright, 1930).

42. Tillie Olsen. "Tell Me A Riddle," *Tell Me A Riddle.* (New York: Dell, 1960).

43. Bonnie Lyons, "American Jewish Fiction Since 1945," *Handbook of American-Jewish Literature: An Analytical Guide to Topics, Themes, and Sources,* ed. Lewis Fried (New York: Greenwood Press, 1988), 73.

44. Bernard Malamud, "Lady of the Lake," *The Magic Barrel* (New York: Farrar, Straus, and Cudahy, 1957).

45. Philip Roth, *Portnoy's Complaint* (New York: Random House, 1969).

46. Saul Bellow, *The Adventures of Augie March* (New York: Viking, 1953).

47. Saul Bellow, "The Old System," *Mosby's Memoirs and Other Stories* (New York: Viking, 1968).

48. Philip Roth, *The Ghost Writer,* 13.

49. Bernard Malamud, *The Fixer* (New York: Farrar, Straus, Giroux, 1966).

50. Leslie Epstein, *King of the Jews* (New York: Avon, 1979).

51. Curt Leviant, *The Man Who Thought He Was the Messiah* (New York: Jewish Publication Society, 1990).

52. Melvin Jules Bukiet, *Stories of an Imaginary Childhood* (Evanstan, Illinois: Northwestern University Press, 1992).

53. Bernard Malamud, "The Magic Barrel," *The Magic Barrel.*

54. Saul Bellow, *Seize The Day* (Greenwich: Fawcett Publications, 1956), 72.

55. See S. Lillian Kremer, "An Intertextual Reading of *Seize the Day*: Absorption and Revision," *Saul Bellow Journal* 10 no. 1 (Fall 1991): 46-56.

56. Irving Howe, *World of Our Fathers* (New York: Harcourt Brace Jovanovich, 1976), 645.

57. Bernard Malamud, "The Magic Barrel," *The Magic Barrel,* 190.

58. Anne Roiphe, *Lovingkindness* (New York: Summit Books, 1987).

59. Philip Roth, *The Counterlife* (New York: Farrar, Straus, Giroux, 1987).

60. Cynthia Ozick, "Bloodshed," Bloodshed and Three Novellas, 72, 67.

61. Isaac Bashevis Singer, *The Penitent* (New York: Farrar, Straus, Giroux, 1983).

62. Philip Roth, *The Counterlife,* 324.

63. Philip Roth, *Deception* (New York: Simon and Schuster, 1990).

64. Cynthia Ozick, "Puttermesser: Her Work History, Her Ancestry, Her Afterlife," and "Puttermesser and Xanthippe," *Levitation: Five Fictions* (New York: Alfred A. Knopf, 1992).

65. Cathy Davidson, "E.M. Broner," *Dictionary of Literary Biography: Twentieth-Century American Jewish Fiction Writers,* ed. Daniel Walden (Detroit: Gale Research, 1984), 28:26.

66. E.M. Broner, *A Weave of Women* (Bloomington: Indiana University Press, 1978).

67. Henry Roth, *Call It Sleep* (New York: Avon, 1964).

68. Anzia Yezierska, *Breadgivers* (New York: Persea Books, 1952), 295.

69. Nessa Rapoport, *Preparing for Sabbath* (New York: William Morrow and Co., 1981).

70. Rapoport, 138.

Images of Jews in Black-Jewish Discourse

Davida J. Alperin

INTRODUCTION

Jews have been represented throughout the ages in a variety of ways, sometimes negative and sometimes positive. In some cases the representations are almost as complex as the reality that is present in such a diverse community of people. In other cases the representations are extremely simplistic, two dimensional stereotypes of evil incarnate or a people just below the angels.

To begin to make sense of some of this variation, it is useful to look at the specific contexts in which these images are presented. Images of Jews are a part of the social, political, and economic worlds in which they are created and perpetuated. Some of the images are more accurate than others, but even when these images do not reflect the truth about Jews, the images themselves become a part of the social reality in which Jews and non-Jews live. The images are real in the sense that they can influence the attitudes and behaviors of people in that social community.

The context in which I have examined images of Jews is the discourse surrounding Black-Jewish relations in the United States. In particular I have examined what we might call "talk about cooperation." When Blacks[1] and Jews try to explain why the two groups have cooperated with each other in the United States, when they discuss reasons Jews and Blacks should or should not cooperate, when they debate the relative value of such cooperative efforts for one group or the other, they often present different images of Jews and of Blacks. While the images of both groups are important, for the purposes of this collection I will focus on images of Jews which are presented in this discourse.

81

The discourse about cooperation which I analyze here comes from two main sources. First, there are writings in published materials. In gathering the discourse from published sources I made every effort to collect a diverse set of materials from a variety of sources. These included books, articles, letters to the editor, and columns published in general periodicals and also periodicals produced within, and primarily for, the Black or Jewish community. The articles were found using computer indexes and print indexes focusing primarily on the years 1979-1990. In addition, academic colleagues, friends, and family sent me articles, some of which were not found in the indexes. Second, there are the thirty-five interviews I conducted between 1988 and 1990 with Blacks and Jews involved in cooperative efforts in Chicago and the Twin Cities of Minneapolis and St. Paul.[2]

My first aim in this paper is to describe and analyze five of the numerous images of Jews that appear in discourse on Black-Jewish relations. My second aim is to discuss the implications of such images for relations between the two communities.

Before delving into the images themselves, it should be useful to consider two assumptions about the use of images as rhetorical tools for social and political aims. First, in this day of negative political campaigns, the notion that images and symbols are used as political tools often carries with it a sinister connotation. Indeed, masters of deception have used images and symbols as political tools for some of the most despicable of goals; take for example Joseph Goebbels, Hitler's Minister of Propaganda. But the use of images and symbols to persuade and motivate need not be directed to immoral, unethical or even purely self interested ends. If we think, for example, about Martin Luther King's use of images and symbols to motivate the thousands of civil rights workers in the 1950s and 1960s, it is clear that they can be tools for constructive rather than destructive goals. In the analysis of Jewish images in this paper, I therefore began with the assumption that writers and speakers who introduce images of Jews into their discourse about Black-Jewish relations may have a variety of reasons for doing so. I do not assume that all uses of such images are carried out with sinister intentions or done so in a way which misleads.

Second, while it is useful to think about choice of image as a rhetorical tool, it is important not to exaggerate the consciously strategic aspects of communications. Some of those presenting a particular image of Jews in their "talk about cooperation" have made a conscious strategic decision about what image to present. Others have not consciously thought about the impact that particular images will have on their audience. In either case, the image itself serves as an important rhetorical device, as I will show in examples which follow.

SELECTED IMAGES

Image 1: Victim of Oppression

A common image of Jews presented in discussions of Black-Jewish cooperation is that of victim of oppression. The "victim of oppression" image is often used in statements which seek to explain past and current cooperation or promote future cooperation between the two groups. Some say that identification with the plight of the other group motivates Blacks and Jews to cooperate with each other. Such individuals often describe a sense of kinship, strong emotional bond, deep empathy, or sense of intimate understanding for members of the other group. Jews and Blacks are said to cooperate because they identify with each other as current or former "underdogs," "outcasts," "victims," or "minorities."

The circumstances upon which this identification is made can be historical or contemporary. Often contemporary struggles of Blacks are compared to historical struggles of Jews. Among the historical parallels raised are those related to the slavery of ancient Israelites and slavery of Blacks in this country;[3] Europe's historical treatment of Jews (before the Holocaust) and America's treatment of African Americans;[4] and the deaths of Africans aboard slave ships and the deaths of Jews in Nazi concentration camps.[5] Frequently members of one community are said to speak up for the other community during a particular crisis because that crisis situation reminds them of their own suffering in the present or past. So for example, pogroms, directed against Jews in Eastern Europe at the turn of the century, were condemned by the editors of many Black newspapers, who noted the similarities of such pogroms to lynchings of Blacks in this country.[6] In another example, a Black attorney in a letter to the editor of the *Chicago Defender* argues that "Jews supported anti-segregation legislation in the 60s . . . because of the tragedy of the . . . holocaust and historical discrimination against Jews in Europe."[7]

Other statements about empathy based cooperation focus less on broad historical events, and more on personal experiences. In written analyses and even more commonly in dialogues between the two communities, individuals will use the rhetorical mode of personal narrative to describe the moment when they started to identify with members of the other group and to see Blacks and Jews as having a special bond. The salience of this identification is perhaps conveyed most clearly in such narratives. In the quotation which follows we learn about that moment of realization for Cherie Brown, a Jewish activist who leads workshops throughout the country on coalition building:[8]

> Her [Cherie Brown's] current commitment to black-Jewish alliance-building reflects a realization that she traces back to a moment during her early childhood in a working-class, largely Orthodox Jewish neighborhood in Cleveland. "I remember walking down the street and being struck by the image of a black woman I passed," she says. "I saw in her face the same pain I saw every day in my father's eyes. Suddenly I knew that, somehow, blacks and Jews must have a special bond."[9]

Beyond similarities in suffering, strong identification is also based on similarities among the two communities in their determination to break their shackles. Their long histories of fighting discrimination and their quests for "deliverance, freedom, liberation" are said to increase empathetic feelings between members of the two communities. Here, too, the common experience of struggle is often couched in biblical metaphors. For as Roberts indicates "the cry of the Exodus, 'Let My People Go!' strikes a responsive and collaborative cord between Jews and Blacks."[10] Or in Zakim's words the "exodus inspired prayers and let my people go liturgies . . . largely created the sentimental hold we have for each other."[11]

Other arguments based on the image of Jews as victims are less concerned with empathy and identification and more concerned with self preservation and group interest. These arguments often focus on Jews and Blacks as victims of "common enemies." These "common enemies," it is claimed, wish to harm both Jews and African Americans and their efforts to harm will be enhanced if Jews and African Americans are fighting each other. An example of this argument is given by Rose:

> Others, seeing that once again Blacks and Jews are targets of reactionary forces, know that unless there are serious attempts to reason together and to reforge the old alliances, both groups will be used by those who have little use for either.[12]

The enemy that is named in these arguments varies somewhat, but generally the reference is to some group on the far right such as "the small virulent nest of neo-Nazis" who bombed a synagogue in Atlanta in 1958,[13] or David Duke and his supporters in more recent times.[14]

A more general variant of this argument is that a tolerant social climate is important for both communities. Blacks and Jews are more likely to become victims when intolerance and prejudice increase in a society. Working to promote tolerance and social understanding is seen to be in the common interest of both. So for example Silberman argues in the following that fighting anti-Semitism is in the interest of Blacks:

> Because of millennia of hatred and destructiveness to which anti-Semitism is linked, not to mention its consequences in our own time, any use of political anti-Semitism goes beyond shouting "fire" in a crowded theater; it runs the danger of lighting the fire itself. And in that fire, blacks, no less than Jews, are bound to be burned. For all the real and imagined conflicts of interests between blacks and Jews, members of both groups have a common interest in maintaining a society in which prejudice and hatred play a declining, rather than increasing role.[15]

An extension of this viewpoint is based on an empirical argument about the connection between poverty and injustice and rising levels of social disorder, instability, and intolerance. At the National Conference on Black-Jewish Relations sponsored by Dillard University in 1989, John Jacob, President and CEO of the National Urban League, argued that "the continuing racial disadvantage that afflicts African Americans" is not only "an affront to traditional black and Jewish values" but also a "source of instability that threatens African Americans and Jews."[16] For both communities, then, true security needs to be measured "not by economic achievement but by social stability and social fairness."[17] It is thus in the interest of Jews to work to eliminate the racial disadvantage of African Americans.

Another version of this group interest argument focuses less on right wing extremists and the climate of prejudice they promote and more on the prejudices of society's elite members and the nation's laws which victimize Blacks and Jews. Several authors described the fact that both Blacks and Jews had a common interest during the 1950s and 1960s in making sure that discrimination in housing and employment was struck down by the courts or made illegal through congressional action.[18] Even though these laws have changed, many argue that society still does not fully accept Blacks and Jews. For example, Reverend Charles Spivey explained in an interview that he sees the "white power structure," which he believes is the "common enemy" of both Blacks and Jews, not as a monolithic thing but as "attitudes, intentions, institutional practices, all of which constitute a milieu, a mind set in the face of which Blacks and Jews have to themselves operate."[19] According to this viewpoint, racism and prejudice are not an aberration, but are built into the structure of American society.

Image 2: Jews as Affluent People Unsympathetic to the Plight of African Americans

This second image contrasts sharply with the first. Rather than looking for similarities between the two groups, differences are emphasized. Jews may have suffered in the past but have achieved so much success economically, socially, and politically that they are no longer allies of African Americans. This is precisely the image given by the *Economist* magazine in trying to explain Black-Jewish relations in the United States to the British public:

> For liberal Jews and mature blacks, the alliance of the two minorities, with their separate histories of oppression, was a natural marriage. But American Jews have moved on and up, leaving the sour legacy of a broken marriage behind.[20]

Similarly Maulana Karenga, in describing Jesse Jackson's 1984 presidential campaign, presents the image of many Jews and particularly the "Jewish establishment" moving to the right ideologically as they have become more powerful and wealthy.[21]

In effect, then, both Karenga and the *Economist* present us with two images. The first is of Jews in the past who had to struggle to make it in America and did so in alliance with African Americans. The second is a image of Jews who have already made it and leave the struggle and alliance behind. Karenga and the journalists at the *Economist* do not rest their entire analyses on these two images, but without the two images their explanations for the supposed breakdown of the grand alliance would be less coherent. For example, Karenga acknowledges that the two groups cooperated in the movement for civil rights. He also argues that one important factor which led to the alliance's breakdown was its very success. He claims that Jews have moved to the right and that this was partially because "the success of the civil rights struggle benefitted Jews more than Blacks, and thus, Jews have become more powerful and wealthy."[22]

The image of Jews working for civil rights primarily when it was most immediate to their interests is not confined to non-Jews. Take for example Albert Vorspan's statement from an essay written in 1969:

> Jewish racial liberalism has operated in inverse relation to the distance from Jewish economic interests. Jewish organizations were strong on desegregating the South; relatively few Jews were involved, and they were safely ignored. Jews supported fair housing and fair employment in the North; it was largely the WASP establishments which were cracked open, both for Jews and for blacks. Jewish organizations supported Mayor Lindsay's referendum for a civilian review board in New York City; that was directed against Irish cops. But the school strike impinged upon large numbers of Jews. Jewish liberalism became confused, distracted and, in the end, blunted.[23]

Karenga and Vorspan claim that economic interests influenced Jews' ideological positions, so that in some time periods and on some civil rights issues Jews are more active allies with African Americans, and at other times and on other civil rights issues Jews are less active allies with African Americans. Neither author seems surprised by such behavior and both acknowledge that cooperation between the two groups has benefitted both. Other individuals, however, only hold the image of Jews as affluent and uncaring, not knowing about or believing that a strong or healthy alliance ever existed. For example, the *Economist* asserts that:

> a generation of blacks has grown up unaware of that old black-Jewish alliance. Individual Jews carry on the tradition but, for young blacks struggling up from the bottom, the Jewish community has blended into the prosperous, uncaring mainstream of white America.[24]

A much more malevolent view of Jews and their behavior suggests that even when Jews join civil rights efforts they do so not to benefit themselves and Blacks, but to benefit themselves at the expense of Blacks.

Take for example this statement of Malcolm X from his autobiography:

> I gave the Jews credit for being among all other whites the most active, and the most vocal, financier, "leader" and "liberal" in the Negro civil rights movement. But I said at the same time I knew that the Jew played these roles for a very careful strategic reason: the more prejudice in America could be focused upon the Negro, then the more the white Gentiles' prejudice would keep diverted off the Jew.[25]

Malcolm X does not explain the exact strategy by which this seemingly paradoxical behavior would focus more prejudice on "the Negro." As Dunbar writes "how would Jews focus prejudice on blacks by fighting to remove it?"[26] Perhaps he thought that Jews actually sabotaged efforts from within the movement, or perhaps he thought they participated in order to generate a backlash against Blacks. What is unusual about his argument is not that he suggests Jews acted out of self-interest or that Jews would be happy to have prejudice diverted to others. Others have made either one or both of these arguments. However, generally an individual who argues that self-interest was the main motivator will either say that Jewish self-interest led some Jews to activities which also benefitted African Americans, or that Jewish self-interest in maintaining a buffer between themselves and the prejudices of white gentile Americans kept some Jews from supporting the civil rights movement. Malcolm X does not argue that Jews deserted Blacks or that they were committed but ineffective allies. Instead he argues that Jews actually were working against Blacks when they claimed to be working with and for them.

Image 3: Landlords of Black Tenants and Shopkeepers of Black Customers

The image of Jews as landlords and shopkeepers located in African American neighborhood is often raised to help explain conflict between the two communities. There are many metropolitan areas in the United States where Jewish neighborhoods became Black neighborhoods. Some of the Jewish merchants and landowners remained in the area after most of the Jewish residents moved away. The new Black residents became the tenants and customers of the

Jewish landlords and merchants. This pattern developed in Harlem in the 1920s and 1930s, but occurred later elsewhere. The situation often promoted hostility between the two groups. Even today, when very few Jewish merchants remain in predominantly African American neighborhoods, these images are still frequently raised in discussion about Black-Jewish relations.

There are sharp contrasts in how the image is presented. Some individuals argue that the basic nature of the relationships between landlords and lower income tenants, and between storekeepers and lower income customers is bound to have its tensions. The Jewish landlords and shopkeepers need not have been more exploitative or disrespectful than others to incur the wrath of their African American tenants and customers. Others acknowledge the potential for the dominant-subordinate economic relationship to generate tension, but also cite the image that Blacks had of specific Jews who were particularly exploitative of their tenants and customers. For example, Capeci, in an analysis of surveys of Blacks and Jews taken in Detroit in 1943, argues that:

> Subordinate-dominant relationships would have generated tension irrespective of the groups involved or their perceptions of fairness, but blacks aware of one or two well-known Jewish proprietors who overcharged for cheap goods or slum dwellings exacerbated the conflict.[27]

An editorial in the African American periodical *Encore* provides a similar image, but generalizes more broadly about Jews:

> The Black man in Harlem knows the Jews as landlord, merchant, school-teacher—not as a Jew *per se*, but as a White person who will, when he can, use his position of relative power to take advantage of the powerless.[28]

Others, including Dinnerstein and Silberman, analyze this image and its origins from a different perspective. Dinnerstein argues that the image of exploiter comes out of "European-American folklore about the cunning and exploitative Jew whose ruthlessly amassed fortune is used to acquire political and economic control of society."[29] From his perspective the image of Jew as economic exploiter became part of Black culture long before the two groups came into daily contact with each other. Silberman acknowledges that direct contact between Jews and Blacks in their relationships as landlords and tenants reinforced anti-Semitism among Blacks and racism among Jews, but he believes that the origins of these prejudices were absorbed by Blacks and Jews much earlier from prejudices embedded in American society.

Finally, in its most extreme versions, the image of the Jews as economic exploiter begins to shed basic human characteristics. While none of the authors of articles I collected went this far, some did report that others had presented such images. For example, Skerry in the *American Spectator* reports that "a young black attorney on her way up told me,' Blacks have learned the hard way about parasitic relationship with whites—er, Jews,'"[30] and "at Michigan State University, in a speech to some 4,000 people," the *Chronicle of Higher Education* reported that Louis Farrakhan "allegedly said Jews 'had sucked the blood of the black community.'"[31]

Image 4: A People In Between

An image closely related to that of landlord and shopkeeper is the image of Jews as a "people in between." This image is presented as part of an interstitial understanding of Jewish history by Rabbi Robert Marx, a long time civil rights activist and poverty advocate in Chicago.[32]

What Marx means by a "people in between" is that in many societies Jews have not been part of the power structure or the masses, but in between the two. Historically in Europe Jews were used by rulers to collect taxes, collect land rents, and sell liquor to the masses. Historically in the United States, Marx sees Jews between the power structure and the masses in economic positions as store owners and landowners in the inner city and in more recent years as teachers, civil servants, and professionals.[33]   What is the result of this interstitial position? According to Marx, even if only a minority of Jews actually occupy these positions at any given time, Jews as a whole find themselves being used by the power structures as scapegoats during periods of rising social anger. The role of some Jews in a society leads to a broader image being placed on all Jews and the consequences can be devastating.

The consequences of this interstitial role, however, need not be totally negative, according to Marx. Jews who take this interstitial image seriously can learn important lessons from it, some directly relevant to Black-Jewish relations in this country. As a people in between, Jews are also "admirably positioned to be prophetically relevant and vibrant."[34] Marx bases this on the idea that the in-between position gives Jews an "independent voice . . . able to challenge conformity patterns."[35] In order to play such a role, however, Jews must *not* "make peace with the powers who . . . repress the masses" in an attempt to obtain protection.[36] This strategy and such "protection" can provide only a false sense of security because historically, "the flames of anti-Semitic violence are fanned, not so much by the masses, as by threatened power structures."[37] Therefore, according to Marx, Jews, for prophetic reasons, but also in their own self-interest, must work to promote societal justice in league with those outside the power structure.

Marx is not alone in seeing Jews as a people in between.[38] A similar position, taken by Cherie Brown, is described by Ellen Stone in her 1984 article on Black-Jewish relations:

> There *is* anti-Semitism in this country, and as Cherie Brown points out, one of its manifestations has been in the roles Jews have been allowed to play in an economic system that is still, after all, controlled by a white Christian majority. What this has meant in concrete terms is that Jews have found themselves in positions that make them visible, middle-level agents of a largely gentile society that oppresses blacks. The history of the supposed disintegration of the black-Jewish coalition is a history of blacks and Jews being set against each other, whether as landlord versus tenant, social worker versus welfare recipient, or, as in the Ocean Hill-Brownsville public schools battle in New York City in 1968, as largely Jewish educators versus largely black people demanding local control of the schools.[39]

Generally those who present this image of Jews, as a people in between, wish to promote greater cooperation between Blacks and Jews. Marx, for example, founded and directed the Jewish Council on Urban Affairs in Chicago based on his understanding of Jews as a people in between. Since its founding in 1964 this organization has worked in coalition with many organizations and individuals in Chicago's African American community on issues of urban poverty and social justice.

Image 5: Jews as Emotionally Dysfunctional or Naive Idealists.

Other images presented during discussions about Black-Jewish relations portray Jews as guilt ridden, weak, emotionally dysfunctional, naive, or some combination of those qualities. Jews are seen as childlike, easy prey, willing to give up too much to an alliance partner. More often than not such images are presented by a Jewish speaker or writer. In addition, the images often come with either an explicit or implicit position that too much effort is expended on cooperation between the two communities, that cooperation is taking place for the wrong reasons, or that cooperation has not, on balance, been positive for the Jewish community.

One example of this type of image was presented during the 1989 mayoral election in New York City. Jackie Mason, a well known Jewish comedian claimed that Jewish support for David Dinkins was based on guilt about "the black predicament":

> There is a sick Jewish problem of voting for a black man no matter how unfit he is for the job. . . . All you have to do is to be black and don't curse the Jews directly and the Jew will vote for a black in a second. Jews are sick with complexes.[40]

Mason's language presents a broad generalization about Jews as psychologically troubled and willing to support Blacks if only they do not curse Jews directly. Furthermore while a specific election is the immediate focus of his attention, the implication of his remarks is that this type of voting is not an isolated occurrence. If readers take the image of Jews he presents seriously, they will look very skeptically at the wide range of cooperative efforts between the two groups.

Mason, as a well known comedian, got a fair amount of publicity when he made these remarks, but as a comedian, it is not clear how seriously he was taken. Still he is not alone in holding such images or describing them to others. For example Martin Plax in the Jewish publication *Midstream* counters Joyce Gelb's arguments[41] for the importance of and possibility of continued cooperation. He claims that Gelb minimizes the conflicts between Blacks and Jews and unrealistically "presumes that coalitions can exist as a political force as long as some similarities in manifest ideology exist."[42] While not generalizing to all Jews, he argues that Gelb, and Jews like her, are in need of "psychological solace":

Her optimism shows how unwilling are other Jews, like herself, perhaps younger, less religious (if not irreligious), and middle-class to face political reality confidently. While their generosity may give them psychological solace, it fails to give them the ability to distinguish a healthy pluralism from an unhealthy one.[43]

The nature of Mason's and Plax's arguments about cooperation between Blacks and Jews are different in important ways. Mason's statements are off the cuff, broad generalizations, and the image of Jews is the centerpiece of his statements. Plax's arguments are developed in a lengthy article, the image is *not* presented as one that pertains to all Jews, and the image is *not* the centerpiece of his article. Furthermore Mason's remarks are covered by a mainstream media outlet with wide circulation (the *New York Times*), while Plax's article appears in a Jewish publication with much smaller circulation (*Midstream*). Still, it is striking that images of Jews are used to develop positions in both types of discourse, despite the differences in the manner in which the images are presented and the medium in which they appear.[44]

IMPLICATIONS

The five images described above do not constitute a comprehensive typology of images of Jews found in discourse on Black-Jewish relations. There are many more images of Jews in this discourse. A number of these images were described to me by Reverend David Chambers, an African American minister who has been involved in Black-Jewish dialogue and cooperation in Chicago and other cities. Jews are seen as a people "connected with business," "they tend to be philanthropic," "a very aggressive, fast-talking, highly competitive group," "always in the books," a people with a "thirst and hunger for knowledge."[45] Still others present images of Jews as paternalistic, a people with strong ethical principles, or a group which exaggerates their underdog status. And the list goes on. However, rather than attempting a more comprehensive listing, I believe that it is more important to look at the implications that the presentation of such different images has on the possibilities for cooperation between these two social groups.

What are the consequences of using one image versus another? When speakers or writers wish to disrupt relations between Blacks and Jews, they may try to present Jews in a very negative light. It is clear that such negative stereotypes can be extremely dangerous. The history of Jews throughout the world suggests that when negative images are believed to represent all Jews, and hard economic times arrive, Jews can easily become targets of hate and violence. These hateful stereotypes have been the focus of considerable academic research, and the consequences of such hateful images are acknowledged by many concerned with human relations. However, the consequences, both negative and positive, of more benign images are rarely studied. Therefore, here I wish to focus on the images presented by the well intentioned. When individuals, who wish to promote solid understanding between the two groups, present particular images of Jews, what are the consequences?

First, it is important to recognize that broad generalizations of negative characteristics of Jews are not the only images which can be harmful. Broad generalizations of positive characteristics can also be dangerous. For example when Jews are portrayed as a group of people with super-human ethical standards, expectations of how actual Jews will behave in any given situation are put at unrealistically high levels. Such expectations are sometimes met, but when they are not met, disappointment and anger (sometimes within both the African American and Jewish communities) can result.

Other generalizations which are neither inherently negative nor positive, can be problematic as well. For example, the image of Jews as victims, if not carefully placed in historical context, has its own potential difficulties. Certainly Jews have been victims of many injustices, but when a relationship with another group is based solely or primarily on a sense of shared underdog status, certain problems can develop.

One such problem could be labeled the "victim's contest." A victim's contest occurs when members of each group try to establish that their group has suffered more oppression than the other group. So, for example, in some dialogue efforts between Blacks and Jews, much time will be devoted to debates about which was worse, the Holocaust or slavery. While it is useful to look at the differences and similarities between the histories of Blacks and Jews, such victim contests can be very destructive. This is particularly true if trust between the participants in the discussion has not yet been established.

Except in situations where a participant is trying to undermine relations between the two groups, it seems that the underlying motive behind such debates is the need for members of one of the groups to have members of the other group acknowledge their pain. In the words of Pat Crutchfield, an African American member of Black and Jewish Women in Dialogue in the Twin Cities:

> We both suffered. That's what it basically is. I don't even know if we should even debate which is worse. We just want to make sure that people know that we really, really suffered.[46]

Therefore it is important that dialogue group members find ways to acknowledge the other groups' pain to alleviate the need for such debates.

A second problem comes from not recognizing that the needs of the two groups differ, even when for both groups those needs are based on some type of underdog status. Jews and Blacks have both faced discrimination, scapegoating, and been victims of other types of social injustice. The current concerns about their vulnerability in this society, which sometimes bring them together into an activist alliance or dialogue group, may, however be very different. Unless those differences are recognized and dealt with, the dialogue effort may not succeed. An example of this is given by Letty Cottin Pogrebin who participated in a Black and Jewish dialogue group in New York City. After wondering why Black participation in the group had dropped off while Jewish participation had remained fairly high, she and a black participant in the dialogue concluded that the discrepancy resulted from the fact that the two groups had different motivations for joining. African Americans were more often motivated to participate in a dialogue effort in the hopes that it would lead to some form of action on issues of employment, affordable housing, and other pressing concerns in the Black community. Jews, on the other hand, were more likely to "invest in dialogue as a form of insurance against anti-Semitism":[47]

> I had suggested there was something wrong with Blacks for dropping out of the dialogue when in fact there was something wrong with the dialogue for failing to serve the needs of its Black participants. Because the Jewish agenda—creating

alliances—was being fulfilled, Jews kept showing up at the meetings. But the Black agenda—cooperative activism—had stalled, so some Black women had stopped coming.[48]

What, then, are people of goodwill to do to avoid the problems of using images even when they are positive? If presenting even positive images of Jews has its pitfalls in trying to build bridges between the two communities, should we avoid the use of any images? I would argue first that this is hardly possible, and second that it is not desirable. Whether we discuss images or not, almost all of us hold images of the groups to which we belong and sometimes of other groups also. The images are part of our interactions whether we describe them explicitly or not. The problems are not a result of the fact that images are made explicit, but that the images themselves are often too simplistic. More complex images can help improve relations. In this final section I will indicate three ways in which the images could be made more complex and useful to the strengthening of relations between Blacks and Jews.

First, to add some complexity to the images, it is important to emphasize the fact that no one image can describe all Jews. Gross generalizations are a problem both when they are critical of Jews or when then are flattering towards Jews. Certainly all Jews are not exploitative business owners, but neither are all Jews highly principled and ethically pure. Disputing negative stereotypes can be more effective if we do not attempt to replace them with positive over-generalizations.   Second, while it may be obvious that a simplistic image cannot adequately describe all Jews, it is also true that a simplistic image cannot adequately describe even a single Jew. For example, the image of a victim does not adequately describe a Jew even if he or she is a victim of some social injustice. There is more to that Jew than that one aspect of his or her social position. Also, consider the image of the affluent Jew. In terms of status that individual may be wealthy, but his or her internal identity may be a that of a vulnerable member of a minority social group. Based on Jewish history, that internal image is very understandable, but only to those who are knowledgeable about Jewish history and know that Golden Ages for Jews in such places as Spain ended very abruptly. Starting with a complex image of a particular Jew can quickly lead to discussions of Jewish history, which in turn allow for a more complex image to be painted of the broader Jewish community.

Third, more complex images include a variety of aspects of a group or person. In the discourse on Black-Jewish relations, some images focus entirely on internal motivations, others on a group or person's place in the social structure, other images include both social position and motives, and still others recognize people may act on the basis of multiple motives. I would argue that greater complexity makes the images more useful in attempting to promote inter-group understanding. Take for example the image of "a people in between" presented by Rabbi Marx. This image includes an analysis of the social position that many Jews have occupied in this and other countries - a place in between. Instead of seeing Jews as shopkeepers and merchants, a closeup shot, focusing only on shopkeepers and their customers or landlords and their tenants, Marx uses a wide-angle lens to show that these relationships existed within a broader community and economic system. In addition, he acknowledges that Jews in the middle position do not all behave in the same way. Some will try to become allies with the powers that be, whereas others will become allies with the down trodden. Finally, Marx acknowledges that the Jews he is describing have a variety of motivations for their behavior including self-interest and ethical principle.[49] They are, in other words, complex human beings who cannot be described in simple ways.

This recommendation for greater complexity runs counter to common sense advice in advertising, public relations, and the media. We have come to believe that to influence people and events we need to keep the message short and the image simple. My advise, though, is not to focus on the main media channels and instead to use such forums as continuing dialogue groups and broad based issue coalitions. My experience and research suggest that there is a much greater chance of inter-group understanding when Blacks and Jews of good-will come into close contact with each other, in a setting of equality, over a continuing period of time. In such settings, sometimes intentionally, and sometimes just in the course of other activities, members of the two groups share their stories with each other. Their stories are complex. They are about their actual lives, after all, and life is rarely simple. It is not only that the Jews will learn that Blacks are not all alike, and Blacks will learn that Jews are not all alike. After all, at some level they already know that. More importantly, they will begin to see where the stereotypes, both positive and negative came from. Instead of replacing one negative stereotype with one or more positive ones, members of both communities will see begin to see the full and diverse humanity of the members of the other community.

NOTES

1. When "Black" is used in this paper as a noun or adjective synonymously with African American, it is capitalized, even though that is not the case in many other publications. A concise argument for its capitalization is found in the 3rd edition of *Minority Organizations: A National Directory* (Garrett Park, MD: Barrett Park Press, 1987): "the word Black is spelled with a capital 'B' on the grounds that it refers to a specific cultural group, in much the same way that Hispanic or Basque would be capitalized." For a somewhat more extensive discussion of the politics of capitalization see Michael Parenti, "Capitalization," (letter to the editor) *PS: Political Science and Politics* 22 (March 1989): 7-8. In addition, since the term "white" does not identify a specific cultural group in the same way that "Black" does, I have not capitalized it. An imperfect analogy, which may help to explain the underlying consistency of capitalizing "Black" and not capitalizing "white" is the use the terms "Jew" and "gentile." Just as Black and white are often juxtaposed, so too are Jew and gentile. "Jew" identifies a specific cultural group and is always capitalized. "Gentile" does not identify a specific cultural group and generally is not capitalized.

2. In the Minneapolis-St. Paul metropolitan area, sixteen interviews were conducted with women involved in a group called Black and Jewish Women in Dialogue. Nine were Jewish and seven were African American. In Chicago, nineteen individuals were interviewed about their participation in a variety of cooperative efforts, most of which related to the work of the Jewish Council on Urban Affairs. Ten were African American and nine were Jewish. No African American Jews were interviewed in either city.

3. John Gibbs St. Clair Drake, "African Diaspora and Jewish Diaspora: Convergence and Divergence," in *Jews in Black Perspectives: A Dialogue*, ed. Joseph R. Washington, Jr. (London: Fairleigh Dickinson University Press, 1984); Christopher F. Edley, (speech presented at the First National Conference On Black-Jewish Relations, Dillard University, New Orleans, LA, 7 April 1989); Charles Kroloff and JoAnne Tucker, "Coalition Choreography," *Reform Judaism* 17 (summer 1989): 18-19.

4. Louis Schmier, "For Him the 'Schwartzers' Couldn't Do Enough: A Jewish Peddler and His Black Customers Look at Each Other," *American Jewish History* 73 (1983): 39-55.

5. Laura Parks, "The First Holocaust," *Chicago Defender*, 3 June 1978, 14.

6. Philip S. Foner, "Black-Jewish Relations in the Opening Years of the Twentieth Century," *Phylon* 36 (1975): 360-62; Johnathan Shamis, "Coalition Builders Meet in Chicago," *Chicago Defender*, 2 April 1984, 4.

7. Roy Carleton Howel, "Blacks and Jews: Old Friends, New Enemies," (Letter to the Editor), *Chicago Defender*, 23 October 1979, 9.

8. Cherie Brown is the founder and executive director of the National Coalition Building Institute and has written guides on coalition building and Black-Jewish dialogues (Cherie R. Brown, *The Art of Coalition Building: A Guide for Community Leaders* [New York, NY: American Jewish Committee, 1984]; Cherie R. Brown, *Face to Face: Black-Jewish Campus Dialogues* [New York, NY: American Jewish Committee, 1987]). She and Arlene Allen led the workshop for a leadership conference sponsored by the Twin Cities Black and Jewish Women in Dialogue.

9. Ellen Stone, "Blacks and Jews—Trying to Rebuild the Old Coalition," *Present Tense* 11 (summer 1984): 6.

10. J. Deotis Roberts, "Let My People Go! The Black/Jewish Ecumenical Dialogue," *Ecumenical Trends* 19 (January 1990): 4.

11. Leonard Zakim, (speech presented at the First National Conference On Black-Jewish Relations, Dillard University, New Orleans, LA, 6 April 1989), 5. See also Allan R. Gold, "Blacks and Jews Share a Night Like No Other," *New York Times*, 12 April 1989, Y7.

12. Peter I. Rose, "Blacks and Jews: The Strained Alliance," *Annals of the American Academy of Political and Social Science* 454 (1981): 69.

13. Janice Rothschild Blumberg, "The Bomb That Healed: A Personal Memoir of the Bombing of the Temple in Atlanta, 1958," *American Jewish History* 73 (1983): 33.

14. Cornel West, "Black Anti-Semitism and the Rhetoric of Resentment," *Tikkun* 7 (January 1992): 15; Ronald Smothers, "Black-Jewish Talks Produce Angry Clash But Some Hope," *New York Times*, 9 April 1989, 13.

15. Charles Silberman, "Jesse and the Jews," *New Republic* 181 (29 December 1979): 14.

16. John E. Jacob, "Towards a New Era of Cooperation," (speech presented at the First National Conference On Black-Jewish Relations, Dillard University, New Orleans, LA, 7 April 1989), 8.

17. Ibid., 6.

18. Glen C. Loury, "Behind the Black-Jewish Split," *Commentary* 81 (January 1986): 23; James A. Thomas, "Time Remembered," *Chicago Defender*, 26 March 1980, 16; Leonard Zakim, (speech presented at the First National Conference On Black-Jewish Relations, Dillard University, New Orleans, LA, 6 April 1989), 4.

19. Charles Spivey, Jr., interview by author, Chicago, Illinois, 15 August 1988.

20. "Blacks and Jews Come Apart," *Economist* 308 (27 August 1988): 16.

21. Maulana Karenga, "Jesse Jackson and the Presidential Campaign," *Black Scholar* 15 (September/October 1984): 65.

22. Ibid.

23. Albert Vorspan, "Blacks and Jews" in *Black Anti-Semitism and Jewish Racism* (New York, NY: Schocken Books, 1969), 216.

24. "Blacks and Jews Come Apart," *Economist* 308 (27 August 1988): 15.

25. Malcolm X (with Alex Haley), *The Autobiography of Malcolm X* (New York, NY: Grove Press, Inc., 1965), 372.

26. Leslie W. Dunbar, "The Old Union, and the New," (speech presented at the First National Conference On Black-Jewish Relations, Dillard University, New Orleans, LA, 6 April 1989), 17.

27. Dominic J. Capeci, Jr., "Black-Jewish Relations in Wartime Detroit: the Marsh, Loving, Wolf Surveys and the Race Riot of 1943," *Jewish Social Studies* 47 (1985): 224.

28. "A Marriage on the Rocks," *Encore American and Worldwide News*, 5 November 1979, 26.

29. Leonard Dinnerstein, "The Origins of Black Anti-Semitism in America," *American Jewish Archives*, 38 (1986): 113.

30. Peter Skerry, "On Edge: Blacks and Mexicans in Los Angeles," *American Spectator* 21 no. 5 (1988): 18.

31. "Black Speakers Spark Protests on Two Campuses," *Chronicle of Higher Education*, 7 March 1990, A2.

32. I learned about Rabbi Marx's interstitial analysis from some of his published writings and from an interview I conducted with him in the summer of 1989 (Robert J. Marx, "The People In Between," *Dimensions in American Judaism* 3 (spring 1969): 11; Irwin Blank and Robert Marx, "The Jewish Option," *Background,* issue 5 [New York, NY: Institute for Jewish Policy Planning and Research of the Synagogue Council of America, November 1972]; Robert J. Marx, "Problems of Coalition Building," [speech presented at the First National Conference On Black-Jewish Relations, Dillard University, New Orleans, LA, 6-7 April 1989]; Robert J. Marx, Interview by author, Chicago, Illinois, 10 July 1989).

33. Marx, "The People In Between," 11; Blank and Marx, "The Jewish Option," 2.

34. Marx, "Problems of Coalition Building," 2.

35. Marx, "The People In Between," 9.

36. Blank and Marx, "The Jewish Option," 3.

37. Marx, "Problems of Coalition Building," 2.

38. In sociological theory Edna Bonacich has developed the "middleman" minority model in which certain ethnic groups tend occupy positions in small business between producers and consumers. She finds that Jews and a number of different Asian American ethnic grouping fit the model: Edna Bonacich, "Class Approaches to Ethnicity and Race," *Insurgent Sociologist* 10 (fall 1980):

11.

39. Ellen Stone, "Blacks and Jews—Trying to Rebuild the Old Coalition," *Present Tense* 11 (summer 1984): 7.

40. Don Terry, "Giuliani Team Drops Comedian After Racial Remarks," *New York Times*, 28 September 1989, B12.

41. Joyce Gelb, *Beyond Conflict, Black-Jewish Relations: Accent on the Positive* (New York: American Jewish Committee, 1980).

42. Martin J. Plax, "Jews and Blacks in Dialogue," *Midstream* 28 (January 1982): 16.

43. Ibid.

44. Members of the Black community have also been portrayed as weak for cooperating with Jews. For example in a 1979 editorial in *Encore*, an African American periodical, Benjamin Hooks and Vernon Jordon were criticized for backing away from "the Black declarations of independence" in which Black leaders declared they would no longer avoid publicly criticizing Israel. Hooks and Jordan were portrayed as hanging their heads and begging forgiveness so as not "to jeopardize the moral and financial support that Jews have contributed to Black causes" ("A Marriage on the Rocks," *Encore American and Worldwide News*, 5 November 1979, 26). In suggesting that some weakness on the part of certain cooperators clouds their vision and impairs their judgement, such criticisms are similar to those made of Jews by Mason and Plax. However, there is also an important difference. In the case of the Black community the criticisms seem to imply that cooperators in certain circumstances behave like "Uncle Toms," in a dependent and servile manner. In the Jewish community the criticisms seem to imply instead that cooperators are behaving like "bleeding hearts," in a sentimental, neurotic, guilt-ridden, and/or naive manner.

45. David Chambers, interview by author, Chicago, Illinois, 13 July 1989.

46. Pat Crutchfield, interview by author, St. Paul, Minnesota, 25 July 1990.

47. Letty Cottin Pogrebin, "From Our Heads and Our Hearts: Connecting with Black Women," *Lilith* (winter 1991): 15.

48. Ibid., 28.

49. For further clarification of this issue see Davida J. Alperin, "Motives for Political Cooperation: The Case of African Americans and Jews in the United States" (Ph.D. diss., University of Minnesota, 1993). In that work I argue that the tendency in Political Science is to search for a single motivation for person's behavior. Competing explanations will include self-interest or ethical principle. Rarely is the possibility that multiple motivations may influence an individual considered. My analysis of the discourse on Black-Jewish relations, on the other hand, suggests that individuals involved in public life frequently understand themselves as having a variety of motivations, which at times conflict with each other, but which at other times reinforce each other.

The Jew as the "Other":
The Image of the Jew in American Films

Yoram Lubling

A Jewish joke tells about two Jewish individuals who are on their way to the firing squad. One of the victims starts yelling "I am innocent . . . I am innocent!" The other Jew turns to him and whispers, "Be quiet, don't make any troubles." This joke epitomizes, I suggest, the psychological condition of the Jew and his/her phenomenological "being-in-the-world."

My intention in this presentation[1] is to argue that the most mature and consistent image of the Jew in American film usually represents an outside perspective of either local culture or the world in general. Early images of the tailors and shop keepers of the Jewish immigrants at the turn of the century to Charles Bronson's portrayal of an Israeli commander in the Entebbe rescue operation depict a mind that looks at his/her environment, as it were, from the outside. This image of the Jew not only emerges out of the themes and characters in the films, but also is shaped by the conduct of the Hollywood Jewish community and its politics and its interaction with the American public.

I contend that such an outer perspective is a culturally engineered one, and furthermore, that such a perspective ideationally defines the concept of a Jew, as well as experientially describes his/her behavior in the world. In other words, ideationally, the concept of a Jew involves a deep metaphysical division between itself and the concept of "gentile." The existence of the "gentile" was required for the appearance of the Jew. It is the Jew that God chose as his moral representative to function as a "light" to the gentile world. In short, the very notion of being a Jew includes the *a prioristic* metaphysical assumption of separation from the non-Jewish realm. This separation is the very meaning of God's act of choice and is sealed in the conditions of the covenant.

Experientially, the living experience follows its ideational counterpart and forces the Jew into a deep division between him/her and the gentile world. Observe, for example, that a contemporary Jew is proud at the fact that during 2000 years of exile, the Jewish community kept its tradition intact, primarily by physical/experiential and ideational isolationism. Notice traditional Jewish resistance to new converts and the contemporary debate in Israel over the question of "Who is a Jew?" It is isolation and outside perspective, not acceptance and cultural integration, that is inherent in the existential condition of the aware Jew.

Before I continue with the Jewish theme of this presentation, I want to say something about the medium of film. As Stanley Cavell argued, movies are a magical reality projected on a screen with a strange metaphysical implication. It is a projected reality from which we are conspicuously absent. As such, the medium of film provides us with a unique opportunity to present and evaluate ourselves and our world without actually risking involvement:

> The depth of the automatism of photography is to be read not alone in its mechanical production of the image of reality. The audience in a theater can be defined as those to whom the actors are present while they are not present to the actors [thus] movies allow the audience to be mechanically absent. . . . In viewing a movie my helplessness is mechanically assured.[2]

In the context of the above discussion, this aesthetic, as well as technological quality, allows us to inspect the Jew's "outsider" perspective because Jewish individuals greatly influenced the American movie industry. From studios to movie theaters ownership, from directors to actors and screen writers, from musicians to song writers and others, the *historical* perspective of the new minority in America was inevitably projected on the screen.

Finally, the medium of film, as Cavell also correctly observed, is restricted artistically. It must project only types of characters or myths of life. In other words, movies cannot project a specific image of an individual, but only the "form" of such an individual. For example, the film about Golda Meier, *A Woman Called Golda* (1982), does not depict the specific image of Maier, but a type of woman. Col. Netanyahu in *Operation Rescue* portrays a type of hero rather than the individual:

> [T]ypes are exactly what carry the forms movies have relied upon. . . . Does this mean that movies can never create individuals, only types? What it means is that this is the movies' way of creating individuals: they create *individualities.*[3]

This artistic limitation, nonetheless, provides a unique opportunity to observe the types or the myths that the filmmakers worked with. This in turn reveals their deepest metaphysical sense of themselves—that of being the eternal other. The historical and phenomenological condition of the Jew as the outsider naturally manifests itself in these films as it has through Jewish poetry, fiction, paintings, and social thought.

AT THE BEGINNING: THE OUTSIDER AS STEREOTYPE

Despite the significant Jewish influence during the silent movie period, the movie makers did not worry about creating exaggerated and straightout insulting images of Jews. Examples are the 1916 image (or even the 1948 version) of Fagin in the film *Oliver Twist,* as well as Shylock in the adaptation of Shakespeare's *The Merchant of Venice* (1908, 1912, 1913). Lester D. Friedman, who researched the Jewish image in American films, observed that: "the predominant portrayal of Jews in such literary adaptations shows them as usurers, villains, cheats, and crooks."[4] Interestingly, Friedman also observes that Jewish filmmakers, as well as Jewish theater owners:

> simply recycle literary presentations that include what today, however, we would label as racist stereotypes. In non-classical silent films the Jew is usually portrayed as a shrewd, clever individual that is inherently obsessed with "making it."[5]

Look at various titles of the period: *Cohen's Advertising Scheme* (1904), *The Yiddisher Cowboy* (1909), *Such a Business* (1914), *Cohen's Fire Sale* (1907), *The Firebug* (1913), *Lucky Cohen* (1914), *Get Rich Quick Billington* (1913).

However, the insensitive attitude towards exaggerated visual stereotypes in the early silent films can be explained. First, as Cavell observed, movies are constrained by the concept of a type, and silent films *had* to visually exaggerate the character in order to communicate meaning. Character development in later sound films replaced the reliance on traditional stereotypes and visual exaggeration to communicate. With the advent of sound, the audience could achieve insight into the introspective thought processes of a character and didn't have to rely on exaggerated images.

Second, early images of the Jews were primarily directed toward the new Jewish community in America. Jewish filmmakers did not understand the dangerous power of negative images. At this early period, little could be imagined about the promethean "meaning-giving" nature of projected moving images. It simply didn't occur to Jews producing these films that these silent images were anything more than entertainment. The power to alter culture and minds was not yet apparent. However, it didn't take long for the American government, movie industry, and people to realize the power of motion pictures in determining our culture. As we will observe later, by the late fifties and early sixties, the film industry and the American government battled over the political influence of films in determining public perceptions.

However, it can be argued that even this early period shows the (unreflective) projection of the "otherness" in the existential condition of the Jew, as I suggested above. In these films it is the cleverness of the Jew that is required to deal with the ordinary world. The Jew is forced to use extraordinary measures to compete in a world which is essentially not his own. It is only in a world in which the Jew is rejected religiously, socially, economically, etc., that the Jew must work harder to negotiate with the surroundings. Even early adaptations of biblical images, such as Samson in *Samson and Delilah* (1949), projected the perspective of the outsider, the Jewish hero as the ultimate victim of the non-Jewish world. Although Samson could have been more clever in his relationship with Delilah, he still succeeds at the end, as does Mr. Cohen in nearly all early films about his business adventures. Although the early films also made attempts to introduce the new Jewish immigrant to the American public, their usage of traditional stereotypes and old myths seem to unreflectively communicate the historical condition and perspective of the Jew.

MERGING SOUND AND FILM:
AMERICAN JEWRY AND THE FEAR OF DIFFERENCE

During the rise of Nazism in the thirties, the Jewish film industry radically changed its presentation of Jews on the screen. No longer did it project exaggerated images; rather, it made great efforts to remove Jewish types and myths from the films. As the historian of films Lester D. Friedman observed:

> The thirties . . . represent the lowest point in the history of Jewish-American films. . . . [T]hirties movies' versions of literary works containing Jewish characters usually rob these figures of all telltale traces: names, mannerisms, issues . . . [and] the most praised film of the decade featuring a Jewish character, *The Life of Emile Zola* (1937), basically ignores Dreyfus' heritage.[6]

I would like to suggest that during the late thirties, it was not only the Jewish community of the film industry that made serious efforts to act quietly, but the American Jewish community as a whole. The anti-Jewish sentiments expressed all over Europe found some sympathy in America. More specifically, anti-Jewish sentiments were directed against the perception that the Roosevelt administration was pressured by the American Jewish community to enter the war. The Holocaust historian, David Wayman, similarly observed that "the anti-Semitism of the time was another factor limiting American Jewish action for rescue."[7] The other factor was the "business as usual" attitude of the American Jewish community. Witness the following warning given to Jan Karski, the Polish underground agent who traveled to England and the U.S. to report the Jewish destruction in Poland and to press Jewish leaders to act:

> Jewish leaders abroad won't be interested. At 11 in the morning you will begin telling them about the anguish of the Jews in Poland, but at 1 o'clock they will ask you to halt the narrative so they can have lunch. That is a difference which cannot be bridged. They will go on lunching at the regular hour at their favorite restaurant. So they cannot understand what is happening in Poland.[8]

However, the failure of the Jewish community in America, including those involved in the influential movie industry, to react forcefully to the events in Europe is a familiar reaction of an historical outsider. Recall the earlier joke about the two Jews who were to be executed. While European Jewry was literally led to slaughter, the free American Jewish community was attempting to "make no troubles." Very few films challenged the plight of European Jews during the thirties. The one American film worth mentioning is *Hitler's Reign of Terror* (1934) by the photographer Cornelius Vanderbilt, Jr. The film directs its attention toward the Nazi attempt to destroy Jewish culture and thought by burning their books and works of art. In short, the absence of Jewish characters and themes during the thirties is a clear manifestation of the Jew as the other. Here too the Jew finds him/herself in a world not his/her own in which he/she needs to maneuver quietly and inconspicuously. The fate of the Jew is projected, I suggest, by its conspicuous absence.

A CINEMA OF CONCEALMENT: THE JEW AS AN AMERICAN

The movie industry faced its most challenging time during the events of the Second World War and the McCarthy period. The discovery that motion pictures could have great influence on public perception, both at home and abroad, created a clash between the movie industry and the American government, in which Jewish producers, writers, and actors found themselves at the center. During the forties and most of the fifties the movie industry became what Friedman described as "a cinema of assimilation." The image of the American Jew became simply that of an American performing his/her civil duties, living a productive ordinary life, and confronting his/her problems openly. Observe Chip Abrams, played by Sam Levin in the 1943 Bogart film *Action in the North Atlantic* as an ordinary American Navy officer, or Asst. Crew Chief Weinberg, played by George Tobias in *Air Force* (1943). In *Gentleman's Agreement* (1947) we see the ordinary law-abiding American Jew confronting his gentile surrounding's anti-Semitism. It is worth noticing that it wasn't until this film that the movie industry addressed the issue of American anti-Semitism.

However, the period also witnessed some of the most destructive years in American politics for the movie industry. As early as 1939,

Sen. Hiram W. Johnson (Republican from California) accused Roosevelt of pandering to "Jewish interests." Sen. Johnson charged that Jews' loyalty was to their group and not to their nation. He claimed that all Jews were "on one side, widely enthusiastic for the President and willing to fight to the last American . . . [to save] . . . their people, who neither live here, nor have anything in common with our country."[9] In 1941, Senator Gerald P. Nye of North Dakota, a known isolationist, directly accused Jews in the movie industry of engaging in a propaganda campaign designed to involve America in the war in Europe. At the same time, Charles A. Lindbergh, in his speech entitled "Who Are the War Agitators?" told the American people that the "three most important groups who have been pressing this country toward war are the British, the Jews, and the Roosevelt Administration. . . . If any one of these groups—the British, the Jews, or the Administration—stops agitating for war . . . [there would] be little danger of our involvement."[10]

Like their counterparts in Europe, the senators and Lindbergh perceived the Jewish population as having its loyalty elsewhere. Again the Jew was perceived as the other who—historically and religiously—must be first and foremost committed to Jewish causes, notwithstanding the Jew's commitment to the rest of creation. In this case, the loyalty of the American Jews was with the fate of the Jewish community in Europe and the Jewish pioneers in Palestine. The fact that during this period very little was done by the movie industry is quite understandable. Not making unnecessary troubles is the way Jews act when they perceive themselves as outsiders in a foreign land, no matter the promise of its democratic institutions.

The uncontroversial movies of this period, such as the remake of the *Jazz Singer* (1953), *The Juggler* (1953), and *Marjorie Morningstar* (1958), attest to such behavior. The general interest of the movie industry at this point was to portray Jewish individuals as ordinary and loyal Americans. The House Committee on Un-American Activities (HUAC) looked into communist conspiracies in the movie industry from 1947 until 1952. Given the Jews' traditional and historical sympathy towards left-wing social ideas, as well as their status as immigrants from *new* communist countries, the industry was an easy target for right-wing paranoia. Six out of the "Hollywood Ten" were Jews, and thirteen out of the first nineteen individuals to be called in front of the committee were Jewish. As depicted by Walter Bernstein and Martin Ritt in their 1976 film, *The Front,* the Jewish writers and actors were making every attempt to conceal their Jewishness and their ideational creativity.

Before moving on to our last period (the sixties to the contemporary period), we can sum up the forties and fifties as follows: we must look at the image of the Jew not only as it was projected on the screen, but also through the actions, or lack of actions, undertaken by the community. Especially deserving examination is the attempt to "cool off" or conceal the Jewishness of characters and themes (note the non-Jewish version of the 1947 *Humoresque*) in order not to make trouble. This is not the behavior of an individual or community that is secure in its new democratic environment. This is a reaction of a community that phenomenologically lives a dichotomized existence, rooted in its commitment to its faith and the consequences of its history.

CONTEMPORARY INTROSPECTION: THE CELEBRATION OF DIFFERENCE

The sixties and the student revolution brought the celebration of differences. There was nothing to be ashamed of in being Jewish or identifying with its history and difficulties. Some of the leaders of the sixties' student revolt were Jewish and the voices of the period—Bob Dylan and Allen Ginsberg—became quintessential American poets. In this period we witness a celebration of Jewish figures and themes: Zero Mostel as Max Bialistock and Gene Wilder as Neil Blum in the *Producers* (1968), Barbara Streisand as Dolly Gallagher Levi in *Hello, Dolly!* (1969), Oskar Werner as the double agent in *The Spy Who Came in from the Cold* (1965), Spencer Tracy in *Judgment at Nuremberg* (1961), to name a few. There were big movies about the young State of Israel such as *Exodus* (1960) and *Cast a Giant Shadow* (1966).

The seventies and eighties continued the sixties' celebration of American Jews as ordinary Americans. In *All the President's Men* (1976) we see a Jewish journalist working as an ordinary American citizen, saving democracy from political decay. In *Norma Rae* (1979) we witness a young Jewish labor activist in the Midwest fighting for workers' unity. They were individuals in mainstream America, not outsiders. They were in-laws in *The In-Laws* (1979) with Alan Arkin, cowboys and Indians in Mel Brooks' *Blazing Saddles* (1975), boxing managers in *The Main Event* (1979), directors in *Funny Lady* (1975), doctors in *Love at First Bite* (1979), eccentric unemployed actors in

Neil Simon's *The Sunshine Boys* (1975), a Jewish werewolf in *An American in London* (1981), Jewish revolutionaries in *Reds* (1981), and an ordinary talented student in *Porky's II* (1984).

However, I believe that this "projected" celebration is not an indication of the final integration of the Jews into American society. The films do not project an already integrated image of the American Jew. If we look at the work of the contemporary filmmaker, Woody Allen, we observe a more accurate representation of the condition of the American Jew. Although Allen doesn't necessarily see himself as a "Jewish filmmaker," ideationally his movies provide us with a unique insight into the contemporary isolated condition of the Jew in America.

There are several reasons for the quality of Woody Allen's work *vis-à-vis* the Jewish image. First, he is an introspective thinker who projects the Jewish stream of consciousness on a much deeper level than most contemporary Hollywood filmmakers. Second, he is unique in utilizing humor to address the difficult issues regarding Jewish-American existence. His humor is capable of disarming the most fundamental and horrifying issues in contemporary Jewish consciousness: (e.g., the Holocaust, alienation, Jewish/Christian relationship, guilt, the value of tradition, American mainstream anti-Semitism, to name a few).

More then any other Jewish filmmaker, Woody Allen's upbringing in a middle-class Jewish area of Flatbush, Brooklyn, is totally revealed in his work and is greatly responsible for his way of thinking, feeling, and creating. As Sam B. Girgus makes explicit in his book, *The Films of Woody Allen:* "Woody Allen was a Jew to the core . . . [for whom] the ambiguities and anxieties of Jewish identity . . . comprise the body of his work."[11]

For example, witness his concern with American anti-Semitism in *Annie Hall* (1978). In particular, observe how it reveals the unchanging condition of the contemporary American Jew as the ultimate outsider:

ALVY:	I distinctly heard it. He muttered under his breath, "Jew."
ROB:	You're crazy!
ALVY:	No, I'm not. We were walking off the tennis court, and you know, he was there and me and his wife, and he looked at her and they both looked at me, and under his breath he said, "Jew."

ROB: Alvy, you're a total paranoid.

ALVY: Wh—How am I a paran--? Well, I pick up on those kind o' things. You know, I was having lunch with some guys from NBC, so I said . . . uh, "Did you eat yet or what?" and Tom Christie said, "No didchoo?" not, did you, didchoo eat? Jew? No, not did you eat, but Jew eat? Jew. You get it? Jew eat?

ROB: . . . you see conspiracies in everything.

ALVY: No, I don't! You know, I was in a record store. Listen to this—so I know there's this big tall blond crew-cutted guy and he's lookin' at me in a funny way and smiling and he's saying, "Yes, we have a sale this week on Wagner." Wagner, Max, Wagner—so I know what he's really trying to tell me very significantly Wagner.[12]

We need to notice here that not only does Woody Allen reveal the unconscious anxiety of the eternal "other" (as *outsider*), but he also reveals the American insensitivity to such Jewish concerns. "You are a total paranoid" answers his gentile friend Rob, displaying the American tendency to avoid unpleasantness. The insensitivity to this Jewish anxiety is further revealed when Annie Hall remarks that Alvy (Woody Allen) is what Grammy Hall, the quintessential Wisconsin wasp, would call "a real Jew." Annie seems to be totally oblivious to the insensitivity and impact of her words:

ANNIE: [*Laughing*] Well, uh . . . [*pausing*] You're what Grammy Hall would call a real Jew.

ALVY: [*Clearing his throat*] Oh, thank you.

ANNIE: [*Smiling*] Yeah, well . . . you—she hates Jews. She thinks that they just make money, but let me tell yuh, I mean, she's the one—yeah, is she ever. I'm tellin' yuh.[13]

More then anything else, the sense of discomfort that Alvy experiences at the diner table at Annie's home in Wisconsin reveals the phenomenological "being-in-the-world" of the Jew in America. This sense of anxiety and feeling of alienation is depicted by Allen through *reading* Grammy Hall's anti-Semitic mind and concluding that she is "a classic Jew hater." Although Allen describes his sense of the "other" with humor, the pain that is felt by the Brooklyn Jewish boy is apparent. He is looking from the "outside-in" at a realm of existence called "American," so distinct and culturally different from his ordinary Jewish immigrant background. By juxtaposing images of his parents' behavior and mannerisms during dinner with the "all-American family," in this scene he beautifully reveals the sense of alienation the Jew feels in his/her contemporary American surroundings.

I want to conclude this discussion by looking into the issue of morality and how it reveals the separateness of the Jewish experience. In his most mature film to date, *Crimes and Misdemeanors* (1989), Woody Allen brilliantly displays the perception of the Jew's ultimate place in the cosmic drama. The film uses the image of eyesight as a metaphor for moral insight and responsibility, as well as projecting the Jew's unique conviction that "the eyes of God see all," especially his/her conduct in life.

The powerful image of the eyes of God seem to be directly focused on the conduct of his chosen children. Through a presentation of several Jewish families, Woody Allen creates a natural separation between their values and perception of their status in the cosmic story, and the American culture. Although they all hold ordinary American occupations (a physician, a shallow Hollywood director, a neurotic filmmaker, a Seventh Ave. gangster, a middle-aged housewife who dates through the personals, etc.), they are a separate community since God sees them all and evaluates them differently (note the discussion around the Seder table regarding the very meaning of Jewish faith, universal morality, and ordinary Jewish doubt).

It is my view, then, that the Jew is authentic only when he/she works from the outside. This is not to suggest that, socially, the Jewish community doesn't work towards the improvement of the human condition. But this work is done from the position of the other. In other words, the Jewish community is bound to look supernally at the shape of creation since it was agreed upon by the conditions of the Covenant (the reason for God's choice).

Finally, such a phenomenological "being-in-the-world" is not without its merits. From a practical standpoint, the position of the Jew is a universally needed function. It represents the idea of a moral structure which is the bedrock of civilization. The Jewish idea of a moral structure supernally imposed on our daily experience is our historical recognition that daily life must be constrained by ideational accomplishments. Like Plato and Aristotle later, the Jewish introduction of man's privileged access into the world of the mind defined their otherness—as the philosophers in Athens were metaphysically separated from the rest of mankind. Such a moral standpoint, I suggest, is a very desirable quality in a short Western history that, despite its intellectual accomplishments, has very little to celebrate morally. As such, a tradition that, regardless of its persecutory past, sees its image as an outsider in charge of the moral shape of the world is something to be celebrated and nourished. Although no perspective is truly capable of transcending the plurality of experiences, it is still a necessary function in our ultimate collective attempt to negotiate with an inevitably changing environment.

NOTES

1. I would like to thank my colleague, Eric Evans, for the helpful comments and suggestions he offered on earlier versions of this paper and for his assistance with the visual aspects during the presentation.

2. Stanley Cavell, *The World Viewed* (Cambridge, Massachusetts: Harvard University Press, 1993), 25.

3. Ibid, 27.

4. Lester D. Friedman, *The Jewish Image in American Film* (Secaucus, New Jersey: Citadel Press, 1987), 19.

5. Ibid., Friedman observed that in 1908, forty-two out of the 120 motion-picture house in Manhattan were located on the Lower East Side.

6. Ibid., 33.

7. David Wayman, *The Abandonment of the Jews* (New York: Pantheon Books, 1985), 330.

8. Ibid.

9. Johnson Papers, cited in Wayne Cole, *Roosevelt and the Isolationists, 1932-45* (Lincoln: University of Nebraska Press, 1983), 308, 607.

10. Deborah E. Lipstadt, *Denying the Holocaust* (New York: The Free Press, 1993), 36.

11. Sam B. Girgus, *The Films of Woody Allen* (New York: Cambridge University Press, 1993), 8.

12. Woody Allen, *Four Films of Woody Allen* (New York: Random House, 1980), 9-10.

13. Ibid., 28-29.

"Jews Don't Hitch": *Northern Exposure's* Depiction of a Jew's Assimilation to the American Religion
—or—
Why the Tip of the Penis is No Longer a Yardstick

David Porush

> Some people erroneously assume that world peace will come about only through sameness of opinion.... Therefore, when they see that intensive study of the Torah leads to a multitude of positions and opinions, they think it is the opposite of peace. The truth is otherwise.
>
> — Rav Kook

My subtitle is a Freudian slip in the truest sense, a line delivered by Maurice Minnifield in CBS's often-brilliant television show, *Northern Exposure*. Maurice is a retired, extremely wealthy astronaut living in the fictional town of Cicely, Alaska. As the benign, right-wing patron, its primary benefactor, landowner, and entrepreneur, he contracts for the medical services of Joel Fleischman, fresh out of a New York medical school. The premise for the television series is this indentured servitude against which Joel often bristles.[1] Although every hour-long episode concerns the intertwined or parallel stories or problems of several different characters, the primary source of the comedy is Dr. Fleischman's displacement (or misplacement). As a quintessential and parochial New York Jew, Joel finds himself a sort of indentured medical servant in America's rugged last frontier, an outpost town in Alaska.[2]

115

One of the many cunning achievements of the program is in its exploration of a Jew's diaspora within the Diaspora. Over the long haul, *Northern Exposure* is Joel Fleischman's *bildungsroman:* he is made increasingly aware that he is exiled from New York to Alaska. In fact, the word *exposure* in the title of the show ironically refers to this ongoing drama about Fleischman. He is continually exposed to and surprised by a non-New York, non-Jewish, non-urban life on the northern frontier of America. And in turn, the Northwestern natives of Cicely are exposed to Joel's strange Oriental (or Eastern) ways, since as the town's only doctor he continually comes into contact with most or all of them. Like most Jews in America, Fleischman may find himself forgetting that he is in Diaspora at all. Yet his exile to Cicely is an emblem of the alienation of Americans from their own native or hereditary culture(s) or their unwitting assimilation to a larger, blander, more ill-defined compromise culture.

I. THE SPECIAL PROBLEM OF THE JEW IN POPULAR FILM AND TELEVISION

The episode I treat in Section II below depicts the final assimilation of this one Jew to what Harold Bloom has called "The American Religion." It reveals in a remarkably striking and subtle way a theme that haunts virtually all American popular depictions of the Jew, and illustrates the larger point I will make in this paper: When a Jew is not an accessory or minor or token character, but rather is the central figure in a popular movie or television show about Jews in America, he (and sometimes she) is frequently shown struggling with his identity *as* a Jew in the religious sense. The Jewishness of the Jew becomes the issue in a way that the "Italianness" of an Italian or the race of an African American is rarely challenged in the pop culture. For instance, *The Cosby Show, The Jeffersons,* or even *Sanford & Sons* did not make an issue of how the characters negotiate their identities as blacks and as Americans. True, these shows played on or against racial stereotypes, but the characters themselves were not concerned with "passing," "assimilating," or being "accepted" as members in the culture around them. In striking contrast, quite often, the Jewish hero of popular entertainment is *forced* to choose between his affiliation with a narrow, confining, and strictly-interpreted Jewish religious identity and the larger, more attractive cosmopolitanism of the American community.

Never is the Jew shown choosing his religion over membership in the wider world. What may be confusing to popular audiences, and even to some Jews, is that the more the Jew gives up his religious identity, the more the depiction may lavishly, humorously, generously — even lovingly— find amusement in the Jew's ethnicity. So the subtle charge I am here exploring is nearly invisible because it is so seductive and reassuring. In fact, it is this very ambiguity — that the Jew is shown at the moment of assimilation as at once very ethnically or stereotypically Jewish and at the same time in the process of trespassing against the fundamental religious laws that make him a religious Jew— that is most important to grasp and most explosive. For the implication of these scenarios is that the Jew can be accepted as a Jew only if he cuts himself off from the most essential source of his Jewishness, his Judaism.

The most common sign of the Jew's choice to assimilate is in the automatic pairing of clearly, almost stereotypically, Jewish men to non-Jewish women. Under Jewish law, a Jewish man must choose a Jewish woman to remain Jewish and, more importantly, to keep his children Jewish. Yet just the shows in the last few seasons illustrating this transgression presents a stunning list of portraits of males Jews chosing non-Jewish women: *Friends, Seinfeld, Mad About You, Murphy Brown, Beverly Hills, 90210.* In persistently showing the Jew in the last stages of divesting himself of his Jewish religion, television has taken over the theme from popular films like *Abie's Irish Rose, The Jazz Singer, Diner, Crossing Delancey, A Gentleman's Agreement, Annie Hall,* and *The Apprenticeship of Duddy Kravitz.* In the meantime, American cinema has simply avoided explicit Judaic content at all, going so far as de-Judaizing the appearance of Jewish characters and changing scripts about Jewish families to ones about Irish or WASP families. An article by Rebecca Ascher-Walsh, "Does Hollywood Have a Jewish Problem?" gives a good review of the entrenched embarrassment over or resistance to showing strongly Jewish characters in recent films.[3] She suggests that:

> Ironically, what paralyzes Hollywood the most may be the ambivalence of its own executives, many of them Jewish, about seeing Jews represented on the screen. "There are so many Jews who came out here and figured out how to pass," says [director Todd] Graff. "It's hard for them to make a movie about the kind of Jewishness they've turned their backs on."[4]

Whatever the motives of the writers, directors, actors, and producers to de-Judaize the Jews in popular depictions of them, the fact is that the tenor of such characterizations remains remarkably constant through the decades. What particularly concerns me in this paper is the extent to which assimilation is made so attractive—even or perhaps especially to Jews—at the very moment that the hero denies the ritual practices of Judaism. This point is made in an extraordinarily subtle and ambiguous—yet potent—fashion in the episode of *Northern Exposure* I would like to examine closely, "Kaddish for Uncle Manny" (Episode 4.22, the twenty-second episode in the show's fourth season, 1993).

II. A CLOSE READING OF "KADDISH FOR UNCLE MANNY"

In this episode, Fleischman receives word that his beloved Uncle Manny has died. Fleischman promised his uncle he would say *Kaddish*, the prayer for the dead. But to properly say *Kaddish*, as Fleischman explains to his Eskimo friend Ed, a Jew needs a *minyan*, ten Jews (in traditional construction, ten adult men). "Why?" asks Ed. "I don't know," Fleischman replies. "Nine guys on a field for baseball, ten guys in a room for a *minyan*." But what is to be done? Of course, Jews are in short supply around Cicely, and for that matter, in all of Alaska. As one character says, "I doubt whether you could find ten Jews within two thousand miles of here."

Maurice is a cartoon of a military man who finds himself surrounded and often bewildered or beleaguered by alien "types": a neo-hippie, full-blooded Inuits, a macho woman pilot, an MTV-generation Californian, and now this New York Jew whom he cannot fathom. Maurice commits himself to helping Fleischman if only to keep sane the doctor in whom he has invested so much. As Fleischman says to his face, "I always thought of you as a loudmouthed, unprincipled bigot . . . but I really appreciate this gesture."[5] Maurice investigates the Jewish rules of mourning. He gathers the other residents of the town in a military-style briefing and orders them to go out and round up "nine other Hebrews."[6] For many in his audience in Cicely, not to mention the wider American viewing audience, the whole concept of "Jew" is rather unsettling to begin with. As the townsfolk talk to Joel about it, they say "a Jewish person," a "Hebrew," "one of your people," "a worshipper," etc., but only once or twice do we hear the word "Jew" from the lips of a gentile. As

Maurice clearly knows, trying to educate the Cicely townsfolk in the subtle skills required to distinguish between *Americans* and *American Jews* is a tricky business. Their problem is "How do you spot one?" Many of them don't know any other Jews besides Fleischman. Maurice anticipates the problem and sets about trying to define a Jew to the residents of Cicely. The trouble is, Maurice, bigot that he is, thinks only in stereotypes. So when he struggles to find an apt description of what a Jew is, the best he can come up with is they're "a lot like your Chinese people, only with a sense of humor." That's not good enough, so he expands, getting himself deeper into the conundrum of How to Spot a Jew.

Jews can look just like everyone else, he notes—they do not comprise a distinct race. Maurice shows the townspeople a photo of a group of *Chasidic* Jews and says, "Jews don't look like this anymore." Then he shows a photo of Kirk Douglas, one of the best known "Jews who pass" (Douglas changed his name, became a Hollywood star) along with Tony Curtis (né Bernie Schwartz).[7] The photo is from Douglas's role in the movie *Spartacus* (1965). The iconography of this snapshot itself would be worth another essay about the Greco-Roman versus the Jewish dichotomies in Western culture. But Maurice is no academic. He has chosen this photo to prove the point that Jews can look just like anyone else. In fact, the photograph suggests that *"they" can look even more American than Americans* to the point that they get cast in roles that embody classical Greek (and therefore classically gentile) ideals of manliness, robustness, stoic speech, and courage. Douglas even has the rugged cleft chin, his "mark." Shelly in her naiveté captures this collapse of distinctions: "Wow!" she exclaims in amazement. "Hercules was Jewish."

In short, Maurice implies, the Jew can even pass himself off as the anti-type of the stereotypical Jew: a muscular, robust, bare-chested classical Roman gladiator, made further ironic by the historical relationship between Roman oppressors and the ancient Israelite Jews. Maurice continues. At other times and in other places, one might be able (were it even possible to arrange to do so) to look for that indelible marker, the circumcised penis. But, as Maurice says, now even that sign has been universalized. As he wistfully puts it, with an oxymoron worthy of Yogi Berra, "with the proliferation of circumcision . . . the tip of the penis . . . is no longer a . . . yardstick." We laugh as Maurice in one stroke unconsciously reveals his own doubts about his masculinity, his nostalgia for a time of clear ethnic divisions, and his bumbling metaphor. It's worth lingering a moment over this wonderfully silly metaphor.

It is a common anti-Semitic fantasy that circumcision is part of a conspiracy of Jewish doctors to either Judaize real Americans or aid Jews in passing as a gentile. Exploring Maurice's Freudian slip further reveals a complement to these dark fantasies. Maurice's literal intent is to suggest that the tip of the penis "is no longer a valid form of ID" as he puts it, distinguishing Jew from gentile. But there is a general male lament lurking in his words: the penis is no longer what it used to be, no longer as long, and therefore, psychically speaking, no longer as potent. And there is also an accusation: because circumcision has been universalized, "[the tip of] my penis [like those of most Americans] is no longer as long as a yardstick. In fact, it's been cut off!" Finally, there is a potential, though admittedly tenuous, implication based on the lurking stereotype of the Jews as sexually more potent and more active: since the Jews have come along as competition, I can no longer use my penis as I once did, when its tip alone—now cut off—was as long as yardstick.

In the end, Maurice is reduced to repeating simple caricatures and platitudes about how one might go about finding a Jew in contemporary America: "They tend to go towards the professions. . . . [When I was an astronaut] I was glad to have a lot of Goldfarbs and Finkelsteins at the buttons. Although," he adds with a sniff of macho condescension, "none of them got into the cockpit of a Mercury capsule."

Arming them with not much more than that, Maurice bids the good people of Cicely go forth across Alaska to scan the phone books. "Look for names with colors in them, like GREENberg and GOLDstein," he says.

One by one, the townspeople bring to Fleischman the Jews they have found. As the process goes on, however, Fleischman grows more depressed and mournful, until he has a nightmare: dressed in late nineteenth century Western clothes, he emerges into the sunlight of Cicely's Main Street. Nine cowboys wearing sheriff's badges (which were, in historical fact, often six-sided like the Star of David) ride up to him and pull their horses to a quick stop. Their leader says, "Dr. Fleischman—we're your Jews." They're the "Minyan Rangers—Have Torah will Travel!" One by one they are introduced, and indeed some, but not all, bear Jewish names. Yet all defy the stereotype in one broad way or another. They look as diverse as America itself and, in fact, embody Americana. There's The Chief, complete with feathered bonnet. He holds open his palm and instead of saying "How" says "Shalom" (a scene lifted from Mel Brooks' film *Blazing Saddles* (1975) and Gene Wilder's *Frisco Kid* (1979) which in turn can be traced back to pre-colonial sources conjecturing that Native Americans were the lost tribes of Israel). There's Yehuda, a black Jew (*Falasha*) from Ethiopia. There's Levi, a converted Eskimo, and there's also Strauss. In this dream sequence, Joel is recapping an incident in his waking life when Ed brings Joel a tall, broad-shouldered lumberjack who arrived in Cicely by hitchhiking. Ed introduces him as "Buck Shane." An incredulous Fleischman can't believe it. Buck can't be Jewish, he says, because "Jews don't hitch. They don't wear red suspenders and slobber tobacco juice in their beards and don't have names like Buck." Furthermore, Shane isn't a Jewish name.

"It used to be Schoen," Buck says.

Joel, still disbelieving Buck, challenges him to recite the *Sh'ma*, the basic prayer in all Jewish liturgy reaffirming a Jew's faith in the singularity and unity of God. In other times and places, being forced to pass this test, uttering this shibboleth,[8] this password, might be a humiliating prelude to martyrdom. At the same time, it recalls the biblical origin of the word "shibboleth." The Ephraimites revealed themselves by mispronouncing this word and therefore were prevented from crossing over the river to join the army of the victorious Jephtaph. Here, Buck recites the *Sh'ma*, confesses he was from a well-known Jewish suburb of Cleveland, and asks whether his fee for showing up for the *minyan* includes breakfast and "money on the barrelhead."

This extraordinary confrontation deserves closer scrutiny. Here we have Fleischman, a stereotypical New York Jew—a whiny, fastidious, ironic, overly-critical, neurotic, tense, superior, liberal, intellectual, anxiety-ridden, self-absorbed doctor in the process of struggling with his own assimilation. He faces a fully assimilated Jew, the anti-stereotype Jew, one who could not get far enough away from his roots and who has successfully adopted the guise of a northwoods lumberjack, down to the red suspenders and the tobacco chaw. But the stereotyped Jew challenges the assimilated Jew to declare and expose his Jewish identity by uttering the shibboleth, the password, in this case, the *Sh'ma*. Yet in exposing Buck, Fleischman exposes himself as a Jew who has taken the final step of assimilation: he believes the same libel about his own people that his hosts like Maurice do. He wants to see a Jew like himself, a Jew who doesn't hitch, who wouldn't enter the cockpit of a Mercury capsule. A Jew, in short, who doesn't pass! So he forces Buck, who fully passes, to expose himself as a Jew, to cross back over the line of assimilation and return to the camp of the defeated Ephraimites. By reciting the *Sh'ma,* Buck exposes his reluctant Jewishness. But by making Buck recite the *Sh'ma,* Fleischman exposes his ambivalence about his own identity as a Jew; indeed, he exposes the extent to which he has already assimilated at the very moment he is trying to assert his Jewish identity.

By uttering the shibboleth of the *Sh'ma,* Buck enables Fleischman to see the line he must cross in the opposite direction, back into the camp of victors to whom Buck has assimilated. It's as if Fleischman has demanded, "Show me the way to cross [back] over to the victorious camp." In this paradox, Fleischman has reached a crisis.

With his nightmare of the Minyan Rangers, Fleischman's crisis reaches a climax. He cannot go through with it, he confesses to Maurice. Maurice is exasperated. Of all the absurd incomprehensible things Fleischman has done, this one takes the cake. This is just one in a string of inexplicable acts by their Jew doctor, whose alien ways are filled with inexplicable contradictions and neurotic ambivalence. The explanation is self-evident, however: Fleischman is renouncing his Jewish community in favor of his adoptive, gentile one. In the history of this television series, this was also a critical turning point.

Now the theme of assimilating the Jew can be consummated. The next day, Sunday, Fleischman shows up in the town church with his *tallis* (prayer shawl) and *yarmulke* (headcovering). In his heartwarming eulogy for Uncle Manny, Fleischman also tells the townspeople his spiritual needs cannot really be fulfilled by the letter of the Jewish ritual, the *Halachic* (prescribed legal) requirement to mourn among ten Jews, even if they are strangers. Rather, he turns to the townspeople and tells them that *they* are his real friends, his real community. Standing at the pulpit of a church he recites the *Mourner's Kaddish,* in Hebrew.

The moment is wonderfully moving, perhaps most moving for Jews. The natural memories we have of our own sadness evoked by the recitation of the *Kaddish* are here amplified by a deep reservoir of longing and fantasy. Yet, when I first saw it, this *Kaddish* scene evoked in me a queer and unsettling mixture of conflicting feelings. On the one hand, I wept, for I felt I had witnessed a long-awaited reconciliation or reunion. On the other hand, I felt a disquieting sense of exposure and revulsion, akin to eating forbidden food. Understanding this longing and this revulsion is the key. To do so, we must examine the paradoxes of anti-Semitism.

III. THE NEED TO ASSIMILATE THE OTHER

One of the achievements of Sander Gilman's excellent work, *The Jew's Body*,[9] is that it shows how, with all matters concerning anti-Semitism, every image and libel and cultural current or theme that tries to set the Jew apart as a separate and reviled race comes loaded with complexity, ambiguity, and paradox.[10] As Gilman shows, the Jew does not comprise a separate race and yet is almost always treated (and, I would add, often treats himself) as one. This is certainly borne out in this television episode of *Northern Exposure*. For instance, it is only in his acceptance—his generous desire to make Fleischman feel at home *in his very Jewishness*—that Maurice exposes his own polite and unconscious anti-Semitism. Maurice is a *country club* anti-Semite: he espouses a doctrine of equality and freedom of religion in public at the same time that he votes against letting Jews on *his* golf course or in *his* cockpit.[11] His image of the Jew, and perhaps even his efforts on Joel's behalf, should be as disquieting and outrageous, were it not so funny, as the condescending cocktail chatter of liberal whites who are eager to show African-Americans how comfortable they are with "you blacks." Yet, Maurice means well, sort of. His feeling of responsibility for Fleischman is genuine. Even his desire to fulfill the letter of Fleischman's religious duty, though he only dimly understands it, is heartfelt and extraordinary.

Yet in the same doubling way, *Fleischman cannot assimilate until he exposes himself as the utterly alien Jew.* As Fleischman moves towards observing the ritual demands of mourning and unpacks his *tallis* and *yarmulke*, his understanding of his own Jewishness becomes increasingly ambiguous and ambivalent. At the end of this tale, Fleischman's identity as a Jew disappears entirely in a very comforting accommodation to universality. But the final effacement of his identity as a Jew cannot occur until he fully exposes himself as a Jew first. As this episode begins, he feels strangely compelled to fulfill the letter of Jewish law concerning the prayer for the departed. In the context of the television series, this compulsion represents a culmination of Fleischman's evolving confrontation with (and exposure of) his own identity as a New Yorker and as a Jew (fulfilling a not-so-subterranean elision of the two cultural types, captured in the disparaging name for The City in folklore: "Jew York"). On the one hand, Fleischman remains throughout the show prototypically New York Jewish: neurotic, uptight, a bit hypochondriacal, singularly unsuited for life in the frontier town. On the other hand, over the many weeks and years of his character's development, Fleischman gives up markers of his Jewish religious identity one by one: he forsakes his Jewish New York girlfriend for Maggie, the feminist wildcat pilot from Michigan. By the end of Joel's stay in Cicely,[12] Joel learns to love native food. He hangs out in Harley's frontier bar and drinks beer. He even unwinds a little. But in the end, he cannot make his peace among these American gentiles; his life among them dooms him to neurotic alienation.

How are we to understand Fleischman's sudden desire to put on a *tallis* and a *yarmulke* and observe the letter of the law? Fleischman's need to say *Kaddish* must derive from some very deep well of his religious identification, one that goes beyond the ethnic or regional characteristics that have marked him in prior episodes. Perhaps it is the return of the repressed religious Jew in Fleischman fighting for life, a sudden burst of psychic energy from an identification in its death throes. After all, like a majority of American Jews, he wasn't concerned with dietary laws or keeping the Sabbath or any other Jewish laws of observance; indeed, there was nothing overtly "religious" about him. This sudden eruption of religious feeling is inexplicable and irrational, except if we understand it only literally in terms of a sentimental pledge to his departed uncle.[13] It is akin to a successful businessman suddenly appearing at a banquet in his honor dressed in women's clothing: Fleischman is coming out of the closet, revealing some hidden essence of his identity.

But it is precisely this sudden revelation, this almost reflexive urge to say *Kaddish* in *tallis* and *yarmulke*, that provides the opportunity for the comforting enactment of purge and ultimate release into final assimilation. Fleischman's religious feeling is universalized. It flows out to merge into the town's gentile, cosmopolitan American culture. Although he is warmed and gratified by the community's desire to help him be a Jew, that very act only further proves that his Jewish identity, now linked to a religious ritual, is obsolete, no longer necessary. In other words, and here is the final paradox that Gilman predicts we will find in all such depictions, the community's acceptance of Joel at his most Jewish— clothed in all the accouterments (the word *outré* lurks in there)—comes at the very moment, is the cause of the moment, of his final move to assimilation and his final denial of his ritual Judaism. This Jew's real community is in Cicely, (this episode implies) among the people, non-Jews all, with whom he has become intimate. And they reciprocate the feeling, welcoming him. Why does Fleischman accept Cicely but reject the Minyan Rangers as his true *minyan?* The Minyan Rangers are Jews who are as diverse as Cicely. They are just as American. The only difference is that Cicely is made up friends-but-gentiles, whereas the Minyan Rangers is made up of Jews-but-strangers. Fleischman has abandoned the letter of the Jewish law (he must mourn within a community of Jews, marked by ten men) in order to embrace the spirit of mourning ritual (mourn among your community and be comforted). The Jewish insistence on insularity and specification of physical practice is erased in favor of the gnostic Christian ideal of embracing the larger community in the spirit of the law, fueled by love. Indeed, if we trace the emergence of early Christianity out of splinter Judaism in the first century CE through Gnostic and Essene texts[14] we discover this is precisely the revolution that Jesus apparently preached: embrace the essence of Judaism's humanistic teaching but abandon the insularity, restrictiveness, and compulsory rules of *Halacha.* And so, Jewish law itself becomes universalized until it dissolves into the larger ideal of America's melting pot multi-culturalism, its warm spirit of community.

In his book *The American Religion* Harold Bloom writes:

> Unlike most countries, we have no overt national religion, but we do have a partly concealed one that has been developing among us for some two centuries now. It is almost purely experiential, and despite what you may expect, it is scarcely Christian in any traditional way.[15]

Bloom characterizes this American Religion as being closest to early Christian gnosticism. Bloom goes on to predict that "only varieties of the American Religion will finally flourish among us, whether its devotees call themselves Mormons, Protestants, Catholics, Moslems, Jews or New-Agers."[16] In "*Kaddish* for Uncle Manny" we see an important step in the conversion of one Jew to The American Religion. Fleischman gives up all essential signs of his Jewishness, his singular attachment to following arcane Halachic rules of mourning, in favor of embracing the larger, non-denominational American religion.

The pleasure this fantasy activates in most viewers, especially I believe in its Jewish viewers, is intense. It fulfills many consummations that are devoutly wished by anyone in America who feels they are caught between the two worlds of their hereditary religion and the less stringent American Religion, even if they are further along in their assimilation to American culture than is Fleischman, as most Jews are. Fleischman's story here represents a "way out" (or a "way across") for the Jew who is proud of his or her Jewish identity, but who is painfully aware that to be a Jew is to embrace difference through physical and material practices: the clothes you wear, the food you eat, even where you live, how you marry, how you die, and the calendar you keep. To retain all the markers of Judaism or even any single one (*kashrut*, *mikvah* observance, modest dress, headcovering, *shomer Shabbos*), especially its religious rituals, is to be set apart, closed out from the mall of American culture. Even mourning requires Jews to live among enough other Jews so that when the time comes you can make ten. That's really at the root of why, as Fleischman says, "Jews don't hitch."[17] Not only are they generally fearful and cautious because of their insular lives in urban centers, the Jew cannot take the risk of taking to the open road alone or of becoming a pioneer, a cowboy riding the range, an explorer, a frontiersman in Alaska, a lumber jack. What if he needs a *minyan?* Jews can be Batman or Superman or Flash or Spiderman, especially given the doubleness of those heroes' urban identity: heroes in disguise, trying to pass as one thing but harboring another, secret identity. But a Jew cannot be The Lone Ranger or Davy Crockett or Buck Schoen and still be a religious Jew: one who observes laws and practices which connect his daily life to the metaphysical.

This *Northern Exposure* episode fulfills the fantasy of many Jews, and indeed of many other ethnic groups, by enacting the total assimilation of a Jew to and his acceptance by a gentile community at the very moment that he has exposed his innermost Jewishness, his most metaphysical tendency, his "easternmost" religious urge to obey an ancient dictum—an urge so profound that it surprises even him. But of course in embracing the community that embraces him *in spite of his differentness*, he gives up the source of his differentness by universalizing it. Bloom predicts this will eventually happen—or indeed has already happened—to all religions that cook for long in the American stew. In the very final moments of this final scene,

Fleischman stands exposed before America, in the pulpit of the church of the American Religion, in all his naked Jewishness, clothed in a *tallis* and a *yarmulke*. As he recites the *Kaddish* all the congregants embark on their own version of mourning: Shelley crosses herself, another character places palms together as a Buddhist, another mutters an ancient Native Indian incantation, others join hands. Fleischman has fulfilled the American dream of the melting pot and finally adopted the American Religion as his own.

NOTES

1. As a man whose profession treats the body, the meat, the pun in Fleischman's name is not lost on us.

2. Although *Northern Exposure* is a true repertory series, as many of American television's best shows have been, dramatic and comic. The history of such great repertory television shows can be traced at least to *MASH, Hill Street Blues, Thirtysomething,* and probably back to the long-lived daytime soap operas like *General Hospital, As the World Turns, One Life to Live, The Young and the Restless,* and the aboriginal 1950s comedy repertory, *Your Show of Shows.*

3. Rebecca Ascher-Walsh, "Does Hollywood Have a Jewish Problem?" *Entertainment Weekly* (August 18, 1995), 28-31.

4. Ascher-Walsh, 31.

5. In one episode, Maurice misses his chance to consummate the romance of his lifetime with an English noblewoman because his stereotype prevents him from seeing her as available. She tells him so at her departure.

6. The inability of liberal gentiles, especially southerners, to use the word "Jew" is another mark of the unconscious anti-Semite. I was once invited to a friend's house in Virginia, on one of the old plantations on the James River, to celebrate her mother's birthday. Her father, in an attempt to show how much he knew about my "people," asked me to sing "one of those old Hebraic songs." He informed me that he knew several Hebrews and other members of the "Old Testamental tradition." Later that night I asked my friend, "Elizabeth, why didn't your father call me a Jew?" "Oh," she replied "he didn't want to insult you."

7. Ironically, both Tony Curtis and Kirk Douglas co-star in that great film *Spartacus* (1965) about a slave rebellion in ancient Rome that is filled with allegorical reference both to revolutionary politics in the 1960s and prefigurements of the Passion of Christ. Indeed, the film ends with a scene of the crucifixion of an endless row of slaves, and finally, that of Spartacus himself, played by Kirk Douglas.

8. See "Schibboleth" translated as "Shibboleth" and reprinted as excerpt in Jacques Derrida, *Acts of Literature*, ed. Derek Attridge (London: Routledge, 1991). An earlier version appears in Sanford Budick and Geoffrey Hartman, eds., *Midrash and Literature*, trans. Joshua Wilner (New Haven: Yale University Press, 1986). Derrida's essay is a brilliant and relevant discussion of the role of "shibboleth" in anti-Semitism and its connection to circumcision.

9. Sander Gilman *The Jew's Body* (New York: Routledge, 1991).

10. "An architecture of complexity and contradiction has a special obligation towards the whole: its truth must be in its totality or its implication of totality. It must embody the difficult unity of inclusion rather than the easy unity of exclusion." Robert Venturi, *Complexity and Contradiction in Architecture* (1966) quoted in Edward Tufte, *Envisioning Information* (Cheshire, Ct: Graphics Press, 1990), 51.

11. Indeed, in a recent episode, Harley, one of Maurice's friends and the town's tavern keeper, is rejected from Maurice's men's-only private club because another member objects to the fact that he is a "Huguenot." "You mean to tell me that because my daddy's daddy's grandaddy going back 300 years was a French Protestant I was blackballed?" he protests (28 Nov 1994). We can imagine how a Jew would have been treated in this most extreme example of the country club exclusiveness.

12. We see this most clearly in Fleischman's "last" episode (14 Nov 1994), which also signalled the beginning of the end of *Northern Exposure's* run on CBS (it was cancelled in Summer 1995). All through *Northern Exposure,* Joel's neurotic style and Maggie's "coolness" clash and become the problem source for many episodes. The friction between Maggie and Joel is a barometer of Joel's alienness, since Maggie is often presented as smoothly un-neurotic, blandly—and then later angrily—uncomprehending of Joel's difficulty and moodiness and twisty psyche. After a painfully prolonged quarrel (Maggie and Joel are trapped on a Russian jet for twenty-four hours, awaiting take off to a conference in Moscow), Fleischman, in an air of utter defeat and resignation, says, "There's nothing else for it, nothing else to do." He impulsively proposes to Maggie. She accepts. Instead of actually getting married, though, they attempt a trial marriage but then separate in one final near-violent clash. In fact, Fleischman retreats to an Inuit village upriver where in a few suggestive scenes we understand that Fleischman has achieved utter contentment out in the wilds, living the primitive life of an Eskimo, a most unlikely fate for the one-time New York Jew. In our last glimpse of him, he has become an outdoorsman and, for him, preternaturally calm and self-assured. In short, he has become an ultra Buck Shane—and Maurice's nightmare: he has crossed over that line into utter assimilation one last time so that Maurice would never be able to pick him out as Jew. But as in all this dreamwork, there is a doubled and ambiguous message: where Joel could not find happiness among American gentiles, he seems at peace among these Eskimos. We can only

understand this if we view Fleischman's Jewishness as a species of Orientalism, the ultimate Back Eastishness.

At the same time, this same final episode consummates the theme of Fleischman's *mésalliance* with Maggie as a death wish. Fleischman proposes to Maggie, they rush to her cabin, try to make love . . . and a shotgun goes off under her bed. Fleischman is spooked. They try again, and Fleischman has another brush with death. Fleischman more or less accuses Maggie of living too dangerously. Maggie, struggling to preserve her love for him, can't help but view him as a neurotic coward. To her, it is all a coincidence. To him, it is a sign of her "danger." She is the ultimate *shicksa*; a sign from Fleischman's repressed Jewish identity, struggling for its life, that any profound connection to Maggie spells death.

13. One can also imagine that the writers of the show were uncomfortable exposing Joel to a national audience in his fullblooded Jewishness, wearing *yarmulke* and *tallis* and praying in Hebrew were this scene not portrayed as alien.

14. Barbara Thiering, *Jesus and the Riddle of the Dead Sea Scrolls* (San Francisco: HarperCollins, 1992). In this book, Thiering also gives an excellent interpretation of Gnosticism, or at least of the nature of the break from Judaism which Jesus espoused: it attempted to release the ethical basis of Judaism from the constraints of its practice and its Temple-centered religion, thus universalizing it.

15. Harold Bloom, *The American Religion* (New York: Simon & Schuster, 1991) 37.

16. Bloom, 49.

17. I wrote the first draft of this paper while living in Israel as a Fulbright Scholar. This line of analysis triggered a whole string of contrasts between the American Jew of Fleischman's (and Maurice's) stereotype and the Israeli Jews, who regularly hitchhike as a holdover of their socialist tradition of mutual help, who are lumberjacks and Indian chiefs, who find the Woody Allen New York neurotic not only alien but a little repugnant, as a marker of intolerable weakness. This entire scenario of exposure and assimilation would be mystifying to the Israeli born and bred Jew, the *sabra*.

Jewish Music: Values
from Within Versus Evaluation from Without

Izaly Zemtsovsky

I. PRELIMINARY REMARKS

I would like to begin this article with a story that reveals the essence of viewing ethnic identity "from within and from without." Although I come from a Russian cultural background, I have always remembered a story told to me by a Jewish musicologist who was born in the Ukraine at the turn of the twentieth century. He had a younger blood brother who was in a *klezmer* group. My story-teller found out that his brother and his group used to play for both Jewish and Gentile weddings in the Ukrainian-Moldavian borderlands. He was amazed to learn that their repertory was the same for both kinds of weddings and that the only differences appeared in some details such as ornamentation (grace-notes, trills, accents, glissandos), small melodic repetitions or truncations, and interpolation.

"Well," my educated musicologist said trying to understand, "if they can recognize your versions. . . ."

"Oh, don't worry about that! If they both pay us, it means they both appreciate what we play for them."

"But what about you?"

"Us! We're professionals—we know how to play—we have to serve everybody!"

"But whose melody is this, really?"

"A good question, my dear musicologist! What does it matter to you? Who knows? Some think that it's their music, others are sure that this music belongs only to them. . . ."

"I'm curious. What do you think?"

131

"You know, I never thought about that. We simply know both faces of the same tune—the Jewish and the Ukrainian."

"A two-faced melody! You're a philosopher, good for you! But how do you feel as a person, as a musician?"

"I don't know. While I'm playing for a Jewish wedding, I feel like a Jew, but while I'm at a Ukrainian gathering—I really don't know."

"I guess you feel that you're 'outside looking in,' aren't you?"

"What a tricky question! I'm not thinking about myself but about the wedding. I know nothing about your theories. I know my music. I know their music. I know Moldavian music and maybe more. We grew up on many traditions. That's my business. It's as if I'm 'in' and 'out' at the same time."

"I felt that he had told the truth," concluded the musicologist.

These brothers were discussing a question of special importance for this article. This is the Jewish dilemma of being in Diaspora, that is, how to be an insider and outsider at the same time. A fundamental aspect of the Jewish mind is the ability to be simultaneously an insider/outsider. This is a basic Jewish quality in music-making and in musicology.

One of the central problems we face today is how to define Jewish musical identity, a task that is not easy because there are many types of Jewish music. Despite the widely accepted idea that Jewish music represents a single indivisible tradition, Key Kaufman Shelemay points out that "myths of continuity are necessarily disputed by scholarly scrutiny of the reality of change."[1] For the first "myth of continuity," this article will focus on the music of the Ashkenazic era of East European Jewry.

The opinion is often expressed that the secular folk song of European Jewry has a relatively recent origin and that "it is usually based upon a mixture of 'traditional' synagogue chants with elements of folk songs or folk dances of the host countries."[2] In actuality, we do not know enough about the Ashkenazic folk song to reach such a categorical conclusion. On the contrary, it would appear that the Ashkenazic musical legacy is much richer and more original than is generally supposed. It is astonishing to note, for instance, that after a millennium of being in a European Diaspora the Ashkenazim have preserved several basic oriental traits in their oral tradition: 1) division into men's and women's repertories, styles, and sometimes even cultures; 2) oral professionalism of wandering bards and minstrels in different epochs as well as men's instrumental ensembles of *klezmorim;*

and 3) monodic vocal music. This hypothetical typology of Ashkenazic folk music should be investigated in detail.

It is difficult to comprehend the Ashkenazic musical culture as a whole. The biblical cantillation, cantorial improvisation of *hazanim*, many folk songs, textless *nigunim*, and *klezmer* music exhibit a deep polarization that also exists even in synagogal music itself (the orthodox, conservative, reform, and reconstructionist types of worship). Nevertheless, the Ashkenazic mentality possesses a cohesiveness and single psychological continuum that is provided by the Yiddish language. Thus, as a second limitation, this article will be devoted only to Yiddish music.

It is commonly claimed that Jewish music, and Yiddish music in particular, has always reflected the influences of other cultures and that the Jews borrowed, absorbed, and then recreated parts of the other traditions with which they came in contact. The question of borrowing is not, in principle, a Jewish question because all civilizations thrive by borrowing and absorbing. Nevertheless, this question has special significance for Jewish musicology. In a letter dated February 11, 1904, the Russian critic Vladimir Stasov (1824-1906) wrote these words to the Russian-Jewish critic and composer Yoel Engel (1868-1927):

> I have always felt that it has long been overdue to introduce the Jewish contribution into the history and repository of modern European music. About half and perhaps more of all Gregorian, Ambrosian and other Christian chants are based on Jewish roots.... I think that a thorough study of Jewish melodies may become one foundation stone in the study of contemporary European music.[3]

However, most musicologists still prefer to study Jewish borrowings instead of investigating the originality of Jewish music.

The key to the concept of musical borrowing can perhaps be explained by the Jewish phenomenon of *gilgul*, meaning the rebirth of a soul in another life and consequently the transmigration or metempsychosis of a tune. This implies that the basis of Jewish music lies in borrowing as a form of transformation, transmutation, or metamorphosis. For instance, Hasidic communities have borrowed melodies from surrounding peasant groups and even considered such borrowings to be a legitimate form of composition and a spiritual act. As Ellen Koskoff has pointed out:

The Lubavitcher, as law-keeper, will not profane the melody, since he cannot, in his view, use it in an appropriate or "worldly" way. The borrowing and transformation of melodies by a Lubavitcher provides a means to eliminate potentially harmful influences and to activate the positive traces of *simhah* (joy) and *hitlahavut* (enthusiasm). Any melody, regardless of its source, is suitable for borrowing if it contains the requisite properties of *simhah* and *hitlahavut*.[4]

The Jewish concept of *gilgul* is surprisingly close to the theory of the Russian musicologist Boris Asaf'yev (1884-1949) about *pereintonirovanie*, that is, "reintoning," musical transformation, or melodic reworking. The history of world music could be viewed as a process of continuous "reintoning." In regard to the Ashkenazic tradition, many Hasidic *nigunim*, the numerous *zemirot*, and folk dance and song tunes belong to the category of borrowed or "influenced" material. Fifty years ago Gershon Ephros wrote about these features:

> They have been so much imbued with the Jewish spirit, that it is now impossible for us to disown them. What is more, the melodic changes, however slight, to which these tunes have been subjected in the course of their adaptation by the Jews, have actually transformed them into new material which, in many instances, has lost all connections with its original foreign source.[5]

The indigenous *gilgul* theory of Jewish music has been introduced in an effort to explain all processes of musical evaluation from within and from without on the basis of a triple concept of making, intoning, and articulating music.[6] I propose that a broad definition of articulation encompasses not only pronunciation but also behavior. The music-maker articulates as a single whole. Therefore, a new term, *ethnophore*, has been coined to name a person who is an authentic bearer of a specific ethnic and folk tradition. We are all, in principle, *ethnophores*, the bearers of some ethnic predilections, customs, habits, knowledge, memory, and music.

Articulation is always ethnically specific and ethnically unique; it belongs to a singer or narrator to the same extent as it belongs to a song or a folk tale. Articulation represents the difference between one ethnic tradition and another. For example, a particular song can be forgotten, substituted for another one, or modified, but the type of articulation is preserved. Articulation can not be falsified. Culture expresses itself through an *ethnophore*. An *ethnophore* conveys signs of the culture by means of his articulation. The "articulatory fund" of an ethnic group constitutes an inalienable, fundamental cultural legacy. Articulation is also a value category since it reflects the culture that an *ethnophore* possesses. By possession of the traditional articulatory fund an *ethnophore* demonstrates a position in life. That is why studying and preserving the articulatory fund has unique significance for scholarship and also for understanding the fate of traditional culture itself.

The memory of oral traditional music is materialized in the articulation of specific "intonational" information. Thus "intoning" may be considered to reflect semantic aspects of music: not "who" or "where," but "what about" and "what for." Intoning denotes the content of musical communication and is, in fact, a specifically musical type of thought. Briefly stated, articulation reflects a specific artistic level in the realization of a given intoning within a given tradition of music-making. In other words, all levels of music-making—creation, performance, and perception—are indissoluble and form an integral whole. Such is the concept that is being proposed to evaluate Jewish music.

The unity of musical thought, utterance, music-making, and perception represents the central concept of this approach. We cannot limit ourselves to just one of these four aspects but have to remember them all if we want to appreciate real music value. As Johann Wolfgang von Goethe wrote: *"Nichts ist drinnen, nichts ist draussen, denn was innen, das ist aussen."* Nothing is wholly "within" or "without" in music, including articulation. The function of articulation is to bring thought into the open and to externalize the internal.

In practice, however, musicologists prefer to emphasize "how" to the detriment of "what"—they do not stress the nature of the material but its treatment as if the "treatment" may be unnatural. Such assertions in general cannot reflect the deeply syncretic essence of the arts. It is impossible to study "how" as the main feature of any music without a dialectical penetration into the consequent "what." Among the many "hows" of Jewish music they list a peculiar manner of singing, articulation and gesticulation, and ornamentation.

Other attempts have been made to define Yiddish music from "without" (i.e., by passing over its distinctive musical content). Max Wohling has proposed the following in this regard:

One can replace the definition [of Jewish music] by statements of preferences, choice and emphasis. Motifs of Jewish music may be traced to other nations but the emphasis, the preference and the choice is what make it dear to us.[7]

One may ask why Jewish musicians and all anonymous creators of the folk legacy have no had other preferences, choices, and emphases? What did all this mean to them from a musical within?

It seems that any "how" might be explained from within by a specific "what." Again the Hasidic tradition presents a good example. Their *nigunim*, sacred but non-liturgical melodies, were and continue to be encouraged by Habad philosophy. These melodies are considered to be spiritual for them and "are felt to be best suited to awaken and sustain the proper atmosphere for *devekuth* [adhesion],"[8] a divine realm that appears to be the most important Hasidic concept of all. Behind every "how" there are a special "what" and "what for." One has to look beyond articulation or preferences to examine their organic unity with the musical content. Anyone who evaluates Jewish music solely from without can permit himself or herself to be limited by articulation, but one who wishes to evaluate this art from within must be aware of the intrinsic gist of its hidden quintessence.

II. EVALUATION FROM WITHOUT

While documentary references to Jewish music in Europe date back to the thirteenth century,[9] in Russia they appear from the very beginning of Russian history in Kievan Rus, the Old Russian medieval state that existed from the ninth through the thirteenth century. Here we find the first and also the most complicated example of the evaluation of Jewish music "from without" through Russian eyes. Close reading of Russian oral epics (*bylina*), which originated from the tenth through thirteenth centuries, reveals extensive interrelations among all Eurasian cultures including Western and Eastern Europe. These epics offer additional evidence to support the attitude in Old Russian chronicles that Kievan Rus had a multicultural life and therefore was a typical medieval European country. This aspect of Kievan Rus has been neglected not only because written sources are contradictory, but also because a certain tendentiousness has been introduced into the discussion. As a result, the question of multiculturalism in medieval Rus has become unduly complicated. Perhaps the most misleading and, unfortunately, widespread hypothesis concerns the idea that Kievan Rus was characterized by geographical and cultural provincialism.

The *bylina* evinces its own historical truth, its own indigenous ethnic heroes, and typical medieval phenomena such as wandering epic singers, narrators, and musicians. The *bylina* also may shed new light on the history of European music, medieval musical instruments, terminology, and even repertory. The *bylina* helps to elucidate the contribution of foreign music and music-making in medieval life, casting light on the perception of such music, especially among the upper classes of Kiev and Novgorod, the two main cultural centers of Kievan Rus. The *bylina* succinctly reflects the cultural wealth and diversity of the Kievan state, its astounding ability to absorb features from outside cultures, and to adopt, creatively and organically, even contradictory ethnic traits.

Russian epics contain references to music, melodies and verses, the tuning of instruments (the "tightening" of strings), and musical genres of various people who performed in many different contexts, for instance, at the court of the Grand Prince. According to these passages, Kievan Rus possessed a culture which resulted from an amalgamation of races, peoples, and cultures, and which enhanced its power and originality. For example, in one epic about Dobrynya Nikitich,[10] perhaps the main hero who performs music, the following lines appear:

> Dobrynya was playing excellent melodies,
> He first covered the area within Kiev itself,
> Then from Kiev to Tsargrad [i.e. Constantinople],
> From Tsargrad to the land of the Saracens [Arabs],
> From the land of the Saracens to that of Italy,
> From the land of Italy to Jerusalem.[11]

In other places we learn about enigmatic "Jerusalem tunes" and even "Hebrew verse," that is, about Jewish melodies which evidently were in use together with other tunes, both native and foreign. The Russian bards enumerate various geographical places from which epic performers supposedly borrowed their melodies. This is a striking confirmation that Russian medieval music (both oral professional and written liturgical) had several cultural sources and, at the same time, that a path for transmission of European and Oriental music existed from Italy and Jerusalem through Byzantine, the Middle East, and the Caspian Sea to Kievan Rus. The *bylina* also shows how professional musicians were the main bearers and transmitters of European multiculturalism in the Middle Ages.

A few epics deal with musical performance during a splendid banquet at the grand prince's palace in Kiev. Vladimir requests Dobrynya to start his presentation with "a melancholy and touching style of playing" and then to offer something joyful:

> Dobrynya played *a Hebrew verse*
> In melancholy and touching fashion;
> The guests were brought to a pensive mood
> And hearkened in silent delight.
> Dobrynya the turned to joyful playing:
> He first proffered an elaborate *melody from Jerusalem*....[12]

In other epics Dobrynya and some other Russian epic heroes also play mysterious songs or tunes "from Jerusalem." For instance, in the bylina about Stavr Godinovich the following lines appear:

> [Stavr] brought out *the Jerusalem tunes,*
> And played, in addition, *a Hebrew verse.*[13]

It is evident that Jewish music was not only recognized in Kievan Rus, but was even well liked there. Of course, it has to be understood that the *bylina* represents a special type of historical source because it is an artistic work and not a factual chronicle. Even though the *bylina* does not usually reflect history directly, many of its motifs and images are nevertheless traceable to historical reality and can be utilized for comparison and reconstruction of actual historical events.

Although little specific knowledge is extant about how the Jewish settlement in Kievan Rus came into being, nevertheless epics may provide a fresh look at this topic. In particular, Kievan data can be connected with the almost forgotten and knotty question about the history of the Khazar Kingdom (650 to 1016) which accepted Judaism as its state religion in 740. The Khazar state, which existed in territory later to become part of southern Russia, had numerous contacts with Russians and Jews, something that has been reflected in Russian chronicles, legends, and oral poetry. All known types of materials, including epic texts, should be studied because they mutually support each other despite the fact that independent methodologies may be involved. The numerous Jewish motifs in Russian epics are not accidental, but represent such independent historical evidence.

By late in the eleventh century Kiev had became an important Jewish center. Close cultural and social ties were established between the Jews of Russia and those of Central and Western Europe. There are grounds for asserting that the Jews constituted an important factor in the cultural and religious life of Kievan Rus. This is in part manifested in epics as "Hebrew verse," a special kind of religious singing which was undoubtedly familiar to people in the multicultural environment of Kiev and which has been symbolically connected by traditional bards with the city of Jerusalem.[14]

Let us leave the ensuing centuries behind and draw nearer to the present.[15] We can cite several evaluations of Yiddish music "from without" which were given publicly. It is amazing that even scorn, disdain and mockery have been transformed by the Jews into power and glory. One instance concerns Mohammed's derisive words "the people of the book" which the Jews have changed into unconditional praise and their best self-definition (*am-hasefer*). Similar things have happened in the realm of music. Let us consider a few other examples.

On 30 November 1908, several Russian-Jewish musicians, who planned to organize a large permanent society for Jewish music in Russia, came to the Governor of St. Petersburg, General Drachevsky, to request legalization of the society. It had been decided beforehand to call the organization "The Society for Jewish Music," and with this in mind (according to the recollection of one of those delegates, Solomon Rosowsky) they presented their case before the Russian bureaucrat.[16]

"What!" he exclaimed, "a Society for Jewish Music! Is there such a thing as Jewish music?"

Whereupon, Rosowsky, who had received a law degree from Kiev University before he came to St. Petersburg, metaphorically put on his judicial robes and stepped before the bar to plead for the defense. He pointed out the Jewish folk song and its inimitable characteristics. He drew attention to many Jewish composers (Anton Rubinstein, Jacques Halevy, and Karl Goldmark) who had occasion to use Jewish thematic material. He pointed to the Russian masters, Mikhail Glinka and "The Mighty Five," who had composed what they called "Jewish songs." As his climatic argument he reminded the General about the melody which was carved on Musorgsky's tombstone and which the composer used in his cantata "Joshua."

To all this the General replied, "Yes, indeed, I recall now having heard a Jewish melody once in Odessa at a Jewish wedding. But that was a folk song. I think your society should rather call itself the Society for Jewish Folk Music."

Although the petitioners took exception to this suggestion, they felt that they had already won so formidable a victory that they let the name stand as the General had recommended.

This eloquent testimony can be read as an open recognition of Yiddish folk music; this was not a defeat ("The Jews have no music of their own"), but a victory ("The Jews do have folk music for weddings!"). This powerful rule of opposites should be kept in mind.

The next example concerns the Hungarian pianist and composer Franz (Ferenz) Liszt (1811-1886) who publicly denied the musical genius of the Jewish people but nevertheless became famous in Jewish musicology because of his enthusiastic praise for Sulzer's art.

Salomon Sulzer (1804 - 1890), a celebrated cantor, was gifted with a phenomenal voice and a fiery temperament. It is no wonder that his appearance in Vienna caused a sensation. However, an authoritative specialist in Jewish music, Abraham Zvi Idelsohn (1882-1938), argued that Sulzer's preparation in Jewishness and his impressions of Jewish life were very meager:

Not a single tune he created anew has a genuine Jewish character. . . . He was more imitator than creator. He did not understand the Semitic-Oriental character of the Jew. . . . He did not feel the Eastern European *hazanut*.[17]

He overemphasized the phase of exultation and holiness in the Synagogue song, neglecting the no less important emotional strain, the sentimental note in Jewish song, an important feature in Semitic-Oriental music. Due to the lack of that element Sulzer's music and style makes an exalted but cold impression upon the pious orthodox Jew. . . .[18]

Sulzer may not have known much about Jewish music, but, Idelsohn continued:

he did instinctively feel or he deduced the fact from the general character of Jewish traditional tunes that the manner of Jewish musical expression was a different one from that of the German. . . . A sacred fire burned in his heart, the light and warmth of which inflamed all his hearers.[19]

Moreover, Sulzer was the first to base the Synagogue song on classical Western European harmony and style (i.e., as far as possible from authentic Jewish traditions). Nevertheless:

> For the first time in Jewish history in the Exile did a cantor become so famous, so honored by kings and princes, by artists and musicians, by magnates of wealth, and by academies of art. For a half century he not only reigned over the entire caste of *hazanim,* but held the veneration of the entire modern rabbinical and scholarly world, esteemed by it as the authority and genius of Israel's song. Hundreds and hundreds of *hazanim* were his pupils.[20]

Compare, however, the non-Jewish perception of Salomon Sulzer offered by Franz Liszt, to that of Abraham Zvi Idelsohn. In his book, *The Gypsies:*

> Only once we witnessed what a real Judaic art could be if the Israelites would have poured out their suppressed passions and sentiments and revealed the glow of their fire in the art forms of their Asiatic genius, in its full pomp and fantasy and dreams —that hot fire which they kept so carefully hidden and they covered with ashes so that it should appear cold. In Vienna we knew the famous tenor Sulzer, who served in capacity of preceptor in the synagogue, and whose reputation is so outstanding. For moments we could penetrate into his real soul and recognize the secret doctrines of the fathers. . . . We went to his synagogue in order to hear him. Seldom were we so deeply stirred by emotion as on that evening, so shaken that our soul was entirely given to meditation and to participation in the service.[21]

The attitude quoted above of one gentile was the standard opinion of all gentiles who heard Sulzer. To them, his song and singing were something foreign, un-German, and even non-European. The same opinion was shared by assimilated Jews whose Jewish sentiments had dwindled to a minimum. Jews from the Ghetto—untouched by foreign influence—were overwhelmed by his powerful and sweet voice and inspiring rendition, but they were unaffected by Sulzer's Jewishness. To them, he was only a wonderful singer. They considered his music to be *galchish* (Church style) and by no means Jewish. They felt that the spirit of Sulzer's tunes was in agreement with the current views of European culture and life but not with their own. Idelsohn has formulated a penetrating thought in this regard:

> Music, the originality of which has so dwindled that it would not be recognized as their own even by its own people, is yet by another people considered foreign.[22]

Thus for authentic Jewish perception it is not enough to have a Jewish manner of speaking and singing. There is the expectation of experiencing genuine Jewish tradition in the music itself (i.e. the indissoluble and organic unity of truly creative "intoning," habitual articulating, and customary music-making).

In the context of an attempt to appreciate the evaluation of Yiddish music from without—by a method of involving a rule of opposites—the Sulzer-Liszt case is a significant one. According to Liszt, in music the Jews have nothing original but Sulzer (i.e., only synagogical music). This is another serious example of lack of proper appreciation, but not a defeat. On the basis of two clear denials of the musical wealth of the Jewish tradition, two forced but irrefutable acknowledgements were voiced: "The Jews have nothing but folk music." And, "The Jews have nothing but synagogical music." Both convey a positive image, that is, the Jews have a national musical tradition of their own in two domains, in secular and sacred music. These two types of music constitute the basis of musical culture in general for all peoples.

III. VALUES FROM WITHIN

Perhaps the fundamental problem of contemporary ethnomusicology in general and Jewish ethnomusicology in particular lies in understanding the "other." There have been many worthwhile attempts to elucidate this problem, but it has not yet received a satisfactory solution. The important question concerning "the musical self-portrait of a nation as a mark of its identity" has remained untouched. Although they do not necessarily constitute a barrier between cultures, different understandings and visions of the same culture from diverse points of view nevertheless exist. Being "from without," we are fated to see differently from those who are "from within" and whose identity has been formed by their birth and culture.

From a psychological standpoint, all people speak more or less the same way but use different languages. Differences of language, form, and imagery hinder mutual understanding of the common spiritual wealth of humankind. To be "from within" means to feel the spiritual wealth of a people organically and fully. The spirituality of other people should be as precious to us as our own spirituality, which is full of subtle associations and imperceptible overtones. To study folk music as the self-portrait of one people may offer a means to get to the heart of the matter (i.e., to penetrate beyond the language, form, and imagery of one people and to discover its spirituality, ideals, and self-perception).

It is natural that the whole world looks at us while we are looking at the whole world. One may say that within human history different musical worlds pulsate by their penetrability/impenetrability, sometimes coming close to each other and sometimes moving apart. And it is understandable that neither "they" nor "we" think about our mutual vision. Most probably "they" recognize us through the most accessible feature in music—through our articulation. They often take us for someone different because they do not know what we have behind our articulated images. We ourselves are used to looking outside through our own glasses, that is, involuntarily through the eyes of our traditional genres. We can see nothing but what and how these genres allow us to see.

At the same time our traditional genres (especially the genres of folklore) might serve as a special document of our own self-perception and self-evaluation. The more we study our music the more we learn about ourselves as a people. But during our involvement in our folklore tradition we tend to forget about the rest of the world with its glances "from outside in." Then we can allow ourselves the liberty of knowing nothing about such glances. We have a right to represent nothing and no one. Folklore is not intended for folklorists. Folklore has its own values, values that form a people's legacy.

To forget about glances from outside means to be at home. Although this is important for everyone, it is especially meaningful for any people in Diaspora. Our music is our home and represents our ideal family, (i.e., a place where we can be ourselves). This is clear because people inside the tradition take much for granted. Your tradition and your music remind you who you actually are. It continuously brings you back to yourself, to what inside you is often greater and better than you actually are. Thus Yiddish music gives back to every Jew a sense of Yiddish culture as a link between the past and the future. To be amidst our distinctive speech and singing intonations, and to be amidst such familiar sounds, rhythms and articulations, traditional music-making, and gestures and mimics means to be at home because all this nurtures your feelings, expectations, dreams, and hopes. You are happy because you discover your own values.

It is said that melodies can go where words cannot. Music becomes a catalyst in our search for spiritual identity. Often one familiar sound is enough to recognize or to remind you who and where you are. This is one reason why sound saves the world—your sound saves your world for you. Jewish music is liberating for Jewish people.

Music is not a mirror of culture, but a mysterious code of special inner cultural information which we are able to decode in the twinkling of an eye. All of us experience such identity feelings as *ethnophores*.

Albert Einstein's moving confession illustrates this liberating feeling:

> The Yiddish folk songs, why are they the most sincere, the most heartfelt I have heard anywhere? They are the truest expression of the soul of a people.[23]

The answer is clear: these songs touched Einstein because he was Jewish. It is impossible to be objective when you are affected by your own music. When you listen to your own music, you have such a different scope of information and associations that the only piece of advice I can give here is do not compare your folklore with others if you do not want to appear to be too naive. While you listen to your music, you can immediately feel your internal sense of belonging to your people and you can even "see" the whole history of your people without any boundary between the remote past and the present. You magically possess everything indigenous and you are filled with those spiritual riches. Nothing similar is possible for anyone who is outside your culture.

"From without" any one who is alien to some other music can evaluate it and some of its values; "from within" one can simply live by and use the values of their own music. At best "from without" they can participate in different ethnic music-making, while "from within" they are nurtured by their own musical values together with values of ethnic dress and style of behavior, food ways and smell, and everyday and holiday ways of passing their time within a given tradition. On the one hand, we take little cognizance of the problematic boundary between a researcher and a participant. On the other hand, we know even less about the exquisitely delicate boundary between a participant and an *ethnophore*.

Actually, evaluations "from without" and "from within" involve the clash of two different ways of hearing. As Abraham Idelsohn has pointed out, we hear much more in our own music because we are familiar with all its earmarks.[24] It is through the use of such signs (termed "intonational vocabulary" by Boris Asaf'yev) that music is recognized and memorized.[25]

It is beyond the scope of the present paper to show how this approach can elucidate all types and genres of Ashkenazic music, that is, to display the self-representation of the Jews through their own music. Instead, I will try to offer an overview of the Ashkenazic musical system.

The main feature of the Ashkenazic musical system is its musical bilingualism. We sing Hebrew and Yiddish, and sometimes a few other local languages such as Russian, Polish or Ukrainian. We have several different pairs of glasses with which to see and to appreciate different depths of our people's history and psychology. This bilingualism blends such opposing traits as old Oriental and modern Western musical features into something uniquely Ashkenazic. There is little sense of eclecticism because the whole is greater than the sum of its parts.

The biblical chant should be regarded as the first and fundamental Jewish melodic idiom. As Joseph Yasser (1893-1981) has pointed out:

> This ancient melodic product has never been challenged in the later history of Jewish music. It represents, perhaps, the only genuine and virtually unalloyed material that ever appeared in Jewish musical life.[26]

The cantillation, *our musical Tanakh,* forms the basic stratum of our legacy.

The second stratum is that of the continuously changing musical comments to the Bible given by *hazonim* (cantors). This can be called *our musical Talmud.* All over the world, Jewish synagogue music consists of three or four types of singing: psalmodies and simple prayer-chant, scriptural cantillation, melodies of *piyyutim,* and florid, melismatic chants. The last form is a particular legacy of cantorial music since it resembles "wordless hymns."[27] These hymns constitute an interesting point of departure for our evaluation "from without" and values "from within." "From within" they represent both our sacred and musical legacy; "from without" they sometimes are similar to an operatic style. For outsiders this music might be appealing because of the strange and haunting beauty of Jewish music. For instance, the French composer Maurice Ravel remarked: "I was so bewitched by the mysterious color and exotic charm of these melodies that for weeks I could not get this music out of my mind."[28]

For gentiles this music sounds more like a concert than a prayer. We have several CDs where the art of famous cantors was taken down in a recording studio. Despite this, we can never forget the inner spiritual essence and religious core of these musical revelations that are addressed to both God and people.

Cantorial music in Eastern Europe had its own distinctive character that was extremely lyrical and emotional. The artistry and astonishing musical imagination of skilled cantors played a central role. A highly gifted cantor-composer and cantor-artist from Southern Russia, Eliezer Gerovich (1844-1913), considered our old synagogue tunes to be "so full of health that they are able to sanitize and to normalize our people provided that Jews understand them."[29]

The era of the great cantors has passed, but in accordance with the law of the eternal return in Jewish history such a phenomenon is bound to appear again.

The third stratum of our legacy is Yiddish folklore which consists mainly of women's and children's genres—often intimate songs without accompaniment. Here we find the spirit and expression of ordinary Yiddish speaking people. Abba Kovner writes:

> More than anything else, the simplicity of their melodies and rhythms brings us closer to understanding the vitality of the Jewish character, the difference between the Jew's feeling-for-life and that of the surrounding peoples, which arose from the abundance of his sufferings and his poor man's joy.[30]

Among other Yiddish musical traditions can be mentioned the *klezmorim,* the only type of male music-making that is performed in public. For instance, everybody recognizes the *klezmoric* way of playing the clarinet and its typical Jewish laughing, dancing sound. I once played a *klezmer* recording for a Moldavian student of mine in Russia. He was sure that this music was the music of his people, but he was shocked to hear the Jewish performance of the same "notes" as in the Moldavian "doina." He admitted that a Jewish kind of performance as well as a Jewish way of musical thinking and behavior existed. *Klezmer* music constitutes a matter of special importance because non-Jewish folk musicians have continued to perform the pre-war Jewish repertory. There is much to be discovered here, but this is a special topic for ethnomusicological study.

My last example pertains to the Hasidic *nigunim*, textless songs or melodies that were sung exclusively by men, usually in public and in groups. According to Hasidic teaching, song comes from an even higher faculty of the soul than reason. Therefore, song has the power to penetrate our "spiritual confusions" and to reach even the most alienated person. A holy melody is redemptive if you are able to grasp it. A holy melody should be perceived not as music but as inspiration from above. Only evaluation "from within," evaluation born from your own inspiration, can reveal the true meaning of these melodies. The power of this music for the Hasidim themselves is immense. Rabbi Nahman of Breslav (1772-1810) taught that:

> There are spiritual confusions from which there is no return. However, the melody of a true *tzaddik*, a holy man, has the power to elevate even the souls which have fallen into them.[31]

Jacob Neusner recently called Jewish theology "sung theology."[32] In the Hasidic *nigunim* "sung theology" has even lost its words so that *melos* replaced the sacred text. Such an emancipation of music implies the type of intoning and articulation that should be equivalent to the spiritual essence of unspoken sacred words. Hasidim have as much faith in this music as they have in their prayers. One of the early masters of Hasidim, Rabbi Pinhas, spoke in high praise of music and song: "Lord of the world, if I could sing, I should not let you remain up above. I should harry you with my song until you came down and stayed here with us."[33]

Jewish (Yiddish) mysticism has created its own great music tradition in which music without words occupies a prominent place. Israel Adler, a renowned Judaistic scholar, once characterized Jewish music as "music without notes": "If, as with all aphorisms, this statement comports a certain measure of exaggeration, it nevertheless contains more than a grain of truth."[34]

But even such exaggeration is inadequate for Jewish spiritual imagination. Jewish thought prefers the spirit to be as high as possible above human beings. When there is less material covering, there is more spirit. Music without words becomes music without notes, even music without sounds!

There are two extremes in Jewish spirituality: on the one hand, we are completely "on the outside" in our gestures, shouts, and debates (this is often the only thing that is familiar to "outsiders"); on the other hand, we are completely "inside" and are afraid of any "reification" as if it were a pagan idol. Our spirituality always prevails over "pagan" form. For the sake of true music a Jew is ready to decline even articulation itself (i.e., to reject life itself). Yitzkhok Leibush Peretz (1852-1915) wrote about such an idea in his story "Kabbalists" (1894):

> There is melody that requires words: this is of low degree. Then there is a higher degree—a melody that sings of itself, without words, a pure melody! But even this melody requires voicing, lips that should shape it, and lips, as you realize, are matter. Even the sound itself is a refined form of matter. Let us say that sounds are on the borderline between matter and spirit. But in any case, the melody that is heard by means of a voice that depends on lips is still not pure, not genuine spirit. The true melody sings without voice; it sings within, in the heart and bowels. This is the secret meaning of King David's words: "All my bones shall recite. . . ." The very marrow of the bones should sing. That's where the melody should reside, the highest adoration of God, blessed be He. This is not the melody of man! This is not a composed melody! This is part of the melody with which God created the world; it is part of the soul that He instilled in it. This is how the hosts of heaven sing. This is how the rabbi, of blessed memory, sang.[35]

In principle, this kind of "hidden music" can be awakened in every spiritual Jew. To be "from within" means to hear before sound, to have a gift for "pre-hearing," to have a presentiment of desired spiritual values, and to hear everything "from within." The essence of Jewish music lies in the fact that it simultaneously is so disputable "from without" and so powerful "from within."

NOTES

1. Kay Kaufman Shelemay, "Mythologies and Realities in the Study of Jewish Music," *The World of Music* 37: 1 (Wilhelmshaven: Florian Noetzel Edition, 1995), 26. She means mythology of continuity vs. reality of diversity.

2. Eric Werner, "Identity and Character of Jewish Music," *Proceedings of the World Congress on Jewish Music (Jerusalem, 1978)*, ed. Judith Cohen (Tel Aviv: The Institute for the Translation of Hebrew Literature Ltd., 1982): 2; Benjamin Harshav. *The Meaning of Yiddish* (Berkeley: Univ. of California Press, 1990), 87: "Yiddish culture served as a bridge between the traditional religious Jewish society and assimilation into western languages."

3. For an English translation see Joachim Braun, "The Jewish National School in Russia," *Proceedings of the World Congress on Jewish Music*, 1982, 200.

4. Ellen Koskoff, "Contemporary Nigun Composition in an American Hasidic Community," *Selected Reports in Ethnomusicology* 3: 1 (Los Angeles: University of California, 1978), 158.

5. Gershon Ephros, "Melody and Jewish Music," *The Jewish Music Forum Bulletin* 7-8 (N.Y.: Society for the Advancement of Jewish Musical Culture, 1946-47): 8.

6. Izaly Zemtsovsky, "The Ethnography of Performance: Music-Making —Intoning—Articulating Music," *Folklor i Njegova Umetnicka Transpozicija*, ed. Dragoslav Devic (Belgrade: Fakultet Muzicke Umetnosti, 1987), 7-20; for the Russian notion *intonatsia* (intonation), see Boris Asaf'yev, *A Book about Stravinsky*, trans. Richard French (Ann Arbor: UMI Research Press, 1982); Gordon D. McQuere, "Boris Asafyev and Musical Form as a Process," *Russian Theoretical Thought in Music*, ed. Gordon D. McQuere (Ann Arbor: UMI Research Press, 1983), 217-252; Izaly Zemtsovsky, "Foundations and Achievements of Ethnomusicology in Leningrad (St. Petersburg)," *Ethnomusicologica* 2 (Siena: Accademia Musicale Chigiana, 1993): 241-249.

7. Max Wohlberg. See *"Proceedings of the World Congress on Jewish Music,"* (1982), 265 (from general discussion).

8. Koskoff, 155.

9. Walter Salmen, *Judische Musikanten und Tanzer vom 13. bis 20. Jahrundert* (Innsbruck: Edition Helbling, 1991).

10. "Dobrynya and Aliosha," see Petr V. Kireevskij, *Pesni* 2, 2nd ed. (Moscow: Society of the Lovers of Russian Literature, 1875), 113.

11. All quotations were taken from Joseph Yasser, "References to Hebrew Music in Russian Medieval Ballads," *Jewish Social Studies* 11: 1 (N.Y.: Conference on Jewish Social Studies, 1949), 21-48.

12. Ibid.

13. "Bylina about Stavr-Boyarin," see Kirsha Danilov, *Drevnie rossijskie stixotvorenija*, eds. A.P. Evgen'eva and B.N. Putilov (Moscow: Nauka, 1958), 96.

14. Presently I am working on a book, *Russian Oral Epics as a Source for the Musical History of Medieval Europe,* in which Jewish materials play the central role.

15. For details about some Jewish themes and images in Russian music, including Modest Musorgsky (1839-1881) and Dmitri Shostakovich (1906-1975), see Richard Taruskin, *Musorgsky: Eight Essays and an Epilogue* (Princeton, N.J.: Princeton University Press, 1993), 379-386; Joachim Braun, "The Double Meaning of Jewish Elements in Dimitri Shostakovich's Music." *The Musical Quarterly* 71: 1 (N.Y.: G.Schirmer, 1985), 68-80. For additional material see Robert A. Rothstein, "Jews in Slavic Eyes—the Paremiological Evidence," *Proceedings of the Ninth World Congress of Jewish Studies,* Division D, 2 (Jerusalem: World Union of Jewish Studies, 1986), 181-188.

16. Solomon Rosowsky, "The Society for Jewish Folk Music: Personal Reminiscences," *The Jewish Music Forum Bulletin* 9 (N.Y.: Society for the Advancement of Jewish Musical Culture, 1948): 9-10; see also: Albert Weisser, *The Modern Renaissance of Jewish Music: Events and Figures, Eastern Europe and America* (N.Y.: Bloch Publishing Co., 1954), 44-45.

17. Ibid., 258.

18. Ibid., 256.

19. Abraham Z. Idelsohn, *Jewish Music: Its Historical Development,* new Introduction by Arbie Orenstein. (N.Y.: Dover Publications, Inc., 1992), 254-55, 253.

20. Ibid., 256-57.

21. Ibid., 253-54.

22. Ibid., 254. It reminds me of a similar reaction by Russian peasants who could not recognize their own songs in a heavy choral harmonization: "They sing in German. . . . They sing in their own way, not in ours." See Eugenie Lineff, "Peasant Songs of Great Russia," Second Series (Moscow: The Imperial Academy of Science, 1911), 49-50. At the same time for all members of the Russian *intelligentsia* who did not know the authentic rural Russian tradition of singing, such a choir sounded quite correct and acceptable.

23. Quoted from the epigraph of "The Yiddish Songbook" by Jerry Silverman (N.Y.: Stein and Day Publishers, 1983).

24. Idelsohn, 27.

25. At the moment I am writing a theoretical paper on this topic where I argue my own notion of the "cultural anthropology of musical hearing" or, in a word, the "ethnography of hearing," as a key to the understanding of evaluation "from without" and values "from within."

26. Joseph Yasser, "The Biblical Chant as Basic Material for Jewish Music," *The Jewish Music Forum Bulletin* 7-8 (N.Y.: Society for the Advancement of Jewish Musical Culture, 1946-47): 9-10.

27. Eric Werner, "The Role of Tradition in the Music of the Synagogue," *Judaism* 13: 2 (N.Y.: American Jewish Congress, 1964), 162.

28. Quoted from the epigraph, *Anthology of Yiddish Folksongs*, by Aharon Vinkovetzky, Abba Kovner, Sinai Leichter, 3 (Jerusalem: Mount Scopus Publications by the Magnes Press, 1987).

29. Quoted from an unpublished manuscript about liturgical music written by Michael Gnessin (1883-1957), a Jewish composer and musicologist, see *The Central State Archives for Literature and the Arts*, Moscow, fund 2154/1. He also wrote that "while we condemn the synagogue for the assimilation of alien sacred art, we should not close our eyes to our temples' fostering of the old Hebrew chant"; see also Lazare Saminsky, "Music of the Ghetto and the Bible," (N.Y.: Bloch Publishing Company, 1934), 187 ff.

30. Abba Kovner, "Folksongs of a Vanished Era," *Anthology of Yiddish Folksongs*, Vinkovetzky et al., xxxvi.

31. Quoted from the epigraph to the CD, "Songs of the Breslever Chassidim: Today," produced by Andy Statman and Dovid Sears (N.Y., Tzefat: Shoresh Production in conjunction with Nachal Novea Mekor Chochma, 1994).

32. Jacob Neusner, *Judaism's Theological Voice: The Melody of the Talmud* (Chicago: The University of Chicago Press, Chicago Studies in the History of Judaism, 1995).

33. Martin Buber, *Tales of the Hasidim: The Early Masters*. (N.Y.: Shocken Books, 1972), 125.

34. Israel Adler, "Problems in the Study of Jewish Music," *Proceedings of the World Congress on Jewish Music* (1982), 20.

35. Ruth R. Wisse, ed., *Yitzkhok (Isaak) Leib Peretz Reader* (N.Y.: Schoken Books, 1990), 153.

"Wicked Jews" and "Suffering Christians" in the Oberammergau Passion Play

Gordon R. Mork

When one teaches a course on the Holocaust, as I do, the historical facts force one to represent European Jews largely as suffering victims. The perpetrators of the Holocaust, the wicked who imposed the suffering upon the Jews, came from the dominant community, a community which was, or which had been, Christian.

When one looks into the traditional representations of Jews and Christians in Western society, however, one sometimes sees portrayals in which these roles are reversed. This paper will describe and analyze the portrayals of Jews as "wicked" and Christians as "suffering" in one such traditional representation. To carry out the task of this paper, the author must make use of a number of stereotypes and therefore apologizes in advance if these portrayals offend. Yet they are part of the historical record, and unless we address them openly and honestly, without resorting to evasion and euphemism, we cannot come to grips with a past which, in some sense or other, burdens us all.[1]

In the year 1633 the villagers of Oberammergau, in the Bavarian Alps, were peacefully hoping to avoid the ravages of the Thirty Years' War, which was tormenting their country. As if the murderous bands of soldiers were not bad enough, the war brought with it an outbreak of the plague. No one knew at the time exactly how the plague was spread, but it was clear to everyone that once the epidemic entered a village it would create a painful death for a large proportion of the population within a few days. Oberammergau, relatively isolated in a mountain valley in southern Germany, made every effort to keep the infection from its doors. But the villagers failed, and it looked like the dreaded disease might totally wipe out the town if nothing were done. In this circumstance the village leaders, Roman Catholics all, met at the church yard and pledged before a large crucifix there that, if God would preserve the remaining villagers from the plague, they would perform a pageant reenacting the suffering of Jesus Christ—the Passion Play—once each decade, forever.

According to the village chronicle, no one died of the plague after that date. Oberammergau was saved. The following year, 1634, the play was performed there for the first time. The Passion Play did not originate in Oberammergau. Indeed, in the seventeenth century passion plays were quite common. But over the years many local passion plays were given up or banned by higher authorities, so that by the twentieth century Oberammergau stood almost alone in Europe as an example of this traditional piety.[2]

Over the years, the play's schedule was adjusted so that (except in times of crisis) the play was performed on zero-numbered years, and instead of being merely a production for the home town folk, it became an international attraction which was of major economic significance to the village and the surrounding area. But to be a part of the production and the performance, one still had to be from the village. No one is exactly sure what text was used for the play in 1634, but we do know that several different texts were used over the next 150 years, and fragments or full editions of them have been preserved in the local archives.[3] During the early nineteenth century the play was established more or less in its current form by two local priests, Father Weis and Father Daisenberger, and the music to accompany it was composed by the village schoolmaster, Rochus Dedler.[4] In the twentieth century it was performed in 1900, 1910, and was planned for 1920. The problems surrounding the First World War and the overthrow of Imperial Germany caused the rescheduling of the 1920 play to 1922. A regular performance followed in 1930 and a special 300th anniversary production took place in 1934, one year after Hitler took power. The 1940 production was in the planning stage when World War II began, and it was cancelled. Productions resumed after World War II in 1950, 1960, 1970, 1980, 1984 (the 350th anniversary), and 1990. The forthcoming play will be in 2000.

The Passion Play is based upon the biblical record. The major thread of the story follows Jesus of Nazareth and his supporters from his joyful entry into Jerusalem on "Palm Sunday," through his "Last Supper" with his disciples on Thursday, his betrayal and quick trial by the authorities, his execution through crucifixion on Friday, to his triumphal resurrection on Easter Sunday morning. Each scene in this drama is punctuated with flashbacks to scenes from Hebrew scripture that Christians call the "Old Testament," such as the expulsion of Adam and Eve from the Garden of Eden, Moses leading the Exodus, the sufferings of Job, and so forth, all interpreted as foreshadowing the story of redemption in the "New Testament." A Prologue Speaker and a choir, with soloists, comment upon the drama as it unfolds. The entire presentation takes a full day, with a single intermission at lunch time.

But the play goes well beyond the mere biblical record itself, incorporating Christian traditions, Roman Catholic theological concepts, and the creative genius of the authors of the play and the villagers themselves. Traditionally, no one may participate on stage who is not a birthright Oberammergauer or has lived there at least twenty years. Although the village still has only around 5000 inhabitants, the quality of the production of this musical drama is remarkably high. The strength of the tradition is so great that families devote themselves to the play, commit their young people to preparing for speaking or singing roles, and compete (sometimes with some bitterness) for the control of the play and the best parts in it. The play is a pageant and a melodrama, performed in the open air, even today in natural light and without an elaborate electronic sound system, before an audience in a covered hall which seats 5,000. The amateur actors, designers, and musicians want to make clear to the audience, many of whom understand little or no German, just what is going on, who is doing what to whom, who are the villains, and who are the righteous.

The play is consciously devoted to the "passion," that is to the "suffering," of Jesus, the Son of God, the Messiah. An important concept of Christian theology is that the long awaited Son of God was not a powerful avenger leading a mighty army, but a suffering servant, who washed the feet of his disciples and who allowed himself to be sacrificed to atone for the sins of all the world.

But the humiliations and physical pain heaped upon the Christ are not the only sufferings portrayed in the melodrama. Jesus' followers, that is his twelve disciples and the women of his entourage, especially Mary, his mother, suffered with him. These people, like Jesus himself, were (of course) Jews. But the traditional Oberammergau Passion Play showed them as "Christians," as one can see in the visual examples.

"The Jews," on the other hand, are presented in the traditional Oberammergau Passion Play as Jesus' enemies. When Jesus drove the money changers from the temple, he was cleansing the House of God from greedy commercial exploiters. These same temple traders, then, took councel on how to get rid of Jesus and contacted one of his dissatisfied disciples, Judas Iscariot. They brought him to the High Priests, Annas and Caiaphas, and the Jewish Council, who had their own reasons to suspect and fear the attractive young preacher from Nazareth. Thus a "Jewish plot" was born to kill the Son of God. The most despicable of the plotters in the play was a man known in the traditional Oberammergau text as "Rabbi," who denounced Jesus, pushed the others to get rid of him, and then scornfully rejoiced as Jesus suffered and died.[5]

The play has not been without its critics. Both Christians and Jews recognized that though it purported to be based directly on the biblical texts of Matthew, Mark, Luke, and John, the play had been written and rewritten so many times in the nineteenth century that it reflected the prejudices of that age. "The Gospel according to Oberammergau," as we might call it, was a melodrama pitting "good Christians" against "wicked Jews." Rather than acknowledging the Jewishness of Jesus and his followers, the play's traditional text and staging perpetuated the myth that the Jews, in general, were Christ killers, and it used standard antisemitic stereotypes for melodramatic effect. Thus it is little wonder that Hitler and his followers saw their version of virtue in the Oberammergau traditions of the first half of the twentieth century.[6]

When Adolf Hitler took power in 1933, the villagers were concerned that they would not be permitted to put on their traditional religious drama and that the newly appointed National Socialist mayor, Raimund Lang, would substitute a specially written version. Indeed, Lang did commission Dr. Leo Weismantel, a writer of popular folk dramas, to work up a manuscript. Several of the leaders of the village, who played major roles in the play, were upset by the attempt to change their tradition. They could not directly challenge the Nazi mayor, but they had connections via the neighboring village of Unterammergau with *Gauleiter* Adolf Wagner of Munich. Wagner had a weekend cottage on the shoulder of a mountain overlooking the villages of the Ammergau and saw himself as something of a protector of the local traditions. When Wagner challenged the mayor's plan, Raimund Lang disingenuously denied that he was making any change. Yet he continued to work with Weismantel on a new text secretly.

The local townsfolk protested to Wagner once more, citing the fact that Adolf Hitler himself had seen the play in its traditional form in 1930 and declared it a German national treasure. They also pointed out, correctly, that Weismantel was not National Socialist. This time Wagner issued a vigorous order to Raimund Lang and the town council of Oberammergau that the traditional text should be used again in 1934, and the local Nazis quickly fell into line.[7]

Adolf Hitler visited a performance of the play again in 1934, to the cheers of the local crowd and the many visitors. Press reports indicated that the Führer once more expressed his delight at the play, and Mayor Lang and the other local leaders responded enthusiastically and awarded him a large album of pictures from the play and the village.[8]

In early 1938 the villagers began to lay plans for the 1940 version of the play.[9] In a lengthy article in the official German publication dealing with foreign tourism, dated August 19, 1939, the play was highly touted. Mayor Lang was quoted as saying that the play is "not a religious matter, but rather a three hundred year old tradition bound to blood and soil." The article quotes an unnamed "leading personality of the NSDAP" as saying that "the Passion Play is the most antisemitic play of which we are aware." And Hitler's utterances of 12 August 1930 and 13 August 1934 were cited as further proof of the legitimacy of the play under the New Order. The *Voelkischer Beobachter* of August 24, 1939, announced "Vorbereitungen für die Passionsspiele 1940: Oberammergau vor neuen grossen Aufgaben, "["preparations for the Passion Play of 1940: Oberammergau stands before new and great tasks"]. Mayor Raimund Lang said that the play would be performed according to the will of the Führer and that the Reich Propaganda Ministry had declared the play to be "important for the Reich."[10] Of course the 1940 play never took place; war intervened. Yet Hitler still recalled his impressions of the play and its portrayal of "wicked" Jews while chatting over dinner in 1942:

One of the most important tasks will be to save future generations from a similar political fate and to maintain forever watchful in them a knowledge of the menace of Jewry. For this reason alone it is vital that the Passion Play be continued at Oberammergau; for never has the menace of Jewry been so convincingly portrayed as in this presentation of what happened in the times of the Romans. There one sees in Pontius Pilate a Roman racially and intellectually so superior, that he stands out like a firm clean rock in the middle of the whole muck and mire of Jewry.[11]

After World War II the people of Oberammergau revived the play. To do so they needed the permission of the American occupation authorities, which they were able to obtain by arguing that their play was in no way tainted by Nazism. The Americans not only gave their approval, but advanced funds to mount the production, and the 1950 play was declared a success.[12]

During the 1960s the Roman Catholic Church articulated a major interpretive shift in its view of Jews and Judaism. Jews were no longer seen as guilty of Jesus' death, and antisemitism in all its forms was explicitly rejected.[13] But the villagers of Oberammergau, who saw themselves as guardians of a local sacred tradition, were loath to change any aspect of their play to conform to the new Catholic guidelines. From their point of view, they had presented a traditional play before, during, and after the Hitlerite period, and they were not going to bow to outside pressure to modify it in the 1960s. The Catholic Church, for its part, took no steps to impose religious conformity on the village. Thus the stage was set for a major struggle in the 1970s.[14] The details of that struggle have been written about at length elsewhere and need not detain us here, except to point out that attempts, both from within the village, and from without, to make a major reform of the play failed.[15]

Traditionalists in Oberammergau allowed only a few editorial changes in the traditional Weis/Daisenberger text for the 1980 play, and then firmly denied that the play was antisemitic in intent or in content.[16] Under the leadership of play director Hans Maier, they continued to control the play for its 1984 production.[17] Only with new and more sensitive leadership from the village, under Christian Stueckl and Otto Huber, did significant reform occur during the late 1980s for the 1990 presentations.

Several examples of the text and the staging, comparing the 1980/84 play with the 1990 play, will demonstrate first of all how the traditional play presented the "suffering Christians" and the "wicked Jews" and, secondly, will demonstrate the areas in which reforms were (or were not) achieved for 1990.[18]

In the traditional play, through 1984, those temple traders and money changers who had been vigorously chastised by Jesus in the spectacular opening scene played a major role in plotting Jesus' death

Figure 1

on the cross. Thus the stereotype of money-hungry Jews as Christ-killers is begun. In the 1984 play, Judas Iscariot meets with the temple traders, who talk him into betraying Jesus.[19] In the reformed play of 1990, the temple traders play no role in contacting Judas; rather he is approached by members of the High Council itself (figure 1).[20] This portrayal avoids the implication that those who desired Jesus' removal were motivated merely by commercialism, and it is much closer to the biblical text.[21]

One of the most vicious of the schemers in the traditional play, through 1984, was the character named "Rabbi Archelaus" and generally referred to in the script and on stage simply as "Rabbi." The idea that a rabbi was especially responsible for the arrest and death of Jesus was both consistent with the most objectionable of anti-Jewish stereotypes and totally inconsistent with the biblical record. Nowhere in the gospels was there such a person as "Rabbi Archelaus"; indeed the only person referred to as "rabbi," meaning teacher, in the gospel accounts was Jesus himself. Protests against this misuse of the word "rabbi" go back at least to the year 1900 and gained more urgency after the Holocaust. Although a few objectionable lines in the traditional play (for example, denouncing the "accursed synagogue") were removed under Hans Maier's leadership before 1984, the offensive use of the so-called "Rabbi" remained. The 1990 reform completely reversed the usage of that word. The wicked character was no longer "Rabbi Archelaus" but merely "Archelaus," portrayed as a member of the

High Council with a Greek name. Jesus, on the other hand, was addressed on stage by his followers not only as "Lord" and "Master" but also as "Rabbi" on several significant occasions.[22]

The traditional Oberammergau play, in both its text and its staging, portrayed the High Council and the High Priests themselves in a very negative light. It can be argued, of course, that the gospels do this as well. It was Annas, Caiaphas, and the others who indeed felt threatened by Jesus and wanted to get rid of him. But the traditional play both heightened the sense of villainy surrounding these persons and portrayed them as the real leaders of the Jewish people, thus perpetuating the myths of collective guilt and deicide. In the 1980 and 1984 play, true to the local tradition, the High Priests met in a council chamber surrounded by major symbols of Judaism, the tablets of the law and the menorah.[23]

The priests wore imposing helmets, apparently topped with great horns. Critics pointed out that anti-Jewish caricatures had long associated Jews with the devil and had pictured Jews with devilish horns. These critics saw the Oberammergau portrayal, with the "horned helmets," as part of this negative stereotyping. Traditionalists in the village defended the local usage by pointing to medieval and early modern paintings which showed Jewish High Priests (and even some Christian bishops) wearing miters turned ninety degrees from the current practice and argued that the Oberammergau costuming was based on these "side-ways miters" rather than on alleged "horns." In the 1990 reform, the stage setting and the costuming were both changed to meet the critics' objections.[24] The High Council meets in an elegant but abstractly decorated chamber, which makes no reference to traditional Jewish symbolism. The High Priests are elaborately robed, but their head-covering show no signs of miters or horns (figures 1 [1922], and 2 [1990]).[25]

From biblical times onward, Pontius Pilate has been an enigmatic figure in the passion drama. It was he who sent Jesus to the cross; as the Apostles' Creed stated, Christ "suffered under Pontius Pilate." Yet, the traditional Oberammergau play presented him, both in the text and in costuming and demeanor, in a rather positive light. Dressed in a toga, and apparently forced by the High Priests and the Jewish crowd in the Jerusalem square to condemn Jesus, he was a noble Roman, attempting to dispense justice as best he could amidst a Jewish plot to kill Christ.[26] Hitler himself took that message away from the two performances of the play he saw at Oberammergau, in 1930 and 1934.

The reformers were sensitive to this criticism. Indeed the Roman governor was the one who held the power of life and death; the Jewish High Council had no legal authority to order or carry out an execution. In 1990, the reformers therefore presented him as a military governor in full armor, first ordering the execution and then cynically washing his hands of the responsibility.[27]

On Pilate's orders, Jesus was sent to be whipped, and graphic pictures of this punishment and suffering have long appeared in Christian art, including paintings familiar to the people of Oberammergau which grace a nearby abbey.[28] Those who administered the whipping to Jesus in the play wore nondescript uniforms, so the audience could draw the conclusion that it was "the Jews" who caused this physical suffering of the Messiah. The actual executioners who forced Jesus to Golgatha with the cross and nailed him to it were, through 1984, also shown in even more ambiguous uniforms, so that one might believe that it was Jewish executioners who actually killed Christ.[29] The 1990 reform put the executioners in Roman uniforms (figure 3).[30]

Judas Iscariot, the one of Jesus' twelve disciples who betrays him to the authorities, is in many respects the most interesting character in the entire Passion Play. One might argue that every other figure plays a static and even stock role, while Judas begins as a loyal disciple, turns against Jesus, and, finally realizing that he had done wrong, takes his own life in despair. For generations, the people of Oberammergau have recognized that this is an extraordinary role, and the men chosen to play it have done so with great pride in spite of the fact that Judas is clearly the major villain of the melodrama.[31] It is in the costuming that the portrayal of Judas most clearly shows him as a "wicked Jew."

Figure 2

Figure 3

While the other disciples wore modest "Christian" garb, through 1984 he wore the yellow tunic and the black cape which was associated with medieval Jewry in general and with the mythological figure known as "the eternal Jew" in particular.[32] The similarity between the Oberammergau Judas and Julius Streicher's Nazi stereotype of the wicked Jew is striking (figure 4).[33] The 1990 reformers finally rejected the black and yellow symbolism for Judas and put him in earth toned costuming similar to that of his fellow disciples.[34]

Part of the 1990 reform was a general effort to assert the "Jewishness" of Jesus and his followers. The reformers recognized that the traditional presentation had permitted the audience to distinguish visually between "suffering Christians," i.e. those who followed Jesus, and "the wicked Jews," by giving the "Christians" a more western or Roman look, and the "Jews" a more "oriental" appearance. Of course, all of these people (with the exception of the Roman occupiers) were Jews. The 1990 reforms abolished the distinction in the costuming and staging. This new costuming of the disciples included the opportunity for them to cover their heads when at prayer, in the manner of prayer shawls in the Jewish tradition.[35]

Most notable among the "suffering Christians" is Mary, the mother of Jesus. The role of Mary, of course, has been traditionally emphasized in Christian, particularly Roman Catholic, symbolism.

Paintings and statues of Mary holding the body of her dead son and grieving over him are frequent, though there is no specific reference to any such scene of suffering in the gospels. The scene of the pieta, nevertheless, is one of the most moving of the scenes from the Passion Play.[36]

Figure 4

The reforms of 1990, which were designed to meet the criticisms that the play was anti-Jewish, were not easily accomplished. In a very real sense the play is the property of the town. In practice, the director of the play does not have control of either the text or the staging. The play is presented by a not-for-profit corporation from within the town, and the Passion Play Committee has the power to approve (or disapprove) any changes from the previous traditions.[37]

For 1990 this Committee selected Christian Stueckl, who came from a well established local family and, though a young man of twenty-six, had training and experience in theater circles in Munich, as well as the deputy director, Otto Huber, also from a well known village family and also with higher education at the university in Munich. It also had the power to dismiss them if it wished to do so. Decisions on the text and the staging were approved (or not) by the Committee behind closed doors on a piecemeal basis. Moreover, other controversial issues also concerned the Committee (such as the role of women in the play), so reformers had to proceed carefully and often had to negotiate changes which would be acceptable to a shifting majority on the board.[38] All this occurred in a context of sometimes bitter personal disputes among factions within the village, disputes which occasionally had their origin decades or even generations earlier. And finally, the changes were not only of artistic, theological, and political significance. If the reformed play was not a commercial success, the economy of the village could be crippled for a decade.[39] Thus the pressure on those concerned was substantial.[40]

It is within this context of complexities that the issue of the so-called "blood curse" must be viewed. The traditional play repeated the verse from Matthew 27 which had been used by anti-Jewish Christians for centuries to show that the wicked plot went well beyond the High Council and to justify ongoing discrimination against, and persecution of, Jews generation after generation. When Pilate condemns Jesus and washes his hands, the crowd replies, "His blood be upon us and our children."[41] The reformers wanted to drop the line, because it had been used to justify persecution of Jews. Such an action would have been consistent with the declaration of the Vatican II council that the Roman Catholic Church rejects the contention that all the Jews of Jesus' time and their descendants were/are somehow guilty for Jesus' death. Moreover, it appears in only one of the four gospels, so (like several other unique biblical references) the reformers argued it could be safely omitted from the play.

Yet the Passion Play Committee refused to let the line be dropped. The issue was discussed in the German and in the American press, and the conflict could well have ended all the reform if the reformers had pressed it and been dismissed or forced to resign. So, a compromise was struck. The words of the "blood curse" remained, but only as one phrase spoken among many. In the published script, the line is spoken not by "all the people" but rather by "Several" (*Einige*).[42]

On stage, the words of the "blood curse" were entirely lost in the hubbub of the crowd scene on the day I saw the play in July 1990. I knew the importance of the line and I was waiting for it, following the script which lay open on my lap. But I did not hear it. Later I asked Deputy Director Otto Huber about the line and he confirmed that the directors intentionally buried it among the crowd noises and the other lines of the multitude, which at that point counted several hundred people on stage.[43]

The National Socialist past still casts its shadows over the Germany of the 1990s. In the village of Oberammergau discussions are now under way concerning the play as it will be next performed, in the year 2000. It took more than forty years after the fall of Hitler for the play to be purged of its most egregious anti-Jewish elements. Some critics argue that cleansing process was itself by nature inadequate, that the changes have been only editorial and superficial, and that the entire concept of the Passion Play is structurally fatally flawed. No amount of textual rewriting and dramatic recasting, they argue, can remove from this tradition the essentially anti-Jewish bias in its heart, which continues to show "suffering Christians" and at least a few "wicked Jews."[44] Others argue that, given the imperfections of this world, the 1990 reformers of Oberammergau succeeded in overcoming the anti-Judaism of the traditional play, while preserving that which deserves to be preserved and presenting it faithfully to the hundreds of thousands of visitors who made their way to the picturesque village in the Bavarian Alps in 1990, and will doubtless do so again in the year 2000.

NOTES

1. Gordon R. Mork was raised in a Christian home and is currently an elder in the Presbyterian Church. He wishes to thank the National Endowment for the Humanities and the Purdue University Jewish Studies Program for supporting the research on which this paper is based.

2. See *Hoert, sehet, weint und liebt: Passionsspiele im alpenlaendischen Raum*, ed. Michael Henker, Eberhard Duenninger, and Evamaria Brockhoff, Veroeffentlichungen zur Bayerischen Geschichte und Kultur, Nr. 20/90 (Munich: Haus d. Bayer. Geschichte, 1990). See also Michael P. Steinberg, *The Meaning of the Salzburg Festival* (Ithaca: Cornell University Press, 1990), for a general approach which emphasizes the broader significance of what appears to be only a local festival. Specifically (p. 23) he notes that Hugo von Hofmannsthal wrote that the Salzburg festival was designed to reestablish cultural roots, like Bayreuth and Oberammergau. But unlike Oberammergau, Salzburg "was to serve a broad, formally secular but inwardly baroque and Catholic theatrical tradition. Salzburg was to emerge 'from the same spirit' as Oberammergau but would be built on 'different fundaments,' those being the 'theatrical ability' of the 'Bavarian-Austrian tribe [*Stamm*].'"

3. A documented chronology of the play's thirty-eight seasons, through 1984, is presented by Otto Huber, Helmut W. Klinner, and Dorothea Lang in "Die Passionsauffuerungen in Oberammergau in 101 Anmerkungen," in *Hoert*, 163-179.

4. The basic play text was written by Father Othmar Weis O.S.B. in 1811/1815 and revised in 1860/70 by Father Joseph Alois Daisenberger. The music, which forms a major part of the production, was composed in 1815/20 by Rochus Dedler, the Oberammergau schoolmaster, and rearranged in 1950 by Professor Eugen Papst. The music is unpublished, but is available on

recordings. Each year the play has been presented a few changes have been introduced. The text has been the subject of careful study, a study made easier by the fact that the townsfolk published and sold copies of the text (in German and English) each year the play was given in the twentieth century. See for example, *The Oberammergau Play of the Suffering, Death and Resurrection of Our Lord Jesus Christ* (Oberammergau: Village of Oberammergau, 1990). Published scripts will be cited hereafter as *Text* or *Textbuch*, followed by the date of the production.

5. As Jesus is dying "Rabbi" says "Has His arrogance still not left Him, although He hangs so helplessly on the cross!" *Text, 1984*, 110.

6. See criticisms beginning with Joseph Krauskopf, *A Rabbi's Impressions of the Oberammergau Passion Play* (Philadelphia: E. Stern, 1908), and more recently Saul S. Friedman, *The Oberammergau Passion Play: A Lance against Civilization* (Carbondale, Ill.: Southern Illinois University Press, 1984).

7. Protest to Adolf Wagner in Munich on the letterhead of Dominik Schwab, Ortsgruppenleiter of the Ortsgruppe Unterammergau of the NSDAP, dated 25 January 1934, and Wagner's reply to the Oberammergau village council, dated 31 January. Bayrische Hauptstaatsarchiv, Munich, M Inn 7274. Published by Gordon R. Mork, in "Oberammergau . . . ," in *Wesenzuege Europas Historische Genese und weltweite Ausstrahlung under geschichtsdidaktischem Aspekt* (Flensburg: Institut fuer Regionale Forschung, 1989), 181-183.

8. The album was captured by U.S. forces after World War II, and is listed in the catalog of the Library of Congress, but it has disappeared from the shelves without a trace.

9. Staatsarchiv Munich LRA 61616, Oberammergau, den (30 January 1938); *Fremdenverkehr: Reichsorgan fuer den deutschen Fremdenverkehr* (19 August 1939).

10. Bayrische Hauptstaatsarchiv, Munich, MWi 2804.

11. Adolf Hitler, *Hitler's Secret Conversations: 1941-1944* (New York: Farrar, Straus and Young, 1953), 457.

12. There were eighty-seven performances before 510,000 visitors, according to Norbert Jaron and Baerbel Rudin, *Das Oberammergauer Passionsspiel: Eine Chronik in Bildern* (Dortmund: Harenberg, 1984), 145. See Friedman for a critical description of the negotiations with the American authorities.

13. Leonard Swidler and Gerard Sloyan, "The Passion of the Jew Jesus: Recommended Changes in the Oberammergau Passion Play after 1984," *Face to Face: An Interreligious Bulletin* 12 (1985): 26.

14. Described well by David L. Kissel in his doctoral dissertation in anthropology, *The Passions of Oberammergau: A Diachronic Study of a Case of Institutionalized Political Factionalism in a Bavarian Village* (Indiana University, 1981) and summarized in his article, "Politics and Play Reform in

Oberammergau: An Anthropologist's View," *Face to Face* 12 (1985): 10-15.

15. *Das Rosner Spiel: Eine Dokumentation ueber die Geschichte und Vorstellung von Oberammergaus barocker Passion anlaesslich des 10 jaehrigen Jubilaeums der Rosner-Probe 1977* (Oberammergau: Ammergauer Spiel-Gemeinschaft, 1987), especially "Documente zur Reform-Geschichte und zur Rosner-Probe," 159-180. See also Friedman, chapter 11. The Rosner play laid blame for Jesus' death on the devil, avoiding the impression that "the Jews" were to blame.

16. See Father Stephen Schaller, "Nie Wieder: Verfluchte Synagogue!" *Schoenere Heimat* vol. 69 no. 3 (1980).

17. Gordon R. Mork, "The 1984 Oberammergau Passion Play in Historical Perspective," *Face to Face* 12 (1985): 15-21.

18. Otto Huber, "Changes of the Oberammergau Passion Play to Avoid Antijudaistic Misunderstandings," typescript in the press packet, Oberammergau 1990, 23 pp., is a carefully detailed list of changes, with a commentary referring explicitly to the recommendations of Professor Swidler and Father Sloyan, cited above. Huber points out that sometimes the actual textual changes in the spoken and sung German text were, in error, omitted from the English-language *Text 1990.*

19. *Passionsspiele Oberammergau, 1634-1984* (Oberammergau: Gemeinde Oberammergau, 1984), 60.

20. *Passion Oberammergau 1990,* 39.

21. *Text 1990,* 17, 28-29.

22. By Simon of Bethany and Mary Magdalene, *Text 1990,* 21 ff.; and by several disciples, including both Peter and Judas. Herod's son and heir was named Archelaus (Matthew 2:22).

23. *Passion Oberammergau* (Oberammergau: Gemeinde Oberammergau, 1980), 46.

24. *Passion Oberammergau 1990,* 54. The "quergestellten Mitraspitzen" are defended by *Praelat* Josef Georg Ziegler, *Das Oberammergauer Passionsspiel* (St. Ottilien: EOS Verlag Erzabtei, 1990), 105-107.

25. One monk from the neighboring Ettal monastery, whom I interviewed, exercised his wit by saying that the former "Mickey Mouse hats" had been replaced by capes which made the High Priests look like "nuns with beards." Interview, 1991.

26. *Passion Oberammergau* (1980), 70. Compare Elaine Pagels, *The Origin of Satan* (New York: Random House, 1995), 28-33.

27. *Passion Oberammergau 1990,* 49. The same photo was included in the Oberammergau press packet, in black and white, with a commentary which states that the staging intends that "the impression of collective guilt is removed through bringing into relief (also visually) the political forces at work." The German-language comment is even more pointed: "Durch die Herausstellung (auch optisch) identifizierbarer politischer Kraefte jeden

Eindruck einer Kollektivschuld zu vermeiden."

28. "Die Geisselung Christi" by Johann Joseph Zwinck, 1725, in the Ettal abbey; *Hoert*, 239-241.

29. *Passion Oberammergau* (1980), 88, showing the executioners reclining before the cross. The headline in the *Kulturwelt* section of *Die Welt* read "Jetzt schlagen Roemer Christus ans Kreuz."

30. *Passion Oberammergau 1990*, 103.

31. A cartoon in the German humor magazine *Simplicisimus* shows two elderly English tourists attacking "Judas" outside the theater after the performance with an umbrella, so moved were they by his "wickedness."

32. *Passion Oberammergau* (1980), 35.

33. *Trau keinem Fuchs Auf gruener Heid, und keinem Jud bei seinem Eid!* (Nuremberg: Stuermer-Verlag, 1936). The text accompanying this picture begins "Von Anfang an der Jude ist, Ein Moerder schon sagt Jesu Christ." ["From the very beginning the Jew is a murderer, says Jesus Christ."]

34. *Passion Oberammergau 1990*, 49.

35. *Passion Oberammergau 1990*, 51. See also Otto Huber's commentary, 12: "The awareness that Jesus lived as a Jew in his people's religious and cultural tradition was not always clearly expressed among Christians. In some respects, Roman traditions had too much influence on ideas, *e.g.*, the clothes worn by Jesus and his followers in the tradition of Christian painting were according to the Roman model, and [before 1990] this was adopted by the Oberammergau Play also. However, if the other Jews were dressed in oriental costume this gave the impression that Jesus was not one of them."

36. 1990 press packet photo. The caption reads "Powerless suffering—one example is a mother's agony at the death of the life to which she has given birth. We encounter Mary's suffering in the Pieta and in the corresponding scene from the Passion Play. . . ."

37. The Committee consists of the mayor, the Catholic priest, the pastor of the Protestant church of the town (though there are relatively few Protestants among the townsfolk), the members of the town council, and six persons selected by and from the persons who have the right to perform in the play.

38. Some insight into the politics of the Committee is given by a handbill circulated in Oberammergau in January 1989 entitled "Im Sorge um das Passionsspiel" [With concern for the Passion Play] and claiming that "fast 1200 traditionsbewusste Buergerinnen und Buerger" [nearly 1200 women and men citizens, conscious of their tradition] had signed petitions calling for Stueckl's dismissal. The young man had narrowly missed being fired by the Committee, according to the handbill, on 18 January 1989 in a vote of 13 to 11. The conflicts were sensationalized in the tabloid press: the Munich *Abendzeitung* of 11 March 1989 displayed banner headlines "Oberammergau: Der schmutzige Krieg um das heilige Spiel" [the dirty war about the holy play]. For the first time

in 1990, married women could appear on stage. Previously Mary, the mother of Jesus, had to be an "unmarried woman of unblemished character", though the men who played Jesus might be fathers of large families. "Oberammergau to star a married Virgin Mary next year," *Koelner-Stadt Anzeiger* (21 March 1989), translated in *The German Tribune* (9 April 1989).

39. A sold out play would bring some 500,000 visitors to Oberammergau, most of them on expensive package tours which has a regional impact in Bavaria, Austria, and even Switzerland.

40. In his introduction to the *Text 1990*, Father Dr. Franz Dietl, the parish priest of Oberammergau and a member of the Play Committee, hinted at the tensions in the Committee when he wrote: "In recent times extensive amendments have had to be made primarily on theological and ecumenical grounds, and these have not always been of benefit to the literary dramaturgical form," *Text 1990*, 9. The issue was aired even in local papers in the American middle west: "Passion Play retains Jewish blood curse," Lafayette, Indiana, *Journal and Courier* (15 February 1990).

41. Matthew 27: 24 and 25.

42. *Textbuch 1990*, 91.

43. The stages of the negotiations are clearly outlined by Father John J. Kelley, SM, a participant in some of the discussions, in "The Dilemma of Oberammergau," *Christian Jewish Relations*, vol 23 no.1 (1990): 28-32. See also Huber in *Passion Oberammergau 1990*, 12, where he alludes to the issue very cautiously. The justification for retaining the line is presented by Rudolf Pesch, a New Testament scholar who served on the text-writing commission of Oberammergau at the request of the German Conference of Catholic Bishops, in an appendix to the *Text 1990*, 109-113. Pesch argues that "The words about blood guilt are not meant to be anti-Semitic. . . . In view of our history we Christians have every reason for accusing ourselves: we also belong to the 'whole people' which spoke the words of blood guilt. . . . The blood from the body of the Messiah which we spilt when we fought each other, burned heretics and gassed Jews not only cries to heaven, it has also 'fallen on us and our children.'" According to Kelley, Pesch favored abandoning the line, but the issue lost on two votes in the Committee, 15-8 and later 11-9. See also Alan Levy in the *New York Times* (Sunday, June 3, 1990).

44. I can recall explaining the whole controversy to a well educated American Protestant woman in my home town of Lafayette, Indiana. She listened politely and then said, "Well, I don't see what all the fuss is about. After all, the Jews did kill him." The myth of deicide dies hard. German press reports in October 1990 spoke of "Reformwilliges Oberammergau" (reform-willing Oberammergau) for the 2000 production.

Inventing the Other: Ambivalent Constructions of the Wandering Jew/ess in Nineteenth Century American Literature

Regine Rosenthal

For centuries, the dominant cultural discourse of the Christian Western world has perceived the Jew as the Other, as an element alien to that culture and consequently to be excluded for his/her difference. This practice of exclusion is not only apparent in the history of the Jews over the ages, it is also reflected in the representation of Jews in the literature of Christian culture. According to Michel Foucault, the author of texts, including literary texts, is not an independent agent; he is subject to an author-function which he adopts, with modifications, from his own times and which is "characteristic of the mode of existence, circulation, and functioning of certain discourses within a society."[1] Discourse, in Foucauldian terms, is related to power. It "is both the object and tool of struggle; it is the power one seeks to get control of."[2] Thus, in writing, an author is both giving voice to and appropriating certain discourses within a society, while these discourses, as Foucault argues, are "practices that systematically form the objects of which they speak."[3] That is to say, the image of the Jew constructed by writers of the dominant Christian culture is a reflection of how that culture has perceived and invented the Jew, and a means of facing, manipulating, and subjugating the Other.

The ambivalence of the dominant culture towards its Jewish Other is clearly demonstrated in its most prevalent representations of Jews as either denigrated or idealized stereotypes: the villainous Shylock, the accursed Wandering Jew, the beautiful Jewess, or the enlightenment-inspired benevolent anti-Shylock, as identified by Edgar Rosenberg in his study of English fiction.[4] Though these concepts of the Jew have their tradition in the literatures of Europe, they were eventually adopted by American writers as well. Thus, by the nineteenth century, the figure of the Wandering Jew is not only widely addressed in European poetry and fiction but has become an integral part of popular culture and literature in America. After the bestselling success of Eugène Sue's French novel *The Wandering Jew* (1844/45), American texts such as F. Marion Crawford's *A Roman Singer* (1884), Nathaniel Hawthorne's *The Marble Faun* (1860), and Herman Melville's *Clarel* (1876) attest to the popularity of the figure in nineteenth century America. This paper will examine how these writers construct the Jew as cultural Other in their appropriation, modification and/or transformation of the mythical figure of the Wandering Jew and how they conceive of his recurring female counterpart, the beautiful and/or Wandering Jewess.

1. EMERGENCE OF THE FIGURE

The accursed figure of the Wandering Jew is based on an extrascriptural legend that probably first emerged, as George Anderson explains in his comprehensive study, *The Legend of the Wandering Jew*, some six hundred years after Christ. In its earliest recognizable shape, it is "the tale of a man in Jerusalem who, when Christ was carrying his Cross to Calvary and paused to rest for a moment on this man's doorstep, drove the Saviour away . . . , crying aloud, 'Walk faster!' And Christ replied, 'I go, but you will walk until I come again!'"[5] The Crusades helped spread the legend all over Europe, while the Christian Church supported it as part of its anti-Jewish discourse and as evidence of the wonder-working power of God. Its central character, the Wandering Jew, appeared under a number of different names, varying according to time, country, and interpretation of his story.[6] His most notable designations are "Cartaphilus" (such as in Roger Wendover's *Flores historiarum* [1228], one of the legend's first written versions), "der Ewige Jude" [the eternal Jew], "le Juif Errant" [the Wandering Jew], and—since publication of a German pamphlet in 1602— "Ahasuerus."

This pamphlet, the *Kurtze Beschreibung und Erzehlung von einem Juden mit Namen Ahaßverus* [*Short Description and Tale of a Jew Called*

Ahasuerus], turned out to be the most influential contribution to the perpetuation of the legend, while clearly reflecting the anti-Semitic discourse of Christian culture at the time.[7] As expressed in Christ's curse, "I will stand here and rest, but you must walk,"[8] Ahasuerus is condemned to everlasting life and eternal wandering. Contrary to the Christian precept of forgiveness, he is punished without pardon. No conversion to Christianity and no repentance can absolve him from his guilt, for his sin basically consists in being a Jew.[9]

The Wandering Jew as cultural Other is thus both a particular figure derived from a specific legend and a stereotype of the Jew. His sin of blasphemy is not only perceived as a personal crime, but in the discourse of the Christian culture it represents the collective guilt of the Jewish people. It has been associated and merged with the crime of Christ-killing of which, in the dominant discourse, all Jews are guilty. But, as Hyam Maccoby points out in *The Sacred Executioner*, this guilt is of a clearly ambivalent nature, for the Wandering Jew as symbol of the Jewish people is performing a task that the Christian faith depends upon. In fact, the Jews are indispensable for carrying out "the great but necessary crime of the Crucifixion."[10] Thus for centuries, the religious discourse of the dominant Christian culture has constructed the Wandering Jew as its necessary, if detestable Other.

By contrast, the idealized image of the beautiful Jewess is derived from Romantic fiction.[11] Based on Sir Walter Scott's historical romance, *Ivanhoe* (1819), it refers to Rebecca, a model of female beauty, maidenly innocence, and daughterly affection, yet an outsider due to her Jewish descent. Her difference stands in the way of marriage to the Anglo-Saxon hero, Ivanhoe, and precludes a happy ending. As a paradigm of Jewish otherness, she is an alien within the community, both belonging to it and doomed to be different. Therefore, as Alide Cagidemetrio observes, her character suggests "a curious adaptation of the Wandering Jew type."[12] True to the traditional pattern of the romance, where fair and dark lady are pitted against each other, the dark lady, Rebecca, the foreign and forbidden Other, is deemed ultimately inferior to the Anglo-Saxon fair lady, Rowena. Thus, "Rebecca's difference, her Jewishness, is presented as a cultural and religious tradition and as exoticism. . . . Her ravishing beauty, exotic as it is, stands out as the mysterious and seductive component of the Other. . . . The Wandering Jew, turned female and British, haunts man's dreams."[13]

2. REPRESENTATIONS IN POPULAR LITERATURE

In fact, the Wandering Jew and his female counterpart, the beautiful Jewess, have captured the American literary imagination. As Louis Harap demonstrates in *The Image of the Jew in American Literature*,[14] the importance of the Wandering Jew for American letters is reflected in the many adaptations of the figure by a wide range of nineteenth century American writers—some of them known, some of them not so well known—in poems, short stories, and novels. Even Mark Twain indicated his fascination with the legend in *The Innocents Abroad* (1869), a travel account of his journey to Europe and the Holy Land. American readers, already familiarized with the fictional rendition of the figure in such English novels as Matthew Gregory Lewis's *The Monk* (1796), William Godwin's *St. Leon* (1800), and George Croly's *Salathiel* (1829), eagerly embraced Eugène Sue's French portrayal in *The Wandering Jew* (1844/45).

This bestselling popular novel, originally published in 1844/45 as *Le Juif Errant* in a Paris paper, was translated into English and became an immediate success in America.[15] Sue's *The Wandering Jew* is extraordinary on several accounts. For one thing, it is remarkable for its sheer volume. In a melodramatic, action-laden plot, it tells, in some 1300 pages, the story of a Protestant French family's fight against the evil forces of the Jesuit order. For another, the novel's title figure actually appears in only very few chapters of the book. In addition, in a surprising move, the lonely figure of the Wandering Jew is reduplicated in his beautiful sister, Herodias, who like him is condemned to eternal wandering and unending life for her implication in a different crime, (i.e., the beheading of John the Baptist). But in this novel of suspense in the dark Gothic tradition, where the forces of evil are forever threatening to annihilate the forces of good, the Wandering Jew and his sister are caught in the middle. Condemned to expiate their crime by their own suffering, they not only spend their restless existence driven on by an unforgiving, vengeful God, but the Wandering Jew as harbinger of cholera is also forced to be an unwilling instrument of death. Yet their victimization is counterbalanced by their unwavering defence of good, (i.e., by their fight for the various family members' survival against the destructive conspiracy of the Jesuit order). In fact, as it is ultimately revealed, the Wandering Jew and his sister are not only the champions of pursued innocence but the critics of modern-day industrial slavery. Both the Wandering

Jew, a one-time shoemaker and artisan himself, and his sister, a representative of female suppression, are conceived as the spokespersons for the socially oppressed. In the end, social progress is the promise of the future, while Herodias and the Wandering Jew find redemption and final rest in death. Thus, Eugène Sue has recreated the myth of the Wandering Jew as negative Other in positive terms. Reduplicating the male figure in the Wandering and beautiful Jewess, Herodias, he has reinvented the Wandering Jew in a series of transformations: from the blasphemous cultural Other of the legend to the mysterious, yet benevolent stranger of the Gothic romance to the champion and spokesperson of social change.

The late nineteenth century novel, *A Roman Singer* (1884), by F. Marion Crawford, a well-known American writer of popular fiction at the time,[16] proves equally influenced by the Gothic romance tradition. Yet different from Sue's conception of the figure, Crawford's Wandering Jew is central to the plot. Set in Italy, where Crawford had spent a good part of his life, *A Roman Singer* uses the wild landscape of the Abruzzi mountains as backdrop to a story of Gothic suspense in the style of Ann Radcliffe. In keeping with this tradition, the beautiful fair maiden, Hedwig von Lira, who is held prisoner by her father in a remote castle high up in the mountains in order to keep her secluded from her Italian lover, Nino, is pursued by the Gothic villain, Baron Ahasuerus Benoni.

As his name, Ahasuerus, suggests, Benoni is Crawford's version of the Wandering Jew. He is first introduced to the reader as a mysterious stranger. Ranging through the nightly streets of Rome, he is conspicuous for his difference "of a pronounced Jewish type. His brown eyes were long and oriental in shape, and his nose was unmistakably Semitic."[17] His age is difficult to assess, as his beard and mustache are "almost dazzlingly white," while his complexion has "all the freshness of youth" (*RS*, 161). He used to be a shoemaker once, taking to traveling the world when obliged to leave home for undisclosed reasons. Apart from these typical of the Wandering Jew, Benoni exhibits some specific characteristics that clearly establish his ambivalent nature. On the one hand, he is a musical genius on the violin and guitar who absolutely enchants his listeners and transforms himself in his play. "I could have listened . . . for hours together," recollects the narrator of the novel. "His features grew ashy pale, and his smooth white hair stood out wildly from his head. He looked, then, more than a hundred years old, and there was a sadness and a horror about him that would have made the stones cry aloud for pity" (*RS*, 194). On the other hand, his marked interest in "pleasures and money, money and pleasures" (*RS*, 174) attest to a cynical outlook on life underscored by his unmistakably strange, "horrid" laughter (*RS*, 294). He turns out to be a selfish liar, incapable of friendship or sympathy, and to be given to random acts of cruelty.

In his fight for the fair lady, Hedwig, Benoni, the arch-villain, is pitted against the courageous hero, Nino. While the latter, "the peasant child," proves to be "the pink of chivalry and the mirror of honor" (*RS*, 263), Baron Benoni, the Wandering Jewish banker, is perceived as the epitome of horror by the fair-haired, blue-eyed, German-born Hedwig, who shudders at the thought of marrying the rich baron. She cannot imagine ever consenting "to belong, body—and soul—to be touched, polluted, desecrated, by that inhuman monster; sold to him, to a creature without pity, whose heart is a toad, a venomous creeping thing" (*RS*, 246). In the end, innocence is rewarded. Nino and Hedwig, "these two virgin hearts" (*RS*, 322), manage to escape from both Hedwig's despotic father and her fiendish suitor.

In his negative construction as the corrupt, cold-blooded rival of the fair lady's lover, the Wandering Jew, Benoni, thus only helps to stress the positive qualities of his antagonist; and as an evil threat to the fair lady's innocence, he underscores the potential destructiveness of his otherness. Thus, contrary to Sue's highly sympathetic treatment of the Wandering Jew, Marion Crawford's Ahasuerus is a representation of the negatively conceived cultural Other. In a surprising twist in the end—an unconvincing attempt on the author's part to demystify the haunting figure of the Wandering Jew—Benoni's alterity is reinterpreted as madness. A suddenly produced newspaper article gives a supposedly "'rational' explanation"[18] of his previous eccentric behavior: "Baron Benoni, the wealthy banker of St. Petersburg, who was many years ago an inmate of a private lunatic asylum in Paris, is reported to be dangerously insane in Rome" (*RS*, 368). But as Foucault has argued in *Madness and Civilization*,[19] madness is only another form of society's definition of difference. If previously for his Jewishness, it is now for his madness that Benoni is shunned. His otherness is only altered in kind, but not in negativity. He thus continues to be perceived as the detested and excluded Other, as "Ahasuerus Benoni, the Jew" (*RS*, 365).

3. HAWTHORNE'S CONSTRUCTION OF JEWISH AND GENDER DIFFERENCE IN *THE MARBLE FAUN*

Some decades earlier, Nathaniel Hawthorne had presented in his work an equally sinister image of the Wandering Jew. While in the two short stories, "A Virtuoso's Collection" (1842) and "Ethan Brand" (1850), he portrays him as a cynical, cold-blooded, Mephistophelian figure, his own deep ambivalence towards the Jewish Other is clearly established in *The English Notebooks*, the journal covering his time as consul in Liverpool. In an entry of 1856, Hawthorne reveals his prejudice in a lengthy description of a Jewish couple he observed at a dinner given by the Lord Mayor of London. Captivated by the woman, he interprets her as the very image of the beautiful, yet darkly ambiguous Jewess. To him, every aspect of her, though extremely attractive, is an expression of her Jewishness: her marble-white, fine complexion contrasting with her black "wonderful . . . Jewish hair,"[20] the "beautiful outline" of her "Jewish" nose (*EN*, 321) and her stately, youthful figure reminiscent of some admirable Old Testament women, such as Rachel or Judith. This ambivalent portrayal culminates in the very revealing final observation:

> I never should have thought of touching her, nor desired to touch her; for, whether owing to distinctness of race, my sense that she was a Jewess, or whatever else, I felt a sort of repugnance, simultaneously with my perception that she was an admirable creature. (*EN*, 321)

Her male counterpart, however, is described in openly hostile, contemptuous terms:

> But, at the right hand of this miraculous Jewess, there sat the very Jew of Jews; the distilled essence of all the Jews . . . ; he was Judas Iscariot; he was the Wandering Jew; he was the worst, and at the same time, the truest type of his race . . . ; and he must have been circumcised as much [as] ten times over. I never beheld anything so ugly and disagreeable, and preposterous, and laughable, . . . so hideously Jewish . . . ; it is as hard to give an idea of this ugly Jew, as of the beautiful Jewess. . . . I rejoiced exceedingly in this Shylock, this Iscariot; for the sight of him justified me in the repugnance I have always felt towards his race. (*EN*, 321)

In this venomous portrayal Hawthorne has merged all the negative Jewish stereotypes of Shylock, Judas Iscariot, and the Wandering Jew into one single representation, the epitome of the negative Jewish Other. The alleged ugliness of all these male figures—both external and internal—results in the "repugnance" Hawthorne expresses and extends towards the female counterpart, despite the fact that she captivates his senses with her beauty. For she is blemished, too: her beauty is distinctly "Jewish" and as such perceived as dark, cold, and potentially deadly.

In *The Marble Faun; or, The Romance of Monte Beni*, written in 1858/59, Hawthorne—in the figure of Miriam and her Model—worked out a pattern of negative dynamics similar to that informing the passage just cited. In Miriam he has created the dark lady of the American romance who is pitted against and brought into relief by her fair counterpart, "the brown-haired, fair cheeked, Anglo-Saxon girl,"[21] Hilda. It is by contrast to this dove-like, innocent maiden that Miriam's dark aspects stand out all the more. Her ambiguity is first revealed in a portrait, painted by Miriam, that carries her features and echoes, in its depiction, the beautiful Jewess of the *English Notebooks*. It is described as:

> the portrait of a beautiful woman . . . ; so beautiful, that she seemed to get into your consciousness and memory, and could never afterwards be shut out, but haunted your dreams, for pleasure or for pain . . . . She was very youthful, and had what was usually thought to be a Jewish aspect; . . . dark eyes, into which you might look as deeply as your glance would go, and still be conscious of a depth that you had not sounded. . . . She had black, abundant hair . . . ; if she were really of Jewish blood, then this was Jewish hair, and a dark glory such as crowns no Christian maiden's head. Gazing at this portrait, you saw what Rachel might have been . . . or . . . what Judith was, when she vanquished Holofernes with her beauty, and slew him for too much adoring it. (*MF*, 47/48)

Here, as in the passage from the *English Notebooks*, Hawthorne insists on Miriam's difference. Both admirably beautiful and deeply disturbing and haunting, the dark lady, Miriam, is a representation of the forbidden Other: she is the epitome of female, sexual beauty; she is an outsider due to her Jewishness, and she carries within her a dark secret of her past adding the Gothic element of an unspeakable crime.

Miriam's origin is gradually disclosed, only to anchor her deeper in the realm of otherness. While in the beginning, some "wild and romantic fables" (*MF*, 22) attaching a racial stigma to her are being cited, Miriam later confirms her partly Jewish descent. Her "mixed race" (*MF*, 430), though promoting independence of mind, has apparently also wrought evil. It contributed to Miriam's stained past, her possible involvement in a most dreadful and mysterious crime.

It is this ominous past that links Miriam to a disturbing figure, her dark alter ego. For months, Miriam has been followed by the "Spectre of the Catacombs" (*MF*, 28) who, according to an old tale, has been wandering for well over fifteen hundred years in the darkness of the subterranean burial grounds seeking to add new victims to his old record of crimes. This stranger looks "dark, bushy bearded, wild of aspect and attire" (*MF*, 19), and "of exceedingly picturesque, and even melodramatic aspect" (*MF*, 30). From now on, he trails Miriam wherever she goes and haunts her imagination to the point of emerging as her model in many of her paintings. Similar to the mystery surrounding Miriam's past, the origin of the Spectre remains obscure. Resembling the demon in Guido's picture of the Archangel Michael, the Spectre/Model exerts a diabolic influence over Miriam "such as beasts and reptiles, of subtle and evil nature, sometimes exercise upon their victims" (*MF*, 93). The utterly negative quality of the figure is reflected in the revulsion he evokes in the innocent, faun-like Donatello, and in the spectre's power to induce murder. For it is Donatello's "repugnance" (*MF*, 90), "disgust" (*MF*, 140), "hatred" (*MF*, 140), and "tiger-like fury" (*MF*, 148) that provoke Donatello to the point of killing Miriam's Spectre.

Miriam's relationship to her persecutor is complex and never entirely elucidated. Like Donatello, she feels "repugnance amounting to nothing short of agony" (*MF*, 97) at his touch and his sombre insinuations about her. Yet she is unable to free herself from the Spectre's spell. Miriam and the Spectre are bound together by an inseparable "bond equally torturing to each" (*MF*, 93)—a mysterious crime from their mutual past—that brings out a spectre-like quality in Miriam herself and seems to be linked to the strangely fascinating portrait of Beatrice Cenci:[22]

> . . . it was the very saddest picture ever painted or conceived;
> it involved an unfathomable depth of sorrow, the sense of
> which came to the observer by a sort of intuition. It was a

sorrow that removed this beautiful girl out of the sphere of humanity, and set her in a far-off region, the remoteness of which—while yet her face is so close before us—makes us shiver as at a spectre (*MF*, 64)

For when Miriam studies this portrait that in the nineteenth century reader/spectator immediately evoked the story of the Cenci incest/murder in which Beatrice Cenci was raped by her father and, in revenge for the outrage, helped to murder him, Miriam takes on an expression almost identical to that of the portrait. In her attempt to solve the question of Beatrice's moral accountability, of "whether she thought herself innocent, or the one great criminal since time began!" (*MF*, 67), Miriam's own moral ambiguity is reflected. Her double role as victim and possible perpetrator of an earlier crime is never unequivocally explicated.[23] What becomes clear, however, is her implication in the present crime, the murder of her spectre-like Shadow, emphasizing her role of serpent-like seducer and her basic resemblance to her dark alter ego.

Thus, like the Jewish couple in the *English Notebooks*, Miriam and her Shadow are representations of alterity both complementing each other and differing in the nature and degree of their negativity. Miriam, the dark lady of the romance, is a complex, ambiguous figure. She is haunted by the Shadow of her past and her role of victim or possible perpetrator in a mutual crime, and she is doomed to suffer forever for her role as instigator in a crime of the present, the murder of that Shadow. In addition, like the strong biblical women, Jael and Judith, she has killed with her beauty and like the daughter of Herodias (*MF*, 44), she has sinned deeply. Thus, as Cagidemetrio has noted concerning Scott's idealized, impeccable Rebecca, Miriam combines the features of the *beautiful* Jewess—though in a much more tainted version—and those of the forever exiled *Wandering* Jew. For though she feels deeply penitent, there is no forgiveness in store for her. She is condemned to eternal restlessness and wandering, excluded from the rest of humanity by a "fathomless abyss" (*MF*, 461).

Miriam's Shadow, however, inspires terror and repugnance. As Gothic villain, supernatural spectre, and guilty, eternal wanderer, he displays all the negative features of the legendary Wandering Jew.[24] Miriam's potential relative and alleged, remorseless companion in a former crime inspires a repugnance similar in kind to that elicited by "the very Jew of Jews; . . . the Wandering Jew" (*EN*, 321) of *The*

English Notebooks. Lacking a proper name that would anchor him in the fictional present, Miriam's Shadow is defined by his spectre-like qualities that, similar to those of the Wandering Jew, emphasize his actual transcendence of the boundaries of place and time. Continuing to haunt others and being driven and cursed himself, he is the paradigm and epitome of the unambiguously negative Other.

4. MELVILLE'S *CLAREL*: PROBLEMATIZATION AND TRANSCENDENCE OF THE FIGURE'S NEGATIVITY

In 1856, some two years before Hawthorne wrote *The Marble Faun*, Herman Melville set out on a trip to the Mediterranean and the Near East, visiting his friend, Hawthorne, on the way. Melville's subsequent journey to Palestine became the basis for *Clarel: A Poem and Pilgrimage in the Holy Land*, a long, four-part narrative poem in iambic tetrameters that was only published in 1876, almost twenty years after the voyage. In *Clarel*, Melville does not only offer his own version of the legend of the Wandering Jew—a much more favorable and less oblique one than Hawthorne's—he also achieves, in terms of the nineteenth century, an exceptionally varied representation of Jewish characters.[25] It is against the background of Melville's own preoccupation with a restless search for belief[26] that the legend of the Wandering Jew gets its specific significance in *Clarel*, and it is in the context of Pilgrimage and Wandering that the legendary figure and all the other characters, among them a number of Jews, are defined.

Clarel, a young American divinity student, has undertaken a pilgrimage to Jerusalem and the Holy Land in quest for the certainty of faith.[27] In Jerusalem, he joins a group of pilgrims on a ten-day excursion through the Judean desert to the Dead Sea, and back to Jerusalem via Mar Saba and Bethlehem. In Mar Saba, a Coptic convent high above the Kedron Valley near the Dead Sea, Clarel and the other pilgrims take part in religious festivities, and it is then that the Wandering Jew appears—not as an actual character, but as the leading figure in the masque of "Cartaphilus, the Jew / Who wanders ever."[28]

True to the legend, the Wandering Jew portrayed in this drama is condemned to a restless, unending life of wandering. He feels alienated and cut off from human companionship not only because his curse is relentlessly driving him on, but because, through his longevity, he is condemned to understand history, accumulate knowledge, and find truth. Thus, the terrible realization Melville's Wandering Jew has to face is twofold: for one, he is, by the nature of his curse, condemned to a life of loneliness. Secondly, and this is even more pivotal, his fate, as emphasized in the Masque, challenges the concepts of love and forgiveness as two fundamental tenets of the Christian faith. Jesus is not, as taught in the New Testament, the forgiving Savior of mankind, but has, in a "voice estranged from love" (C, 351), condemned the Wandering Jew till the end of time, however repentent he may be: "Just let him live, just let him rove / . . . / Long live, rove far, and understand / And sum all knowledge for his dower; / For he forbid is, he is banned; / . . . / Ruthless, he meriteth no ruth, / On him I imprecate the truth" (C, 351).

The Masque of the Wandering Jew thus exposes some basic ironies and contradictions inherent in the legend and the curse: the Wandering Jew is sent on an endless journey in the course of which he will accumulate knowledge at the expense of love; he has been sent on his wanderings in punishment for his own lack of faith in a saving God; and, most ironic and devastating of all, his assumption about the Messiah may have been correct: there is no certainty that the compassionate Savior of mankind ever arrived at all.

It is this deep-seated doubt expressed in the masque of the Wandering Jew that serves as a thematic link to the rest of the poem. Similar to this lonely, driven figure, Clarel and most of the other characters are travelers and pilgrims in search of certainty of belief. The actual performance of the Wandering Jew's tale is thus both a dramatic realization of the myth itself and of the poem's major theme, the plight of the restless pilgrims, Wandering Jews themselves. They are those, as Bernard Rosenthal maintains, "who have been told that Christ would return and who fear that He had never come at all."[29] By extending the symbolic significance of the figure to include all those who are doubters and seekers after faith, Melville has clearly transcended the anti-Semitic connotations of the Wandering Jew. In Clarel, the figure has evolved into a concept of the outsider or cultural Other both encompassing a much broader range of religious/cultural backgrounds and reflecting Melville's own doubts and concerns.

Among the various people Clarel meets on his pilgrimage through the Holy Land, there are a number of Jews, intricately linked with the theme of the Wandering Jew as well as envisioned as a remarkable variety of Jewish individuals. Foremost among them is the family of Nathan, Agar, and Ruth. Clarel meets them in Jerusalem, when he first arrives, and returns to them, under dramatically changed conditions, after his pilgrimage to the Dead Sea and Mar Saba. The many discrepancies and ironies in their lives are both a commentary on and an anticipation of the masque of the Wandering Jew positioned in the middle of the poem. Nathan, the father, is another variation, yet full of ironic twists, on the theme of the Wandering Jew. An American Puritan turned Zionist, he is presented as an admirable yet controversial figure whose religious zeal as well as his lack of tolerance, sympathy, and understanding bring on his own destruction.

In contrast to Nathan, the two Jewish women—Agar, the mother, and Ruth, the daughter—are portrayed as unequivocally sympathetic. They welcome Clarel into their home and their hearts, irrespective of his Christian otherness. Yet their portrayal, similar to Nathan's, is ironically undercut. In a reversal of the concepts of Jewish Diaspora and Eretz Israel, Agar, the American Jewess, feels an outsider in the Promised Land. In allusion to her biblical namesake Hagar,[30] she is condemned to taste the bitterness of exile in her alleged homeland. She thus turns out to be another variation of the central theme: she is both a positive and highly complex (in)version of the figure of the Wandering Jewess.

Ruth is in many ways a replica and younger version of her mother. Endowed with the same gentleness, virtue, and charity, and, in addition, with attractiveness and youth, she perfectly exemplifies the beautiful Jewess in the tradition of Scott's Rebecca. Even though she falls in love with Clarel, their passion for each other is shown to be pure and untainted. And though she is clearly identified by her "Hebrew . . . profile, every line" (C, 56), thus defining her as the cultural Other in relation to the protagonist Clarel, she remains a model of maidenly innocence with none of Miriam's ambiguous, sinful passion in *The Marble Faun*. Neither tempted nor temptress, she has transcended the Romantic opposition of dark and fair lady.

Homesick for America like her mother, Ruth finds Palestine "a bad place" (C, 89), where women are deprived of their freedom. She inwardly rebels against what she considers involuntary exile. She and Agar welcome Clarel for the memories he evokes of their sorely missed home country and for bringing the promise of a better life. Thus there is a hidden ambiguity in Ruth full of ironies similar to those related to her mother: though she has supposedly come home to the Promised Land of the Jews, she secretly yearns for America, her birthplace. Not daring to openly question the male authority of father and rabbi, she and Agar, for that matter, adhere to the Jewish law, yet "with hearts but chill and loath" (C, 89). Not finding the craved-for warmth and love in the Jewish religion, she looks for fulfillment in works of charity and in the love for Clarel, thus assuming the role of savior herself.

Ruth, like Agar, thus turns out to be an ambivalent figure whose simplicity is deceiving. Combining the traits of a loving Savior and the beautiful, yet innocent Wandering Jewess, she is both an ironic inversion of the legend of the Wandering Jew and, in her opposition to the rabbi, a critical commentary on Judaism. For it is the rabbi who in his cold learnedness and heartless adherence to the Jewish law undermines the love relationship that transcends the barriers of religious otherness.[31] Ruth and Clarel fail to find the saving grace they had been longing for. While Ruth had hoped for love as an escape from exile, as a liberation from the limited life in Palestine, Clarel had hoped for love as an escape from religious doubt. Both expectations are thwarted—Ruth dies and Clarel departs in distress. Yet a last message to Clarel transcends the general despair of the poem: "Emerge thou mayst from the last whelming sea, / And prove that death but routs life into victory" (C, 523).

Thus while in the Masque, Melville makes "a reverent and compassionate restatement of the plight of the eternally suffering Wandering Jew,"[32] Clarel as a whole serves to creatively reinvent the significance of the figure in the discourse of Christian culture. In his construction of otherness, Melville has transcended the stereotypes of ethnicity and religion to denote difference as defined by the individual.

5. AN END TO AMBIVALENCE?

If nineteenth century representations of the Wandering Jew and his female counterpart in both popular and major works of fiction are highly ambiguous at best, they basically reflect the dominant culture's deep ambivalence towards the Jew. While the bestselling success of Eugène Sue's voluminous novel, The Wandering Jew, attests to the popularity of the figure, it also transforms the negatively conceived Christ-killer into two conflicting, yet positive views of the Other: the mysterious, spectre-like stranger of Romanticism and the socialist rebel dedicated to the struggle for equality of the classes and the sexes. By contrast, F. Marion Crawford in The Roman Singer insists on the negativity of the figure by portraying him as the prototypical Romantic villain. Even though the Wandering Jew's pervasive threat to the fair lady's innocence is defused and "rationalized" in the end, the negativity of his cultural otherness continues.

The discussed works by Hawthorne and Melville express a similar ambivalence. Thus in *The Marble Faun*, Hawthorne's Wandering Jew evolves as a cynical, repugnant figure whose evilness and alterity become even more prominent by juxtaposing him to his female alter ego, Miriam—the dark lady of the romance and beautiful, yet guilty Wandering Jewess. Melville, however, in *Clarel* has overcome his "conventionally anti-Semitic" attitude[33] of earlier works and drawn a more positive portrait of the Wandering Jew. Here pilgrimage as the controlling metaphor does not only refer to the forever exiled Wandering Jew and Ruth, the beautiful, yet innocent Wandering Jewess, but also to a group of pilgrims, all of them exiles from the certainty of faith. So in *Clarel* Melville has transcended the negative connotations of the figure by generalizing its significance. However, the deep ambiguity expressed in all of these works points beyond nineteenth century American literature; for the dominant culture's troubled invention of the Jew has persisted into the present century, its problematic perceptions of cultural otherness still unresolved.

NOTES

1. Michel Foucault, "What is an author?" *Modern Criticism and Theory: A Reader*, ed. David Lodge (London and New York: Longman, 1989), 202.

2. Michel Foucault, *Die Ordnung des Diskurses* [*L'ordre du discours*, 1972], trans. Walter Seitter, with an essay by Ralf Konersmann (Frankfurt/Main: Fischer, 1992), 11. Translation into English by Regine Rosenthal.

3. Michel Foucault, *The Archaeology of Knowledge* [*L'archéologie du savoir*, 1969], trans. A.M. Sheridan Smith (London: Routledge, 1994), 49.

4. Edgar Rosenberg, *From Shylock to Svengali: Jewish Stereotypes in English Fiction* (Stanford, CA: Stanford University Press, 1960).

5. George K. Anderson, *The Legend of the Wandering Jew*, (Providence, RI: Brown University Press, 1765), 11.

6. Both Anderson's study and the collection of essays by Hasan-Rokem and Dundes present a variety of European and American versions of the legend and the protagonist's name. Anderson, *The Legend of the Wandering Jew*; Hasan-Rokem and Alan Dundes, eds. *The Wandering Jew: Essays in the Interpretation of a Christian Legend* (Bloomington: Indiana University Press,

1986).

7. Stefan Heym's novel, *Ahasver* (1981), a contemporary reinvention of the Wandering Jew, is based, to a large extent, on the *Kurtze Beschreibung* of 1602. For a more detailed discussion of Heym's ironic reinterpretation of the legend and the figure see Regine Rosenthal, "Still Restlessly Roaming: Versions of the Wandering Jew in Two Contemporary Jewish Novels," in *ZAA: Zeitschrift für Anglistik und Amerikanistik, A Quarterly of Language, Literature and Culture* 43, no. 2 (1995): 161-176.

8. In his comprehensive study, Anderson offers an English translation of the *Kurtze Beschreibung* and its version of Christ's curse. Anderson, *Wandering Jew*, 46.

9. Both in the *Kurtze Beschreibung* and in Roger Wendover's *Flores historiarum*, Ahasuerus/Cartaphilus becomes a pious, God-fearing pilgrim and though Cartaphilus is not specifically identified as a Jew, the earlier Italian version, on which this story is based, stresses his Jewishness. Anderson, *Wandering Jew*, 18.

10. Hyam Maccoby, *The Sacred Executioner: Human Sacrifice and the Legacy of Guilt* (New York: Thames and Hudson, 1982), 166.

11. The tradition of the non-idealized "Jew's Beautiful Daughter"—see Rosenberg, *From Shylock to Svengali*, 384—is in fact much older. Shakespeare's Jessica, for instance, Shylock's beautiful, yet disobedient daughter, succumbs both to the pleasures of sex—eloping, as she does, with her Christian lover—and to the temptation of abdicating her Jewish faith.

12. Alide Cagidemetrio, "A Plea for Fictional Histories and Old-Time 'Jewesses'," *The Invention of Ethnicity*, ed. Werner Sollors (New York, Oxford: Oxford University Press, 1989), 21.

13. Ibid., 21-22.

14. Harap actually devotes a whole chapter to the "American Journeys of the Wandering Jew" in *The Image of the Jew in American Literature: From Early Republic to Mass Immigration* (Philadelphia: The Jewish Publication Society of America, 1974), 239-255.

15. An indication of *The Wandering Jew's* sustained success in America is its publication by Random House as a Modern Library Giant. Eugène Sue, *The Wandering Jew* (New York: The Modern Library, n.d.).

16. For critical evaluations of Crawford and his work see *An F. Marion Crawford Companion* by John C. Moran, with introductory essays by Edward Wagenknecht, Russell Kirk and Donald Sidney-Fryer (Westport, Conn. & London, England: Greenwood Press, 1981).

17. Francis Marion Crawford, *A Roman Singer* (Boston: Houghton Mifflin, 1884), 169, subsequently cited as *RS*.

18. Harap, *Image of the Jews*, 248.

19. Michel Foucault, *Madness and Civilization: A History of Insanity in the Age of Reason* [*Histoire de la Folie*, 1961] (New York: Vintage Books, 1988).

20. Nathaniel Hawthorne, *The English Notebooks,* ed. Randall Stewart (New York: Russell and Russell, 1962), 321; subsequently cited as *EN.*

21. Nathaniel Hawthorne, *The Marble Faun: or, The Romance of Monte Beni,* vol. 4 of *The Centenary Edition of the Works of Nathaniel Hawthorne,* ed. William Charvat, Roy Harvey Pearce, Claude M. Simpson, and Matthew J. Bruccoli (Columbus, Ohio: Ohio State University Press, 1968), 389; subsequently cited as *MF.*

22. In the mid-nineteenth century, this portrait was among the most sought-after attractions of Rome. It fascinated many nineteenth century writers, among them Hawthorne and Melville. Though it was attributed to Guido Reni and believed to represent Beatrice Cenci, it is well established today that both assumptions were mistaken.

23. While Greenwald maintains that "Miriam, like Hilda, is 'innocent'"— Elissa Greenwald, "Hawthorne and Judaism: Otherness and Identity in *The Marble Faun,*" *Studies in the Novel* 23, no. 1 (1991): 134—Vallas, consistent with my own view and with Hawthorne's strategy of mystification as an integral part of the romance, holds that Hawthorne "sets her [Miriam] up to be found potentially guilty." Stacey Vallas, "The Embodiment of the Daughter's Secret in *The Marble Faun,*" *Arizona Quarterly* 46, no. 4 (1990): 78.

24. Harap also finds Miriam's rejected suitor to be "invested with features of the Wandering Jew." Harap, *Image of the Jew,* 114.

25. Harap therefore claims that "in symbolic significance, in variety, in awareness of Jewish matters, and in humanistic depiction this work is without parallel in all of American literature before our century." Thus, despite the first phase in Melville's writing career (up to the year 1856), where the treatment of Jews was stereotypical and ambivalent, the Jews in *Clarel* "are depicted with humanity and understanding." Harap, *Image of the Jew,* 118.

26. Hawthorne, on the occasion of Melville's visit, took note of Melville's troubled search for certainty: "[He] will never rest until he gets hold of a definite belief. It is strange how he persists . . . in wandering to and fro over these deserts . . . He can neither believe, nor be comfortable in his unbelief." *EN,* 432-433.

27. Goldman suggests that "the title of the poem . . . explains Melville's theological task" in that the name 'Clarel' intimates a semantic compound of 'clarity' and the Hebrew word 'el' for 'God,' thus implying "a quest for the clarity of God." Stan Goldman, *Melville's Protest Theism: The Hidden and Silent God in Clarel* (DeKalb: Northern Illinois University Press, 1993), 3.

28. Herman Melville, *Clarel: A Poem and Pilgrimage in the Holy Land,* ed. Walter E. Bezanson (New York: Hendricks House, 1960), 349; subsequently cited as *C.*

29. Bernard Rosenthal, "Herman Melville's Wandering Jews," in *Puritan Influences in American Literature,* ed. Emory Elliott, Illinois Studies in Language and Literature, vol. 65 (Urbana, Chicago, London: University of

illinois Press, 1979), 171.

30. Hagar, Sarah's Egyptian slave girl, was the mother of Abraham's first son, Ishmael. When Sarah finally gave birth to Isaac, Abraham's second son and rightful heir, Hagar and Ishmael were turned away. Condemned to wander in the desert, Ishmael was, however, comforted by God with the promise of being the future founder of a great nation (Genesis 16, 21).

31. The rabbi in his unquestioning adherence to "empty forms," seems to represent Melville's critical comment on "the mind infertile of the Jew," with respect to religion (C, 64). The rabbi's austerity and stern abidance by the Jewish law knows neither tolerance for difference, nor compassion.

32. Harap, *Image of the Jew*, 243.

33. Ibid., 121.

Henry James' Fictional Jew

Greg W. Zacharias

Henry James' fiction and other writings have struck a chord of interest with contemporary Americans. Over the past fifteen years, at least, there has been more professional scholarship published on James' work than on that of any other American writer. At the same time, one notices roughly the same number of references to James in the popular press as to Shakespeare.[1] A revival of "The Heiress," a play written after one of James' novels, *Washington Square,* is popular now with Broadway audiences and critics. Last January *The New Yorker* ran an ad for Anita Brookner's new novel, *A Private View.*[2] In using James' status and reputation as a selling point, the ad affirmed them. "If Henry James were alive today," the ad proclaimed, "the only author he would read would be Anita Brookner." Leaving James' posthumous reading preferences aside, attention given to his work and imagination signal their importance in American culture. No less important is his idea of the Jew, which he uses in his fiction and non-fiction to advance his vision for twentieth-century American society.

In James, the idea of the Jew is always related to his view of private identity, cosmopolitan culture, and language. Thus in James the idea of the Jew rests at the center of his thinking and writing on the individual's relation to culture in general.

In an 1888 letter, written at about the mid-point of his career, Henry James wrote of the "melting together" of English and American cultures to such a degree that he could speak of "the life of the two countries as continuous or more or less convertible, or at any rate as simply different chapters of the same general subject." More, James wished to represent himself as a fiction writer "in such a way that it would be impossible to an outsider to say whether I am, at a given moment, an American writing about England or an Englishman writing about America . . . and so far from being ashamed of such an ambiguity I should be exceedingly proud of it, for it would be highly civilized."[3]

James' insistence on the inevitable "melting" together of the English and American "worlds" and the benefits such a melting would bring to "civilization" says a great deal about his view of all national identities and cultures. I contend that his remarks also explain his central and Jewish characters. For the civilized cosmopolitan identity James mentions in the letter, the idea of the Jew, and his literary characters, all cohere around and issue from James' particular conceptualization of identity, which cherishes the individual but also prizes social coherence and cohesion.

James' idea of the Jew points to a picture he gives of himself.[4] For like the new Jewish immigrants he saw at the turn of the century in New York City and represents in *The American Scene*, and like his best fiction characters, James lived for much of his life in foreign countries. And like his best characters, who, like James and the Jews of New York, find themselves to be strangers in strange lands, James and James' central novel heroes work to find a way of living, a kind of public mode of performance or self-presentation, that will allow them, in James' words, to "melt" into the new culture. But, at the same time, such performances would allow the immigrants to preserve their own conceptions of identity, culture, and heritage.

James' idea of assimilation, difference, and identity was like that of Amy Levy, an Anglo-Jewish writer and James' contemporary, who argued strongly that Jews in fiction ought to be "thoroughly English although singular in many ways."[5] Like James, Amy Levy saw an essential place in life and in fiction for citizens with hyphenated, cosmopolitan identities, who lived as cultural natives but also preserved differences from the dominant culture which defined their particular identities.

Such a conception of the cosmopolitan identity was James' way to face and overcome what Alex Zwerdling calls an "Anglo-Saxon panic"[6] in the United States as immigrants from southern, central, and eastern Europe poured in at the end of the last century.[7] But James' point is not to discuss these immigrants for their own sake. He uses them in *The American Scene* as he would characters in fiction, that is, to represent ideas. Because in James' day there was no Jewish state and national biases defined even Jewish families who had lived in one place for generations as outsiders, James could use fictional Jews as literary symbols of immigration, thus of alienation. But another side of the idea of the fictional Jew is that that alien, that immigrant, also must represent cosmopolitanism because of the Jews' history of compulsory migration and domicile, which forced Jews at once to live within a larger culture and also, by their enforced separation, encouraged them to preserve the Jewish tradition and identity.

Jewish immigrants in *The American Scene,* central characters in novels, and James in the letter all dramatize the complex relationship of identity and language. When in the letter which I excerpted earlier James explains that "I aspire to write in such a way that it would be impossible to an outsider to say whether I am, at a given moment, an American writing about England or an Englishman writing about America," he underlines the significance of language in terms of self-presentation, assimilation, and identity. It is important to remember that James only wants to *appear* or *perform* as both English and American. He never expresses a desire to *hold* both identities. Thus "cosmopolitan" characterizes best James' attitude. Such cosmopolitanism is an attitude that Adeline Tintner says James developed at least in part to counter those who "felt that cosmopolitanism was a disease of modern society with roots in Jewish capitalism and that it corrupted morals. . . ."[8]

In addition, however, James' discussion of Jews (and also of immigrant Italians, for that matter) in the *American Scene* can be understood as a response to contemporary calls for total assimilation, which Teddy Roosevelt summarized thus: "a hyphenated American is not an American at all. . . . Our allegiance must be purely to the United States. We must unsparingly condemn any man who holds any other allegiance."[9] Through the fictional Jew, James responds to such calls for total assimilation by issuing his own declaration to those immigrants *not* to abandon their deeply held cultural and thus personal identities, but to develop a Jamesian public performance, which would enable their integration into the larger culture without forcing them to renounce their identities.

Such a process of Jamesian assimilation may at first seem impossible because, in general, Teddy Roosevelt's idea of assimilation governs our thinking. James' fictional Jew counters it and offers another way of living.

James' cosmopolitanism never implies that appearing English requires a rejection of his core identity as an American. But James puts a premium on his ability to control through a non-threatening public performance with language *how* others perceive him. At the same time, he maintains through that control his sense of himself as an individual. Thus, James' ability to choose when to conform to a given culture, to decide when and how to "melt" into it, also is a marker of his difference from it. For only by seeing himself as an outsider to a new culture could he make the changes necessary to perform as if he were an insider.

James' characters who fail to gain a perspective of themselves from another point of view live disappointing lives. Some characters, especially Miriam Rooth of *The Tragic Muse*,[10] learn, as James himself did, to see themselves from an outside perspective and thus find a way to use that knowledge to live better with others.

James' central character in *The Tragic Muse,* Miriam Rooth, has a gentile mother and a Jewish father, who changed his name from Roth. Even with the name change and the lack of a Jewish mother to affirm her identity, Miriam Rooth is identified by others in the novel as Jewish, which tends to push her into the margin of English society. In order to gain acceptance, Miriam Rooth must perform a life. But she must perform without losing her fundamental identity. For if she should lose that, she would have no anchored place from which to act out her other parts.

James' depiction of Jewish immigrants in *The American Scene* advances a similar recommendation not only to all immigrants, but to all resident or "Yankee" Americans living for the first time in what we would call a multi-cultural society. James worked thus to shape a twentieth-century world in which one could be both a part of a large cosmopolitan culture and yet still preserve individual sovereignty.

Like America's greatest poet, Walt Whitman, and like Amy Levy, James thus celebrates the individual large enough to "contain multitudes."[11]

For the mainly Jewish immigrant population James represents in *The American Scene,* the pressure to conform through the kind of assimilation Teddy Roosevelt favored and James opposed is relentless.

James, having lived most of *his* adult life away from his native United States, must have felt deeply the immigrants' difficult circumstances, judging from his description of the effects of assimilation that coerced them to separate from their pasts and thus from a vital element of their private identities. Linking the immigrants' manners or ways of living with their very identities, James was acutely aware of their crisis under the pressure to abandon their past, their manners, their identities. Thus he wrote that under the pressure of total assimilation the immigrant "presents himself . . . as wonderingly conscious that his manners of the other world . . . have been a huge mistake. . . ."[12] "There are categories of foreigners," James continues, "of whom we are moved to say that only a mechanism working with scientific force could have performed this feat of making them colourless."[13] Thus the problem James sees with a dehumanizing and "scientific" assimilation that operates through humiliation is that it aims to produce "colourless" Americans.

Americans who are stripped of their local or home "color" or "culture" only contribute to a homogeneous society which threatens James' cosmopolitan ideal in two ways. First, because a culture that lacks foreign influence cannot be cosmopolitan, it can only be nationalistic. (Writing less than ten years after the Spanish-American War, and facing a rise in German nationalism that would lead to two world wars and the Holocaust, muscular nationalism was a problem for James as it was for others.) Second, a homogeneous American culture threatens Jamesian cosmopolitanism because James sees the vitality of the United States exactly in the "melting" together of the various identities into something new, vibrant, unique, interesting, and cosmopolitan. For it is exactly in that cosmopolitan version of American culture, which he projects through his image of Jewish immigrants in turn of the century New York City, that James sees the "future," as he calls it, of the western world.[14]

It is in New York City, which James names "the city of redemption" for immigrants,[15] and which he uses as a metaphor for the United States, that immigrants living on the Lower East Side find their "New Jerusalem," as James put it. James elaborates "the particular identity of 'The New Jerusalem'" thus: "What struck me in the flaring streets . . . was the blaze of the shops addressed to the New Jerusalem wants and the splendour with which these were taken for granted."[16] Here, in this picture of the ethnic shops of the "New Jerusalem," is the possibility for a cosmopolitan culture that resembles in type—though not in kind—the ideal cosmopolitanism James sought for himself. *New* Jerusalem, like *New* York and *New* England, maintains some of the old traditions within the new. Such a description of the place that has adapted to "the New Jerusalem wants" and displayed easily identifiable markers of Jewish cultural "color," but was still incorporated into the commercial American scene, suggests that James sees a possibility for the new cosmopolitan United States on the Lower East Side.

The culture of cosmopolitanism which James represents in his "New Jerusalem" is central to his notion of living best. James' representation of New Jerusalem cosmopolitanism does not differ significantly from the crowded London streets he himself walked at great length as he prepared his novel *The Princess Casamassima*,[17] whose central character, Hyacinth Robinson, is one of his most profoundly alienated. James wrote in the preface to *The Princess* of his own long London walks: "to a mind curious, before the human scene, of meanings and revelations the great grey Babylon easily becomes, on its face, a garden bristling with an immense illustrative flora."[18]

A cosmopolitan United States is a great change for the American Henry James, who faces the prospect and the startling personal implications of such a cosmopolitanism as he listens to the speech of all Americans. That speech, that use of language, whether from the mouths of Yankees or new immigrants, signals differences which in turn create the kind of intensely human and humane circumstances that characterize London's "grey immensity" and the allure of New York's Lower East Side. But, at the same time, the differences shake and disorient James, an American "Yankee," by forcing him to reexamine his sense of the American identity, thus his own. He asks, "Which is the American, by these scant measures?—which is *not* the alien . . . and where does one put a finger on the dividing line . . . ?"[19] As he rethinks and refashions his idea of his native city and nation and thus refashions his idea of himself and of the American character, he must, standing on the Lower East Side of New York City, surrounded by Jewish immigrants from central and eastern Europe, accept the Jewish contribution to his sense of his national identity, of his personal identity. That particular contribution may be extended as an idea of how all immigration affects identity itself.

James observed that both the culture and the history of the United States are, using his word, "invented."[20] Such a concept of cultural and historical invention is important because, like performance, it implies the control of the inventors or performers. It also implies that what has been invented once may be improved. I take all of James' writings that relate to history and culture, then—and all of them, to me, *are* linked directly or indirectly with history and culture—as parts of his effort to contribute to that national "invention." Moreover, since writing is James' act of representing himself, of *performing* his ideas, his fiction and non-fiction, and letters such as the one I quoted from earlier, constitute James' cultural action, his civic performance. In

James' cosmopolitan community, the particular identities of individuals are preserved when they work through their public use of language and manners to integrate themselves into the larger community. At the same time, the larger community must respect from a distance those private identities which define the individual. In *The American Scene,* James himself preserves such distance, even as he recognizes how unusual it is for a Yankee to *have* to act to create a space for tolerance or to perform that creation in writing or in everyday behavior.

James' own words on the power we all have to understand ourselves and thus to control our ever-changing identities, which may be even more complex today than in James', end my paper: "these adventures [in the Lower East Side] of the critical spirit were such mere mild walks and talks as I almost blush to offer, on this reduced scale, as matter of history; but I draw courage from the remembrance that history is never, in any rich sense, the immediate crudity of what 'happens,' but [it is] the much finer complexity of what we read into it and think of in connection with it."[21]

NOTES

1. Adeline Tintner brought this point to my attention during a telephone conversation on August 8, 1995, about her forthcoming book, *The Legacy of Henry James.*

2. "Advertisement" for *A Private View* by Anita Brookner. *The New Yorker* (Jan. 23, 1995), 8.

3. Henry James, *Henry James Letters,* ed. Leon Edel, 3 (Cambridge: Harvard UP, 1980): 244.

4. See Jonathan Freedman, "Trilling, James, and the Uses of Cultural Criticism," *Henry James Review* 14 (1993): 141-150.

5. Linda Hunt, "Amy Levy and the 'Jewish Novel': Representing Jewish Life in the Victorian Period," *Studies in the Novel* 26 (1994): 236.

6. Alex Zwerdling, "Anglo-Saxon Panic: the Turn of the Century Response to 'Alien Immigrants,'" *Ideas from the National Humanities Center* 1, no.2 (1993): 33-45.

7. Ibid.

8. Adeline Tintner, *The Cosmopolitan World of Henry James: An Intertextual Study* (Baton Rouge: LSU Press, 1991), 2.

9. Zwerdling, "Anglo-Saxon Panic," 40.

10. Henry James, *The Tragic Muse,* 2 vols. (Boston: Houghton Mifflin, 1890).

11. Walt Whitman, "Song of Myself" *Leaves of Grass* (New York: Random House, n.d.), 78.

12. Henry James, *The American Scene* (London: Chapman and Hall, 1907), 127.

13. Ibid., 128.

14. Ibid., 139.

15. Ibid, 133.

16. Ibid., 135.

17. Henry James, *The Princess Casamassima*, 3 vols. (London: Macmillan, 1886).

18. Henry James, "Preface to *The Princess Casamassima*," in *The Art of the Novel*, ed. R.P. Blackmur (New York: Scribners, 1934), 59.

19. Ibid., 124.

20. James, *The American Scene*, 77.

21. Ibid., 182.

Hans Schweitzer's Anti-Semitic Caricatures: The Weimar Years, 1926-1933

Russel Lemmons

Since the Middle Ages Judeophobic caricatures have been among the most important forms of popular anti-Semitism. Emerging in a Europe characterized by mass illiteracy, visual representations became the preferred method of creating negative stereotypes of Jews. The images first developed in these drawings, complete with hook-nosed figures committing a variety of violent acts against innocent Christians, are still with us today. Surprisingly, with a few notable exceptions, there has been little research done regarding this phenomenon, especially about its twentieth-century manifestations.[1]

Among the political movements to make extensive use of anti-Semitic caricatures was the National Socialist German Workers' Party (NSDAP or Nazi Party). Joseph Goebbels, the party's propaganda chief, believed that caricatures were a more effective method of political propaganda than the written word. Political drawings could be understood more easily, he insisted, and visual images made a more lasting impression. Under his influence, the anti-Semitic caricature became a mainstay of Nazi propaganda during the Weimar Republic and the Third Reich.[2]

It was during the Weimar Republic that National Socialist cartoonists developed a particularly vicious type of anti-Semitic caricature that envisioned the Jew as the racial enemy of the German *Volk*. Although their hatred of Jews was not unique among right-wing political cartoonists, these "artists" were unsurpassed in the brutality of their attacks upon Germany's Jewish population. Philip Ruprecht ("Fips"), whose semi-pornographic anti-Semitic caricatures appeared in

Julius Streicher's infamous hate sheet, *Der Stürmer,* became one of the most widely-known political cartoonists of the Weimar Republic.[3] While Dennis Showalter has done an extensive analysis of Ruprecht's anti-Jewish drawings, historians have largely ignored other Nazi cartoonists. Among the most important of these caricaturists was Hans Schweitzer, one of the NSDAP's most influential political cartoonists and poster artists.[4]

Hans Herbert Schweitzer, who was born in Berlin in 1901, is of interest for a variety of reasons. Like so many future leaders of the Third Reich, his parents inculcated him with a far-right ideology, especially a virulent anti-Semitism. Having never received his *Abitur,* from the ages of seventeen to twenty-two he attended an art school in Berlin. Even before he joined the NSDAP in January 1926, he began drawing cartoons and posters for Berlin's *völkisch* organizations. Shortly after Schweitzer joined the party, Joseph Goebbels became the Gauleiter (Regional Leader) of the Nazi Party in Berlin. For the next seven years, Schweitzer's career was inextricably linked with the fortunes of Goebbels and the Berlin NSDAP.[5]

Schweitzer and the Gauleiter became fast friends, often spending the evening together, attending the movies or the theater, or just drinking in one of Berlin's numerous pubs. This friendship naturally advanced Schweitzer's career as a political cartoonist, and he began to perfect his "craft" under the tutelage of the future propaganda chief of the Third Reich. Goebbels' violent anti-Semitism dramatically influenced the cartoonist's work. Schweitzer continued to produce his political posters, fliers and caricatures for the Berlin NSDAP, and when, in July 1927, Goebbels established a weekly newspaper, *Der Angriff (The Attack),* Schweitzer became the organ's political cartoonist. Most of the illustrations appearing in *Der Angriff* and a book Schweitzer and Goebbels published in 1928, *Das Buch Isidor,* were dominated by a viciously anti-Semitic motif. The cartoons were simple and their point was always obvious: the Jews were responsible for all of Germany's misfortunes. Goebbels considered Schweitzer "a fabulous illustrator. He has the great gift of being able to make a vital point with only a few lines. Only a master can do that." Following the Nazi "seizure of power," Schweitzer went on to become one of the leading illustrators of the Third Reich. He had an important effect upon the development of the regime's propaganda techniques, and he became a Reich Senator of Culture, making him one of Nazi Germany's cultural elite. He drew many of the most famous propaganda posters of the

Nazi years, urging the German people on to victory at all costs. In spite of two appearances before denazification courts after the war, Schweitzer never paid for his actions.[6]

But it is his activities during the last years of the Weimar Republic that are of interest here. It was during this period that the rabid anti-Semitism of the Nazi Party matured, and Schweitzer developed his distinctive style of Judeophobic caricature. His cartoons reflected the unrelenting violence that had come to characterize political life in Berlin during the 1920s and 1930s. An almost palpable brutality permeated Schweitzer's cartoons, which he published under the pseudonym Mjölnir, the name given to the god Donner's hammer in German mythology. Contending that his cartoons were "sharp and uncompromising . . . hammer blows" on behalf of the German people, Mjölnir waged an unrelenting assault upon Berlin's Jewish population, playing a vital role in the Nazi effort to dehumanize the "racial enemy."[7]

Schweitzer published hundreds of political cartoons, most of which were anti-Semitic in focus. The vast majority of his caricatures appeared in two places. First, as already stated, from 1927 he was the cartoonist for Goebbels' organ, *Der Angriff*. This newspaper began publication as a weekly with a modest circulation of around 2000. By the end of 1932, *Der Angriff* was a daily with a circulation of 110,000, making it the second-largest National Socialist newspaper. Established in response to a ban on the Berlin NSDAP, Goebbels insisted that the paper recreate the frenetic political violence for which the Nazis had become infamous over the previous several months. Whether Goebbels achieved this goal or not is debatable, but there is little doubt that Mjölnir's caricatures played a vital role in giving *Der Angriff*'s attack upon the Weimar Republic—especially its Jewish citizens—a thoroughly vicious tone.[8]

Another important collection of Schweitzer's cartoons can be found in a book he co-authored with Goebbels, *Das Buch Isidor: ein Zeitbild voll Lachen und Hass*. Published in 1928, it is a collection of ninety-one of Mjölnir's early drawings—most of them anti-Semitic caricatures from *Der Angriff*—accompanied by texts written by the Berlin Gauleiter. The book's point of departure is an attack upon Bernhard Weiss, the Jewish vice president of the Berlin police force, whom Berlin's *völkisch* movement had dubbed "Isidor." But the brutal assault upon Weiss had a more general goal than discrediting one of the republic's leaders and most prominent Jewish citizens. The police vice president became, to both Goebbels and Schweitzer, a symbol for everything the Nazis hated about the so-called Weimar system. As Goebbels stated in the opening motto of the book:

> Isidor is not one person, not a person in the legal sense. Isidor is a type, a spirit, a face or, more correctly, a visage. Isidor is that republic, created in cowardice and hypocrisy, which, on 9 November 1918 seized empty thrones and today swings rubber clubs to keep us in line.

Isidor was an idea; he was the personification of the Jew, of hatred of all things German, of all that had gone wrong since 1918. This contention can be seen not only in Goebbels' text, but also in Schweitzer's anti-Jewish caricatures.[9]

Mjölnir's drawings incorporated most of the prominent forms of early twentieth-century anti-Semitism: racial, economic, religious and political Jew hatred. As a convinced National Socialist, Schweitzer was a racial anti-Semite, as can be seen in the physiognomies of his figures, especially their faces. To Schweitzer, like other racial anti-Semites, a Jew was immediately recognizable by his hooked nose, weak chin, beady eyes, grotesquely enlarged ears, and sloped forehead. In general, Schweitzer, like other Nazi caricaturists, emphasized racial anti-Semitism at the expense of more traditional approaches, especially religious ones. Although, as a National Socialist, Schweitzer looked upon religious anti-Semitism as "old-fashioned," he did occasionally make use of this centuries-old motif.[10]

Two excellent examples of Schweitzer's very occasional use of religious anti-Semitism can be found in *Das Buch Isidor*. The first of these, originally published in *Der Angriff* on 26 December 1927, was entitled, "If he celebrated Christmas" (Figure 1). It shows a caricature of Police Vice President Weiss smoking a cigar and hanging dead Nazi storm troopers on a Christmas tree. The tree has a Star of David at the top, and a record player in the background is playing "Daughter of Zion be Joyful." This cartoon is an excellent example of Mjölnir's religious anti-Semitism in that it not only appeals to the traditional Judeophobic belief that Jews have no respect for Christian religious customs, but it also combines this theme closely with one emphasizing political violence. Weiss, so Schweitzer claims, is glad to see Nazis die; indeed, as vice president of the police, he is responsible.[11]

Another of Schweitzer's political caricatures that combines a religious assault with the theme of political violence is one entitled

"The New Nero" (Figure 2). This cartoon depicts Weiss as the Roman emperor Nero standing before an SA man tied to a stake with the word "Prohibition!" appearing at its apex. Behind him are several policemen, one of them carrying a standard with the Star of David upon it. The implication is clear: just as Nero and the Jews persecuted first-century Christianity, Isidor is persecuting the Nazi movement. Not only is Weiss associated with a longstanding Judeophobic stereotype—Jews allegedly persecute practitioners of Christianity—but the Nazis are favorably compared with the early church, a movement that was once persecuted but ultimately emerged triumphant.[12]

Cartoons and caricatures that emphasized religious motifs appear rarely among Schweitzer's drawings and only in combination with themes emphasizing political violence, and political themes were ultimately paramount. Mjölnir's cartoons reflected the Nazi view of politics as a violent confrontation between the forces of right, the German *Volk*, and the legions of darkness and barbarism, the Jews. In this fight the Jews, who dominated the hated Weimar system, had all the advantages. It was they, through the machinations of a government that they dominated, who caused the brutality so characteristic of German politics during the late 1920s and early 1930s. The Nazis were the righteous victims of the Jew-led assault upon the spirit and wellbeing of the German *Volk*.[13]

Closely coupled with Schweitzer's political attack upon the Jews was a more traditional economic anti-Semitism. Just, according to Mjölnir, as they dominated Weimar politics, the Jews controlled the German economy. Jewish capitalists exploited the German people to fill their bank accounts. At the same time, and somewhat paradoxically, Jewish Communists fomented class conflict, the goal of which was to weaken the German *Volk* and keep it enslaved. In the end, both the socio-economic status quo and the Marxist parties were dominated by the Jews. Only the Nazi Party recognized this and was willing to do something about it. All of these themes can be seen in Schweitzer's political cartoons. Of the hundreds that Schweitzer produced, restrictions on space dictate that only a few can serve as representative examples.

That the Jews' supposed responsibility for political violence was an important theme in Schweitzer's cartoons can be seen in a 1931 political cartoon that appeared under the rubric "Three assassinated National Socialists in two days!" (see Figure 3). This drawing depicts three SA men who had recently been murdered, one shot in the lung,

Figure 1: *Der Angriff,* 26 December 1927, "If he celebrated Christmas"

Figure 2: *Das Buch Isidor,* "The New Nero"

Figure 3: *Der Angriff,* 21 January 1931, "Three assassinated National Socialists in two days!"

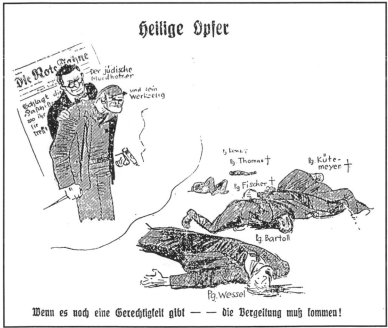

Figure 4: *Der Angriff,* 23 January 1930, "Holy Sacrifices"

Figure 5: *Das Buch Isidor*, "Merchants, skilled workers! Only one is willing to help you!"

Figure 6: *Das Buch Isidor*, "Merry Christmas"

Figure 7: *Der Angriff*, 30 July 1928, "'Tolerance,' pleads the creeping plant to the tree, as it chokes it [the tree]"

Figure 8: *Das Buch Isidor*, "Paragraphs against freedom fighters"

Figure 9: *Der Angriff*, 5 March 1928, "An excellent seed"

Figure 10: *Das Buch Isidor*, "His sweetest dream"

another stabbed in the heart, and the third stabbed in the back. To the side is a Jewish caricature representing the "Jewish press," and behind him is a murderer wielding a knife. The implication is clear: the so-called Jewish press is behind the killing, even going so far as to shield the perpetrators, who are under Jewish control if not Jews themselves. The Jews are responsible for the deaths of these three Nazi heroes.[14]

"Holy Sacrifices" (Figure 4) a January 1930 cartoon appearing in *Der Angriff,* adopted the same theme. It shows six storm troopers who had died as a result of political violence. To the side stands a Jewish Communist, as can be seen by the *Rote Fahne* masthead behind him, who is labeled as a "Jewish instigator of murder." In front of him stands a sinister-looking member of the Communist Party's paramilitary organization, the Red Front Fighters' League (RFB). The RFB man is labeled as "his [the Jew's] tool." Once again, the implication is clear: the Jews are behind the murder of Nazis.[15]

Schweitzer often tried to link alleged Jewish violence against the German people with economic anti-Semitism. This can be seen in his efforts to appeal to Germany's middle classes. One of Schweitzer's cartoons links the damage that "department store capitalism" has done to the middle classes with Judeophobia (Figure 5). In this cartoon, a "department store capitalist," with a "Jewish" face and a moneybag for a body, is crushing "the little merchant, the commercial middle class, [and] the skilled worker." While this is going on, a Social Democrat, a Nationalist and a Communist stand idly by. Coming to the rescue, however, is a National Socialist, rolling up his sleeves. The caption reads, "Merchants, skilled workers! Only one is willing to help you!" Only the Nazis understand the true—(i.e., Jewish)—nature of big business and are willing to fight against it for the benefit of the middle classes.[16]

Yet another way the Jews struck at the German people, according to the NSDAP, was through their control of Germany's international relations. In the area of foreign policy, the Weimar Republic, dominated by the Jews, had abandoned Germany's wellbeing for the benefit of its enemies. One of Schweitzer's cartoons (Figure 6) shows an overweight Jewish banker, representing the Dawes Plan (under which Germany agreed to pay reparations resulting from its defeat in the First World War), and a French soldier sitting on a shackled man symbolizing Germany. The implication is, as always, clear: Jewish finance capital, in league with the former Entente Powers, was determined to crush Germany. The republic's acquiescence in the

Dawes Plan is to be taken as further evidence of this fact. The caption reads "Merry Christmas." The Dawes plan is to be seen as a cruel Christmas gift offered by the enemies of the German people. The Jews have used their control of the economy and foreign policy to do violence to the *Volk*.[17]

Even efforts to promote tolerance and unity among the German people were interpreted as examples of Jewish savagery. A 1928 cartoon attacks tolerance of Jews along these lines (Figure 7). It shows a creeping plant—with a Jew's head—strangling a tree. The caption reads: "'Tolerance,' pleads the creeping plant to the tree, as it chokes it [the tree]." The willingness of so many Germans, Schweitzer clearly implies, to tolerate the Jews is one of the things that enables them to do so much harm to the Fatherland and its people.[18]

According to Schweitzer, the Nazis had proven so effective at exposing and fighting against Jewish violence aimed at the German *Volk*, that the Jews had repeatedly used their control of the Weimar system to get the NSDAP banned. But, in the end, because the Nazis had truth on their side, such prohibitions would ultimately prove fruitless. This is a frequent theme in Mjölnir's caricatures. One of these (Figure 8) shows a storm trooper standing in front of two Jewish caricatures, one of them a lawyer and the other Bernhard Weiss. The caption reads: "Paragraphs against freedom fighters." The Jews are saying to the storm trooper that "The law is ours—to you belongs justice!" The Jews have been using their control of the Weimar Republic's legal machinery to thwart the NSDAP, Germany's only defender of justice in the face of the Jewish onslaught.[19]

Another cartoon (Figure 9) that develops this contention shows Bernhard Weiss as a farmer sowing "persecution, prohibitions, prison sentences [and] battery." His crop is an increasing number of SA men. The caption reads, "An excellent seed." On the bottom right it reads, "Whoever sows the wind, will reap the whirlwind!" Weiss' efforts to crush the Nazis will, in the end, prove counterproductive and only contribute to the inevitable victory of the NSDAP.[20]

The most disturbing of all of Schweitzer's caricatures also depicts Bernhard Weiss (Figure 10). Entitled "His sweetest dream," it shows the vice president of the Berlin police dreaming of using poison gas on Nazi men and women. The accompanying text reads: "Mr. 'Bernhard' Weiss' police force has considered the introduction of poison gas in the struggle against National Socialists." This is, of course, the ultimate example of Schweitzer's efforts to depict Germany's Jews as bent upon the destruction of the NSDAP and, by extension, the German people. Bernhard Weiss, as the representative Jew, will stop at nothing to continue the enslavement of the German people. The question remains: What should Germany do in the face of such enemies?[21]

There was little doubt concerning Mjölnir's answer to this question. His caricatures painted Germany's Jewish population as engaged in a systematic brutal assault against the German *Volk*. In their efforts, they made use of all tools they had at their disposal as the dominators of the system. The Weimar Republic, in keeping with this alleged Jewish influence, pursued savage policies against the Fatherland. Given this assumption, Schweitzer's caricatures intimated that violence against the Jews was an act of self defense. Every "true German" in his cartoons is the victim of Jewish brutality who must be rescued by the Nazi Party. The NSDAP became the source of Germany's salvation; only it recognized the threat posed by the Jewish conspiracy ruling the Fatherland. At the same time, the racial enemy—the Jew—has been demonized. He is no longer human; indeed, to fight him, even to kill him, is a service to humanity.

Schweitzer's caricatures appealed to the worst in the people of Berlin. The population of Germany's capital did indeed suffer during the Weimar Republic. Political violence caused havoc in the streets, economic misery characterized their lives, and political instability only added to their misery. Naturally, they looked for someone to blame, and Mjölnir's cartoons provided a popular scapegoat: the Jews.

While the Nazis did not invent anti-Semitism, they were its most violent practitioners. Preparation for the systematic persecution of the Jews began during the Weimar Republic, even before the Nazis came to power. Even if they did not cause every German to become a rabid anti-Semite, the caricatures of Hans Schweitzer and other National Socialist cartoonists helped anesthetize the German people to the suffering of the Jews. After it came to power, the NSDAP persecuted the Jewish people with a cruelty unparalleled in history, going so far as attempting to exterminate them. Ultimately, it was Jews, not Nazis, who would be gassed. Hitler and his supporters justified their horrific crimes as acts of self defense. Hans Schweitzer's anti-Semitic cartoons played a role in making this possible.

Notes

1. On the medieval origins of the anti-Semitic caricature see Frank Felsenstein, *Anti-Semitic Stereotypes: A Paradigm of Otherness in English Popular Culture, 1660-1830* (Baltimore: Johns Hopkins University Press, 1995), 15. Studies of anti-Semitism still tend to concentrate upon political and intellectual elites. See, for example Peter G.J. Pulzer, *The Rise of Political Anti-Semitism in Germany and Austria* (New York: Wiley, 1964) and Jacob Katz, *From Prejudice to Destruction: Anti-Semitism, 1700-1933* (Cambridge: Harvard University Press, 1980). Some more recent contributions to the intellectual origins of German anti-Semitism include Paul Lawrence Rose's two books: *Wagner: Race and Revolution* (New Haven: Yale University Press, 1992) and the controversial *Revolutionary Antisemitism in Germany: From Kant to Wagner* (Princeton: Princeton University Press, 1990). For recent studies of popular anti-Semitism, see Bruce F. Pauley, *From Prejudice to Persecution: A History of Austrian Anti-Semitism* (Chapel Hill: University of North Carolina Press, 1992); and Dietz Bering *Der Name Als Stigma: Antisemitismus im deutschen Alltag, 1812-1933* (Stuttgart: Ernst Klett, 1987). This book has recently become available in an English translation, *The Stigma of Names: Antisemitism in German Daily Life, 1812-1933*, trans. Neville Plaice (Ann Arbor: University of Michigan Press, 1992). On twentieth-century anti-Semitic caricatures see Dennis E. Showalter, *Little Man, What Now?* Der Stürmer *in the Weimar Republic* (Hamden, CT: Archon Books, 1982); and Sander Gilman, *The Jew's Body* (New York: Routledge, 1991).

2. Joseph Goebbels, *Kampf um Berlin: Der Anfang* (Munich: Eher Verlag, 1934), 201-202.

3. On Ruprecht see Showalter, *Little Man What Now?* 59-67.

4. Peter Paret has written an excellent overview of Schweitzer's entire career. He does not, as I do here, analyze the anti-Semitic motifs in Schweitzer's caricatures. See Peter Paret, "God's Hammer," in the *Proceedings of the American Philosophical Society* 136, no. 2 (1992): 226-246.

5. For Schweitzer's biography, see "Lebenslauf," and "Mjölnir—ein Kampfbegriff," in Hans Schweitzer's Personnel File, Berlin Document Center, Berlin, Germany. See also, Paret, "God's Hammer," 226-227. On Goebbels becoming Gauleiter of Berlin, see Gau Gross-Berlin to Dr. Joseph Goebbels, 16 October 1926, and "Abschrift! Rundschreiben No. 1 der Gauleitung Berlin Brandenburg der NSDAP," 9 November 1926, both in folder 199a of the Schumacher Sammlung, Bundesarchiv, Koblenz, in the Federal Republic of Germany. See also, Peter Huettenberger, *Die Gauleiter: Studie zum Wandel des Machtgefüges in der NSDAP* (Stuttgart: Deutsche Verlag, 1969), 39-42.

6. On the friendship between Goebbels and Schweitzer, see numerous entries in *Die Tagebücher von Joseph Goebbels: Sämtliche Fragmente*, ed. Elke Froelich 1 (Munich: K.G. Saur, 1987): including 13 May 1928, 223; 30 May

1928, 229; 7 June 1928, 231-232; 21 June 1928, 237; 12 July 1928, 244; 5 April 1929, 355; 21 September 1930, 605. For an example of how his connections with Goebbels furthered Schweitzer's career, see Propaganda Abteilung to Hans Schweitzer, 25 March 1931, file 5017, in NS 18 (Reichspropagandaleiter), in the Bundesarchiv. On the creation of *Der Angriff*, see Hans-Georg Rahm, "Der Angriff," *1927-1930: Der nationalsozialistische Typ Der Kampfzeitung* (Berlin: Eher, 1939), 8-9; Franz Hartmann, "Die statistische und geschichtliche Entwicklung der N.S. Press, 1926-1935," (Unpublished manuscript held in the Library of Congress, 1937), 96. For a comprehensive history of Goebbels' newspaper during the Weimar Republic, see Russel Lemmons, *Goebbels and Der Angriff* (Lexington: University Press of Kentucky, 1994). On Schweitzer's career during the Third Reich, see "Mjölnir—ein Kampfbegriff," "Lebenslauf," and Paret, "God's Hammer," passim. For examples of Schweitzer's posters during the Third Reich, see Peter Paret, Beth Irwin Lewis and Paul Paret, *Persuasive Images: Posters of War and Revolution from the Hoover Institution Archives* (Princeton: Princeton University Press, 1992), vii, 109, 145, 176, 184, 209.

7. "Mjölnir—ein Kampfbegriff."

8. Hartmann, "Statistische und Geschichtliche Entwicklung der NS. Presse," 496, 504; Lemmons, *Goebbels and* Der Angriff, 21-42.

9. Goebbels, *Tagebücher* 1 (12 May 1928): 223; (12 July 1928): 244. Mjoelnir and Dr. Goebbels, *Das Buch Isidor: ein Zeitbild voll Lachen und Hass* (Munich: Eher Verlag, 1929), 9-12. On "Isidor" as an anti-Semitic appellation, see Bering, *Stigma of Names*, 169-177. For an excellent comprehensive account of Goebbels' anti-Semitic assault upon Weiss and the latter's response, see Dietz Bering, *Kampf um Namen, Bernhard Weiß gegen Joseph Goebbels* (Stuttgart: Klett-Cotta, 1991).

10. On the physiognomies of Jewish caricatures, see Gilman, *The Jew's Body*. On Nazi views of religious anti-Semitism, see Pauley, *From Prejudice to Persecution*, 190-191; and Adolf Hitler, *Mein Kampf*, trans. Ralph Manhein (Boston: Houghton Mifflin), 232.

11. See Mjoelnir and Goebbels, *Das Buch Isidor*, 40. The cartoon, which was originally entitled, "Isidor, if he would have celebrated Christmas," can also be found in *Der Angriff* (26 December 1927), 5.

12. Mjoelnir and Goebbels, *Das Buch Isidor*, 31. The use of the Star of David is, in itself, indicative of religious anti-Semitism.

13. The most detailed account of the motives—from a Nazi perspective—of the Berlin NSDAP's anti-Semitism can be found in "Warum sind wir Judengegner?" *Der Angriff* (30 July 1928), 1-2.

14. See *Der Angriff* (21 January 1931), 1.

15. See *Der Angriff* (23 January 1930), 5. For more of Schweitzer's cartoons on this theme, which was a prominent one, see, for example *Der Angriff* (21 November 1929), 5.

16. Mjoelnir and Goebbels, *Das Buch Isidor,* 146. See 34 for another example of a "Mjölnir" caricature employing economic anti-Semitism.

17. Mjoelnir and Goebbels, *Das Buch Isidor,* 149. For other cartoons concentrating upon this theme, see 119, 161.

18. See *Der Angriff* (30 July 1928), 1. For another example of how Jews supposedly used tolerance to dupe the German people, see Mjoelnir and Goebbels, *Das Buch Isidor,* 125.

19. See Mjoelnir and Goebbels, *Das Buch Isidor,* 82.

20. *Der Angriff,* (5 March 1928), 5; for a cartoon along a similar line, see Mjoelnir and Goebbels, *Das Buch Isidor,* 23.

21. Mjoelnir and Goebbels, *Das Buch Isidor,* 26.

Radical Islamism and the Jews:
The View of Sayyid Quṭb

John Calvert

It is generally acknowledged that the erosion of Arab-Jewish relations following the consolidation of political Zionism in the first half of the twentieth century elicited, in some quarters, a radical revision of Arab-Jewish history.[1] Choosing to ignore the relatively amicable relations which existed between Jews and Muslims throughout the pre-modern period, many Jewish and Arab writers have characterized twentieth century tensions between the two groups as indicative of ancient visceral antagonisms. Among the most vociferous proponents of this trend are the Islamists,[2] both moderate and radical, from whose pens has emerged a plethora of pamphlets and tractates which are readily available for sale at bookstalls and bookstores throughout the Arabic-speaking world. Briefly, these writings reduce the policy and behavior of the state of Israel to one residual category—that of its Jewish essence. From the Islamist perspective, Zionism is the inevitable consequence of a duplicity inscribed in the Jewish soul since ancient times. From the time of the prophets until the present day, Jews have opposed God's will as revealed in holy scripture and have done everything in their power to undermine the welfare of others, including Muslims. In the pre-modern period Jews falsified the traditions of the Prophet Muḥammad so as to lead Muslims away from their faith. In today's world Jews operate as imperialist spies, agents, and fifth columnists intent upon world conquest.

It is an unsettling view, yet one which enjoys the patronage of respectable Beirut and Cairo publishing houses and the approval of many Islamist-leaning academics, such as the University of Cairo professor whose negative assessment of the Jews has recently been examined by Rivka Yadlin.[3] The themes of Jewish deception, conspiracy, and exclusiveness, basic to these writings, have led many to suppose that their authors have drawn extensively upon the repertoire of European anti-semitism, including the infamous late nineteenth-century Czarist tract, *The Protocols of the Elders of Zion*.[4] However, upon closer inspection it is clear that most of these writings, while they might selectively incorporate specific elements from the European anti-semitic tradition for purposes of reinforcement, are shaped by a discourse of cultural authenticity which is basic to Islamism as a whole. In common with other forms of communalist and populist expression, Islamism rests upon an ontological distinction between the moral self and its corruption by otherness, especially groups, such as the Jews, which have willfully turned away from God's guidance.

This paper explores the origins and nature of Islamist anti-Jewish rhetoric by analyzing the representations of Jews and Zionism put forward by the Egyptian Islamist ideologue Sayyid Quṭb (1906-1966).[5] Quṭb is an obvious figure upon whom to focus in this regard. He is Egypt's most revered Islamist thinker, exceeding in reputation even Ḥasan al-Bannā (1906-1949), founder of the Muslim Brotherhood. In his overall standing as an Islamist ideologue, he may be compared with Turkey's Bediuzzman Saʿīd Nursi (1873-1960), Pakistan's Abū Al'a Mawdūdī (1903-1979), and Iran's Alī Shariatī (1933-1977), all of whom are regarded by the partisans of the Islamist movement as having addressed the maladies affecting the twentieth-century Islamic world in ways authentic to the cultural sensibilities of Muslim peoples. Throughout his career Quṭb was a prolific writer who wrote over fifteen books and dozens of journal and magazine articles.[6] Quṭb's writings on the Jews were composed immediately before and after the creation of the state of Israel in 1948. Although these writings represent only a small portion of his total output, they constitute the earliest explicit treatment of Jewry by an Islamist writer and, for this reason, are exemplary of all that follows in this vein. Little has been added to the Islamist conceptualization of the Jews subsequent to the publication of these works.

Quṭb's Islamism, and thus his image of Jewry, was formed against the backdrop of the political struggle which enveloped Egypt in the 1930s and 1940s.[7] At issue was the legitimacy of the country's semi-independent liberal regime, dominated by the Wafd party, which came to power in the wake of the 1919 anti-British uprising. Initially the absentee landowners who controlled the Wafd enjoyed the overwhelming support of the people. However, the inability of it and the other parliamentary parties to rid Egypt of the remaining traces of British power and diminish the gulf between rich and poor prompted many Egyptians to withdraw their allegiance to the political establishment. For these Egyptians, careers, livelihoods, and national dignity were all seen to be short-changed by a system mired in endless negotiations with the British and in the self-serving policies of the parliamentarians. Increasingly, the optimistic tone of the early 1920s gave way to a mood of despondency and malaise which, by the late 1930s and 1940s, translated into anti-regime demonstrations and clashes with the Egyptian police.

Conceptually, disaffection with the political order was expressed in terms of an alternative mode of nationalist imagining which eschewed the liberals' view of Egypt as a singular nation-state formed around the unity of the Nile Valley in favor of an identity which emphasized civilizational links with other Asian and Arabic-speaking Muslim countries.[8] Many critics of the regime added a specifically Islamic dimension to this eastern orientation by devoting special attention to meanings and symbols derived from the era of the Prophet Muhammad and his Companions (al-Sahaba).

For dissident intellectuals, the effort to tie Egypt's cultural autonomy to an eastern or Islamic framework was simply a way of expressing pride in the national heritage which, in their view, the Wafd and its sister parties had ignored. While critical of the political establishment, they did not envision a radical rupture with the long-established secular orientation of Egyptian politics. This kind of cultural nationalism was typical of men such as Ahmad Hasan al-Zayyāt, who wrote articles and critical reviews celebrating the Arab-Islamic heritage against the unguarded adoption of Western cultural models; and ʿAbd al-Qādir al-Māzinī, co-founder of the modernist Dīwān School of poetry, whose mounting distaste for the policies of the Wafd was displayed in a growing predilection for pan-Arabism.

However, for many more Egyptians, especially the middle social strata of students, civil servants, and shopkeepers, Arab-Islamic cultural reassertion was based on a sincere conviction that only Islam, as a divinely-mandated system of belief and practice, could provide remedies to the on-going problems of poverty, "backwardness," and foreign interference. In this Islamist perspective, the political struggle taking place in Egypt was in essence a contest between competing systems of values, between the Party of God (*Ḥizb Allāh*) and the Party of Satan (*Ḥizb Al-Shaytān*). Like their contemporary Islamist legatees, they believed that it was imperative that the imported secular law codes which had dominated Egyptian legal affairs since the middle decades of the 1800s be replaced with a comprehensive system of laws derived from the Qur'ān and the *sunna* (example) of the Prophet Muḥammad.

The most important expression of the Islamist trend was Ḥasan al-Bannā's Society of the Muslim Brothers (*Jamaʿat al-Ikhwān al-Muslimīn*), founded in the Canal Zone in 1928.[9] From the outset al-Bannā's goal was the creation, first in Egypt and then in other Muslim countries, of an "Islamic order" (*al-nizām al-Islāmī*). To this end he adopted a strategy of advocacy and gradualism aimed at reawakening Egyptians to the faith which lay "dormant (*nā'im*) within their souls."[10] In his view, ideological "acquaintance" (*taʿrīf*) and organizational "formation" (*takwīn*) were to precede the actual "execution" (*tanfīdh*) of the Society's reformist vision.[11] He called upon Egyptians to forsake the political factionalism (*ḥizbiyya*) which he felt was destroying the social fabric of the country in favor of a cross-sectional unity based upon the "credal bonds" (*ribat al-ʿaqīda*) of Islam.[12] Numbers are far from certain, but by its own estimate the Society had over a million members and supporters by the end of World War II.

Quṭb was an active participant in the tide of cultural politics washing over Egypt at this time, first as an independent intellectual and then as a member of the Society of the Muslim Brothers. Quṭb's drift to political activism began in 1921 when, as a boy of fifteen, he left his native village in the underdeveloped southern province of Asyūṭ for Cairo to further his education in the system of state schools.[13] After a number of years spent in preparatory schools, Quṭb was admitted to Cairo's Teachers' Training College (*Dār al-Ulūm*), and graduated in 1933. For the next six years Quṭb taught primary school in the provinces. In 1939 he accepted the first of a series of administrative postings with the Ministry of Education in Cairo, where he remained employed until his resignation in 1952.[14]

After arriving in Cairo, Quṭb quickly established himself as a junior member of the generational cohort of nationalist intellegensia which emerged after World War I to lead Egypt to its national awakening. While still in his teens Quṭb established a professional relationship with ᶜAbbās Maḥmūd al-ᶜAqqād (1899-1964), one of the most important literary luminaries in the post-World War I era, and under his influence made modest contributions in the fields of Arabic poetry and literary criticism.[15] At the Teachers' Training College Quṭb became aware of the currents of anti-regime protest underway in the 1930s, and joined other students in developing a strong commitment to the political and cultural independence of Egypt. Quṭb abandoned his allegiance to the Wafd Party and helped establish a student-teachers association to guard against Western influences in the curriculum. Although Quṭb thereafter professed support for the opposition Saᶜdist Party, he in fact regarded himself as an independent thinker free of party entanglements.

Quṭb's first substantial contribution to the inter-war cultural debate was a lengthy review article, published in 1938, of *Mustaqbal al-thaqāfa fī Miṣr* (*The Future of Culture in Egypt*) by Ṭāhā Ḥusayn (1883-1973), Egypt's great secularist litterateur. In the review Quṭb challenged Ḥusayn's famous contention that in ancient times Egypt had been an integral component of Hellenic-Mediterranean civilization and that, in the present era, it ought to reclaim the rationalist elements of that heritage to foster modernity, just as the West had done in the Renaissance. In Quṭb's estimation, Ḥusayn's thesis obscured the fact that history in general, and the Qu'rān in particular, imbued Egyptians and other Muslim peoples with a spiritual dimension to their lives which stands in stark contrast to the materialist ethos of the modern West. Quṭb makes it clear that there is nothing preventing Egypt from adopting the ethically-neutral technical expertise of the West. Its political and cultural independence, however, depends on the integrity of its Arab-Islamic heritage. According to Quṭb, Egypt should stand with other Muslim countries against the political and cultural encroachments of the West, and must keep in mind the fundamental distinction between culture (*thaqāfa*) and material civilization (*al-madaniyya*).[16]

The imposition of press censorship by the British during World War II prevented Quṭb from continuing his cultural critique of the liberal political establishment. Quṭb therefore spent the war years writing criticism, including several important studies on the literary and aesthetic aspects of the Qur'ān.[17] When martial law was lifted on 4 March 1945, Quṭb resumed his oppositional posture. Yet rather than continue as before, he came increasingly to fuse the notions of cultural uniqueness and common destiny exhibited in his critique of Ḥusayn with the politically programmatic discourses of the Muslim Brotherhood.

In turning to a political, as opposed to a purely cultural, understanding of the role of Islam in society, Quṭb was typical of oppositional Egyptians in the post-war era who sought a definitive solution to Egypt's political impasse. In the face of the precipitous decline of the political establishment at this time, Islam appeared to Quṭb, as it appeared to many, as the only viable alternative. Consequently, Quṭb's "Easternism" was supplemented with a vision of a political order in which the *umma,* or Muslim community of believers, was privileged as the basis of collective identity.

The theoretical bases of Quṭb's new-found Islamism were articulated in a number of works written between the late 1940s and early 1960s.[18] Building, in part, upon intellectual foundations laid by Ḥasan al-Bannā, Quṭb's Islamism hinged upon the premise that Islam is a "system" (*manhāj*) of belief and social practice which provides Muslims with complete "freedom of conscience" (*al-taharrur al-wijdānī al-mutlaq*), which Quṭb defined as liberation of the mind from subservience to anyone, or anything, other than God.[19] According to Quṭb, once humans are released by Islam from the shackles of material greed, priestcraft, and political sycophancy, they will be able to rise above their base desires and bodily appetites to do what is best for themselves and for society as a whole. In Quṭb's words, "complete social justice cannot be assured, nor can its efficacy and permanence be guaranteed, unless it arises from an inner conviction of the spirit."[20] Quṭb believed that the state's role is simply to ensure that social and economic affairs are conducted according to Qur'ānic principles. The range of public and private expression is thus radically circumscribed in Quṭb's thought by the need to abide by the directives of the divine mandate. There is no room, in any of Quṭb's Islamist writings, for non-Islamic political groups or belief systems to operate. Although religious minorities, such as the Jews, can maintain their faiths, they cannot organize politically. Ideologies motivated by non-Islamic principles, or by interpretations of Islam which do not accord with Quṭb's own understanding, are forbidden.

Quṭb's theoretical statements were supplemented by dozens of articles written for the influential journal *al-Risāla* (*The Message*), founded in 1933 by Aḥmad al-Zayyāt as a forum in which the partisans of the heritage could editorialize and express their concerns. In these articles, Quṭb displays the hostility and paranoid style which are characteristic features of Islamist discourses. Influenced by the general mood of anti-colonial revolt current throughout much of Afro-Asia at the War's close, Quṭb heaps scorn upon the intransigent policies of the imperialist powers. Time and again, he castigates Britain for its duplicity and callous behavior in the countries in which it wields influence. "The history of France in the East," Quṭb writes, is likewise characterized by "savage barbarism [al-barbariyya al-mutawaḥḥisha] and pools of blood."[21] From Napoleon's invasion of Egypt until the gallicization of the Maghrib in his own time, France has been intent upon the subjugation of Arab lands.[22] According to Quṭb, the Muslim world has been reduced from a proud and strong community to "colonies and zones of interest" (mustaʿmārāt wa manāṭiq nufūdh).[23] At times, Quṭb's negative criticism of the Western powers takes on explicit racist overtones as, for instance, in his focused attack upon the "white man" who is the Muslims' "first enemy" (ʿadūwanna al-awwal).[24]

In many cases, Quṭb tells us, the imperialists have been aided by "fifth columnist" collaborators, for example, the "brown English" politicians, landowners, and industrial magnates who control Egypt's political establishment and economy. Linked with the West in a web of conspiracy, they seek to lure the Muslim community away from its religion, the source of its worldly strength, by means of their control of schools, universities, publishing houses, and newspapers. Like their British mentors, these colonized elites disparage Islam as a "relic of backwardness and decline" and work assiduously for its demise. For they realize that any increment in Islam's influence can only come at the expense of their own power within the existing system of secular politics.[25] In Quṭb's view, the intelligent observer should focus on the hidden connections which bind the Europeans with the Egyptian establishment; only then can one understand the hidden agendas, identify the true enemies, and follow the plot as it unfolds. Quṭb makes clear his feelings about the West and its native allies. He writes:

> How I hate and disdain those westerners! All of them, without exception. . . . But I [also hate] those Egyptians and Arabs who continue to trust the West's moral conscience in general, and the conscience of colonialism in particular.[26]

It is within this framework of collusion and anti-Muslim sentiment that Quṭb assigns a particularly sinister role to world Jewry.

In Qutb's view, the Jews have worked hard behind the scenes to secure the West's cooperation in the establishment of an independent Jewish state in Palestine, home to close to a million Muslims and site of the Haram al-Sharīf, the third holiest sanctuary in Islam. As evidence of the Zionist-Western collusion, Qutb points to Britain's 1946 plan to float the old idea of partition, even though partition flew in the face of Britain's 1939 White Paper which guaranteed a majority Arab population in Palestine.[27] He also discerned Jewish influence behind American support for the Zionist project, including U.S. President Truman's impassioned plea to the British in 1946 to allow the immediate entry into Palestine of 100,000 European Jewish refugees.[28] Qutb tells us that he was initially surprised by the U.S. commitment to Zionism, since he had shared with other Arabs the belief that the United States was a country dedicated to justice, and would therefore support the self-determination of the Palestinian Arabs after the War. In Qutb's opinion, the United States' refusal to support the establishment of an independent Arab-Muslim Palestine demonstrated that the Americans were no better in this regard than their European cousins.[29] During the course of Qutb's 1950-51 Egyptian government-sponsored visit to the United States to study educational administration, the widespread popular and media support for the recently created state of Israel confirmed further his suspicions of American support for Zionism.[30]

In Qutb's view, the question of Palestine was at the heart of the Afro-Asian reaction to the colonial order and, as such, merited the full attention of Muslims everywhere. In Qutb's words, the struggle for Palestine is "an issue not only of the Arab people, but rather of all of the peoples of the East. It is a struggle between the resurgent [al-nāhid] East and the barbaric West, between God's law [Sharīʿat Allāh] for mankind and the law of the jungle [Sharīʿat al-ghāba]."[31] In 1953, Qutb displayed his concern by attending an Islamic conference in Jordanian-controlled East Jerusalem, convoked to explore the possibility of establishing an Islamic university in the city and to discuss the threat of Israeli irredentism to the Muslim character of the Haram al-Sharīf.[32]

In Qutb's mind, the tyranny of the Western imperialists and their native and Jewish agents was a direct consequence of their lack of a transcendent moral conscience (damīr).[33] Having willfully turned away from the divine guidance, they have adopted policies dedicated to materialism and the usurpation of God's rightful sovereignty (al-

ḥakimiyya) over the world. In the face of unbelief, Quṭb believed that it was imperative that Muslims override the inaction of their governments and adopt whatever measures, including violence, necessary to liberate their lands from the control of internal and external exploiters. Writing in 1946, Quṭb pointed to the impact made on British policy in Palestine by the tactics of terror and sabotage carried out by the maximalist Zionist organization Irgun Zvi Leumi. The Arabs, according to Quṭb, must learn from the Zionists and likewise adopt the tactics of positive action, even if it earns them the censure of the international community.[34] For it is only through praxis, concerted effort and struggle in the material world, that the Islamic ideals of freedom and social justice will be able to take root and triumph over the forces of barbarism and unbelief. For Quṭb, it was significant that the most active opponents of the Egyptian regime and of Zionism throughout the 1930s and 1940s should be the Muslim Brothers who, almost alone among Egyptians, kept their faith intact.[35] Indeed, Quṭb's admiration for the Muslim Brothers' faith-driven activism, exemplified in their activities in the Arab-Israeli war of 1948 and in the anti-British Canal Zone insurgency in 1951, was instrumental in leading him to embrace the organization in 1953.

Quṭb's basic drive was to create a strong state in Egypt capable of protecting the Muslim community from the decadent and enervating forces of immorality and disbelief. His attempt, with others, to generate from out of the symbols of the Islamic heritage a sense of common purpose and identity led inevitably in the direction of chauvinism and exclusivism. Yet, it was not intrinsic to Quṭb's Islamism that any particular group, such as the Jews, should be singled out for special condemnation. In Quṭb's works, as in the writings of other Islamist ideologues, Jews stand with British, French, and American imperialists as enemies of Islam. As in other varieties of nativist and communalist expression, including fascism, the object of Quṭb's ire was dependent on contingent factors, such as the existence of imperialist intervention or of inter-communal tension between Jews and Arabs, which he then incorporated as an integral part of his vision and as an instrument of mass mobilization against the Egyptian regime.

That being said, Quṭb's representations of the Jews do stand out from those of other non-Muslim peoples for the textual support they receive in the Qur'ān and the Islamic tradition. Jews figure in the canonical sources of the Islamic heritage in ways that Christians and other religio-cultural groupings do not. And the reason has to do with history, namely, the Prophet Muḥammad's troubled relations with the Jewish tribes of the oasis town of Medina, site of the first Islamic community in the seventh century C.E.

The great ninth century compilations of redacted tradition, upon which historians rely for a reconstruction of Islam's sacred history, relate how Muḥammad attempted to incorporate the three Jewish tribes, which had long been settled there alongside two pagan Arab tribes, into the nascent *Umma* (Muslim community).[36] Muḥammad, we are told, went so far even as to allow the Jews to retain their distinctive religious beliefs and practices, provided they recognize him as religio-political leader of the Medinan tribal ensemble. The Jews, however, dismissed Muḥammad's claim to be a prophet in the tradition of Moses and the Torah, and refused to cooperate with him against his pagan Meccan enemies. Moreover, the Jews stood behind the Arab "hypocrites" (*al-munafiqūn*) of Medina, who publicly supported Islam while secretly conspired against it. Resentful of the Jews' rejection of him and believing them to be a security risk, Muḥammad had two of the Jewish tribes exiled (one to the nearby oasis of Khaybar, where Muḥammad later had them killed) and had the males of the third tribe massacred, although in circumstances which absolved him of culpability.

Muḥammad's break with the Jews prompted the Qur'ānic revelations to distinguish Islam more explicitly from the religion of the now discredited *Banū Isra'īl* (Children of Israel). Within a space of four years Muḥammad received a series of revelations which changed the *qibla*, or direction of Muslim prayer, from Jerusalem to Mecca, substituted the month long fast of Ramadan for the one day fast of Yom Kippur, and introduced the figure of Abraham as the first Muslim in order to establish the priority of Islam over Judaism.[37] Subsequently, Muḥammad's relations with the Medina Jews formed the basis of traditions, liberally represented in the juridical and theological literature of the medieval period, which emphasized their perfidy and the debased nature of their religion. Typical in this regard is the portrayal by the fourteenth-century jurist Ibn Qayyim al-Jawziyya of the Jews as falsifiers of God's truth and as proponents of religious exclusivity.[38]

What is notable, however, is the fact that these negative images did not, for the most part, translate into an entrenched persecutory posture on the part of the Muslim authorities. Despite the inauspicious beginnings of Jewish-Muslim relations, the Jews appear to have enjoyed a relatively secure position as a recognized and tolerated grouping within pre-modern Islamdom, especially compared to the situation faced by their co-religionists in the Latin West. Along with indigenous Christian groups, who in fact attracted far more attention from Muslim polemicists and political authorities, Jews were allowed to practice their religion in return for their acquiescence to a number of discriminatory regulations which included the payment of a poll tax (*jizya*) and public acknowledgement of their inferior status within the social order.[39]

Several reasons may be cited for this relative tolerance. For one thing, unlike the case in Christianity, there did not exist in Islam a strong theological justification for Jewish persecution: while Christians could, and often did, condemn the Jews for the crime of deicide, Muslims could not accuse the Jews of an equivalent "propheticide" (Muḥammad died a natural death). A perhaps more significant factor was the diverse and pluralistic nature of Islamic society which mollified Muslim opprobrium by the practical need to govern numerically significant religious minorities.[40] Few scholars today would suggest that the situation for Jews within Islamic countries was ideal or utopian. Episodes of persecution of Jews, often accompanied by violence, did occur, most notably in Egypt and Syria under the Fatimid Caliph al-Ḥakīm (996-1021), and in North Africa and Spain in the twelfth century under the Berber Almohads, but these were the exception, not the rule.

Secular Arab nationalists, particularly those inspired by the liberal ideal current between the world wars, drew attention to the relatively good relations which pertained between Jews and Arabs in the pre-modern period as a way of spotlighting the disharmonious effects of Jewish settlement in modern Palestine. According to this line of argument, best represented by the Christian Arab writer George Antonius, "Arab hatred and anti-semitism would end, and the ancient harmony would be restored, when Zionism abandoned both its 'colonialist' and 'neo-crusader' quest."[41] The apologetic underpinnings of this argument are clear in the assumption that the institution of protection (*dhimma*) for Jews and Christians in pre-modern Islam approximated the modern liberal value of equal citizenship which these writers wanted to see applied to the Palestine of their own day.

Quṭb's interpretation of Arab-Jewish history, on the other hand, was prompted by other considerations. Quṭb saw himself as living in an age in which the divinely ordained order of Muslim supremacy had been overturned. Muslim land was occupied and its Muslim inhabitants humiliated by Jewish scriptuaries who, in league with others, were intent upon engineering Islam's demise. In these circumstances, Qutb focused his attention, not on the alleged inter-faith utopia of the medieval period as did the Arab liberals, but upon the history of inter-faith contestation as exemplified in the relations between Muhammad and the Jewish tribes of Medina. In Qutb's view, the obstinacy of the Medinan Jews in the first century of the *Hijra* had a direct analogy in the nefarious purposes of Zionism in his own age.

Qutb's compulsion to recapitulate the Arab-Jewish present in the guise of the past is fully exposed in a tractate, written in the early 1950s, entitled *Marakatna Maʿa al-Yahūd* (*Our Struggle with the Jews*).[42] It constitutes Qutb's only focused treatment of Jewry. Qutb begins the work by observing how "the Muslim community continues to suffer from the same machinations and double dealing which discomfited the early Muslims."[43] Like the Jews of Medina, the Jews of today work tirelessly to distort God's truth and seduce Muslims from their faith in order to weaken and, ultimately, destroy the Islamic community.[44] Muslims should take seriously the Qur'ānic verse which states that: "One segment of the People of the Book shall lead you astray" (3:69).[45] Qutb reiterates medieval exegetical materials which accuse the Jews of inventing bogus tales (*Isrāʿiliyyāt*) about the Prophet's life and career, and of falsifying Qur'ānic commentary. Today, Qutb tells us, this distortion of Islamic doctrine is performed by a vast array of Jewish philosophers, writers, and Orientalists, whose proteges are to be found throughout the Muslim world sowing lies and deception.[46] Indeed, the Jews stand behind an entire range of modern-day calumnies, including Freudian psychology and Marxist socialism.[47] Expanding on references in the Qur'ān and the tradition, Qutb writes how the Jews are naturally ungracious: selfishness lives strongly in them. They do not feel the larger human connection which binds humanity together. The Jews have always lived in isolation. They harbor hatred for other people. All of this evil arises from their destructive egoism grudging that "Allah should send his bounty to whom he pleases" (Qur'ān 2:90).[48]

The gist of Qutb's message is clear. Zionism is rejected not on account of its policies or its behavior, as disagreeable as these might be to Qutb, but because of the vileness of its Jewish nature which has been manifest throughout history. For Qutb, the struggle is one between two rival civilizations, one grounded in truth and virtue, the other in falsehood and impiety. There cannot, in this scenario, be any compromise with the Jews and other forces of disbelief. The Jews did not honor their compact with Muhammad.[49] Therefore one cannot expect of them compliance with treaties in the present age. Inter-group struggle is therefore reduced, in Qutb's mind, to a zero-sum game in which dedication to faith and action is seen to be the prime criterion for success.

The moral categories which undergird Qutb's representations of Jews are fundamental to the conceptual universe of Islamism. Qutb's Islamist worldview, we have suggested, emerged initially from drawn-out political struggle between the liberal elite and its detractors in which the resources of the heritage were mobilized by the latter to legitimize their anti-regime dissent. By turning to the divine word of the Qur'ān, Qutb and other Islamists were able to inject into their discourse a measure of religio-cultural authority which was instrumental in forging the Manichaean divisions between *Hizb Allāh* (Party of God) and *Hizb al-Shaytān* (The Party of Satan) which are fundamental to this thought.

When the Old Regime of notable politicians finally did fall in July 1952, it was not to the Society of Muslim Brothers whose ideology Qutb had enhanced, but rather to a group of young military conspirators led by Jamāl ʿAbd al-Nāsir. Qutb, like many Islamists, was at first encouraged by the Free Officers' coup d'etat. As a recently appointed member of the Muslim Brotherhood's Guidance Council and head of its Propagation of the Call Department (*Qism Nashr al-Daʿwa*), Qutb worked tirelessly to encourage ʿAbd al-Nāsir and the other Free Officers to begin working towards the implementation of an Islamic state based on the Sharia. When it became clear that ʿAbd al-Nāsir was intent upon taking Egypt in the direction of secular republicanism, tensions between the Brotherhood and the new regime mounted. In 1954, in response to a failed assassination attempt by a Muslim Brother, ʿAbd al-Nāsir had Qutb and other members of the Society imprisoned.

During his internment, Qutb was provided with writing materials, thus enabling him to elaborate his Islamist doctrine in light of the new circumstances. In a spate of forcefully written "prison works," Qutb reacted to the Free Officers' betrayal of the Islamist cause by excluding them from membership within the Muslim community (*umma*). In Qutb's estimation, although ʿAbd al-Nāsir had performed the valuable service of ridding the country of corrupt politicians and the last remaining traces of British domination, his unwillingness to rule according to God's will made him no better than the imperialists and their wily Jewish agents. Henceforth, Egyptian republicanism was equated, in Qutb's mind, with the *Jāhili* culture of ignorance which prevailed in the Arabian peninsula prior to the revelation of the Qur'ān. Released from prison in 1965 on the grounds of ill health, Qutb was soon after implicated in an alleged conspiracy against the ʿAbd al-Nāsir regime. Tried and condemned to death, he was sent to the gallows with two other alleged conspirators on 21 August 1966.

Throughout his career as an Islamist ideologue, Qutb attempted to create in Egypt a new sense of community by means of a twofold process: the conceptual distancing of certain groups such as the Jews, whose otherness he highlighted and mythologized, and the elaboration of a set of common cultural attributes appropriated from the past in order to provide the illusion of continuity. For all of its cartoonish imagery of the Jews and other "enemies of Islam," Qutb's Islamist discourse is not without a certain perverse logic. Beneath the exaggerations and historical reductionisms there lie a number of truths which discomfited Qutb and other Muslim Egyptians. These truths included the dominance at the political level of the British and the elite echelon of middle and large landowners, and the Zionist settlement of Palestine which Qutb and others equated with the larger phenomenon of European imperialism. As Terry Eagleton has said of the myths which undergird other forms of communalist struggle, "however retrograde and objectionable [these might be] they are not pure illusions: they encapsulate, in however reductive, hyperbolic a form, some substantial historical facts."[50] Following Eagleton, we may regard Qutb's Islamism as providing groups of Egyptians with a motivating mythology for their struggle against the forces which they considered responsible for the condition of Muslim peoples in modern times. For "men and women engaged in such conflicts do not live by theory alone . . . it is not in defense of the doctrine of base and superstructure that men and women are prepared to embrace hardship and persecution in the course of political struggle."[51] They require collective symbols which encapsulate and define their social being. Qutb appears to have recognized this fact in his negative portrayals of Jews which facilitated the setting of community boundaries and defining the nature of the political struggle in which he was enmeshed.

NOTES

1. On this point, see the discussion by Mark R. Cohen, *Under Crescent and Cross: The Jews in the Middle Ages* (Princeton: Princeton University Press, 1994), 3-14.

2. I choose in this paper to use the term "Islamism" to refer to the phenomenon widely known in the West as "Islamic Fundamentalism." The term "fundamentalism" was invented and self-applied by a party of American evangelical Protestants in 1920. It referred specifically to a theological position of biblical inerrancy developed between 1910 and 1915 in a series of booklets entitled "The Fundamentals: A Testimony to the Truth"; see James Barr, *Fundamentalism* (Philadelphia: Westminster Press, 1978), 2. In more recent times the terms have been loosely (and unjustifiably, in my view) applied to a wide variety of religious groups or movements which seek the authority of scripture as a basis for socio-political mobilization; these include, in addition to Muslim groups, the Gush Emunim in Israel, Sikh nationalists, Tamil liberationists in Sri Lanka and others. See Lionel Caplan, ed., *Studies in Religious Fundamentalism* (Hampshire: Macmillan, 1987). In contemporary French academic discourse the term *intégrisme*, originally referring to a tendency in the Roman Catholic Church to restore full obedience to dogma and ritual, has been adopted to denote the same phenomenon. The term "Islamism," it seems to me, avoids undue comparison with Protestant fundamentalism and Roman Catholic *intégrisme*. At the same time, it captures the ideological character of the phenomenon.

3. Rivka Yadlin, *An Arrogant Oppressive Spirit: Anti-Zionism as Anti-Judaism in Egypt* (Oxford: Pergamon Press, 1989). The academic in question is Hasan Hanafī.

4. For instance, Ronald L. Nettler, *Past Trials and Present Tribulations: A Muslim Fundamentalist's View of the Jews* (Oxford: Pergamon Press, 1987), 21.

5. Studies on Qutb include: Salāh ʿAbd al-Fattāh al-Khālidī, *Sayyid Qutb al-Shahīd al-Hayy* (ʿAmmān: Maktabat al-ʿAqsā, 1981); Yvonne Haddad, "Sayyid Qutb: Ideologue of Islamic Revival," *Voices of Resurgent Islam*, ed. John Esposito (Oxford: Oxford University Press, 1983), 67-98; Emmanuel Sivan, *Radical Islam: Medieval Theology and Modern Politics* (New Haven: Yale University Press, 1985), 21-28 *et passim*; Muhammad Hafiz Diyāb, Sayyid Qutb al-Khitāb wa al-Idiyūlūjiyya (Cairo: Dār al-Thaqāfa al-Jadīda, 1989); Ahmad Moussalli, *Radical Islamic Fundamentalism: The Ideological and Political Discourse of Sayyid Qutb* (Beirut: American University of Beirut Press, 1992); and Ibrahim Abu-Rabi, *Intellectual Origins of Islamic Resurgence in the Arab World* (Albany: SUNY Press, 1996), 92-219.

6. The most complete bibliography of Sayyid Qutb's work is to be found in Muhammad Diyāb, *Sayyid Qutb al-Khitāb wa al-Idulājiyya*, 201-250.

7. The most detailed account of this struggle is Marius Deeb, *Party Politics in Egypt: The Wafd and Its Rivals* (London: Ithaca Press, 1979). For the 1940s, see Tāriq al-Bishrī, *al-Haraka al-Siyāsiyya fī Misr, 1945-1952*, 2nd ed. (Cairo: Dār al Shurūq, 1983).

8. On this point see Israel Gershoni and James Jankowski, *Egypt, Islam and the Arabs: The Search for Egyptian Nationhood, 1900-1930* (New York: Oxford University Press, 1986).

9. al-Bannā's early life is recorded in his *Mudhakkirāt al-Daʿwa wa al-Dāʿiya* (Cairo: Matābiʿ Dār al-Kitāb al-ʿArabī bi-Misr, n.d.). The most complete study on the Society remains Richard P. Mitchell, *The Society of the Muslim Brothers* (London: Oxford University Press, 1969).

10. al-Bannā, *Majmuʿat Rasāʾil al-Imām* (Beirut: Dār al-Andalus, 1965), 98.

11. Ibid., 15-16, 254.

12. Ibid., 105.

13. Qutb's childhood in the village of Mūshā, Asyūt Governate, is traced in a partial autobiography, *Tifl min al-Qarya* (Beirut: Dār al-Hikma, n.d. [1946]).

14. Khālidī, *Sayyid Qutb*, 94-98.

15. Ibid., 99-109; and A. Musallam, "Sayyid Qutb's Literary and Spiritual Orientation (1932-1938)," *The Muslim World*, July-October 1990, 176-189. See Qutb's glowing appraisal of al-ʿAqqād in his *Kutub wa Shakhsiyyat* (n.p., n.d. [1946]), 84.

16. Sayyid Qutb, "Naqd *Mustaqbal al-Thaqāfa fī Misr*," *Sahīfat Dār al-ʿUlūm*, (April 1939), 28-79.

17. "al-Taswīr al-Fannī fī al-Qurʾān al-Karīm," *al-Muqtataf* (February 1939), 206-222, con't (March 1939), 313-318; *al-Taswīr al-Fannī fī al-Qurʾān* ninth printing (Cairo: Dār al-Shurūq, 1987); *Mashāhid al-Qiyāma fī al-Qurʾān* (Cairo: Dār al-Maʿārif bi-Misr, 1946).

18. These include: *al-ʿAdāla al-Ijtimāʿiyya fī al-Islām* (Cairo: Maktabat Misr, n.d. [1979]); *Maʿrakat al-Islām wa al-Raʾsmāliyya* (Cairo: Dār al-Ikhwān li-al-Sihafa wa al-Bāʿa, 1951); *Khasāʾis al-Tasawwur al-Islāmī wa Muqawwimātuhu* (Cairo: Dār al-Shurūq, n.d.); and *Maʿalim fī al-Tāriq*, 15th printing (Cairo: Dār al-Shurūq, 1991).

19. *al-ʿAdāla*, 6.

20. Ibid., 36.

21. *al-Risāla*, no. 624 (18 June 1945), 632.

22. Ibid.

23. *Maʿarkat*, 63.

24. *al-Risāla*, no. 1009 (3 November, 1952), 1217.

25. *Maʿarkat*, 6.

26. *al-Risāla*, no. 694 (21 Oct. 1946), 1155.

27. *Filastīn fī Fikr Sayyid Qutb*, ed. Yaha Ghārib (n.p., n.d.), 47.

28. *al-Risāla*, no. 661 (4 March 1946), 238.

29. *Filastīn fī Fikr Sayyid Qutb*, 50.

30. Quṭb's impressions of America are recorded in a series of articles in *al-Risāla* (nos. 957-961), which came under the title *"Amrīka allatī Ra'ayt"* (*The America I Saw*).

31. *al-Risāla*, no. 694 (4 March 1946), 1157.

32. al-Khālidī, *Sayyid Quṭb*, 143.

33. *al-Risāla*, no. 649 (3 December 1945), 1309.

34. *al-Risāla*, no. 672 (20 May 1946), 549-555.

35. "Aqīda wa Kifāḥ," *al-Daʿwa*, 27 Nov. 1951, 3.

36. For recent accounts of Muḥammad and the Jews, see: Norman Stillman, *The Jews of Arab Lands: A History and Source Book* (Philadelphia: Jewish Publication Center of America, 1979), and F.E. Peters, *Muhammad and the Origins of Islam* (New York: SUNY Press, 1994), 111-124, 180-182.

37. Peters, *Muhammad*, 121-125, 207-218, et. passim.

38. Ibn Qayyim al-Jawziyya, *Aḥkām Ahl al-Dhimma*, part 1 (Beirut: Dār al-ʿIlm, 1983), 238 ff. See also the apposite remarks of Mark R. Cohen, *Under Cross and Crescent*, 23-29.

39. See Cohen, *Cross and Crescent*, 52-74, and Bernard Lewis, *The Jews of Islam* (Princeton: Princeton University Press), 21-44.

40. Cohen, *Cross and Crescent*, 23-25.

41. Ibid., 6. Antonius was the author of the classic study of the origins of Arab nationalism, *The Arab Awakening* (Philadelphia: J.B. Lippencott, 1939).

42. Sayyid Quṭb, *Maʿrakatna maʿa al-Yahūd*, 8th printing (Cairo: Dār al-Shurūq, 1987); trans. by Ronald Nettler in *Past Trials and Present Tribulations*, 72-89.

43. *Maʿrakatna*, 20-21.

44. Ibid.

45. Ibid., 22.

46. Ibid., 23.

47. Ibid., 34.

48. Ibid., 27.

49. Ibid., 28.

50. Terry Eagleton, *Ideology: An Introduction* (London: Verso, 1991), 190.

51. Ibid.

A Lie and a Libel:
The *Protocols of the Elders of Zion*
Since the Holocaust

Richard S. Levy

This paper deals with the most widely distributed antisemitic work of all time, a work that contains what I think of as the most potent negative representation of Jews in the modern era. In the twentieth century, the Jew as deicide and the Jew as usurer have been absorbed by the Jew as world-conquering conspirator.

The work in question is the *Protocols of the Elders of Zion*, a forgery that purports to be the record of twenty-four speeches delivered by the "Chief Sage of Zion" to a secret conventicle at the first Zionist Congress, held in Basel, Switzerland, in 1897. Together the individual protocols comprise a Jewish plot to take over the world, reduce non-Jews to abject slavery, and destroy Christian states and peoples. Employing the world association of Freemasons, their slaves unto death, the Jews conspire by means of liberal institutions, modern culture, and both capitalism and communism gradually to destroy all nations and to erect upon their ruins the Jewish world state, with a Jewish despot at its summit.

The *Protocols* was created in Paris, in all likelihood, at the behest of the Russian secret police, the Okhrana, near the turn of this century. It surfaced in Russia a few years later, first as a manuscript, then as an appendix to a larger book prepared by a Russian mystic who added to it a heavy dose of his own lunatic theology. Thereafter, although published under many different titles, the forgery retained its essential character as a slapdash patchwork composed of several earlier and unrelated writings, namely: a French political satire of the mid-

231

nineteenth century which had nothing to do with Jews; a trashy German novel of the same period; and a well-developed strain of anti-Freemason literature. The *Protocols* was written in French, translated into Russian, then back into French, German, English, Spanish, Italian, Swedish, Danish, Norwegian, Finnish, Romanian, Hungarian, Lithuanian, Polish, Bulgarian, Greek, Arabic, Chinese, Japanese, and Turkish. Despite its lowly pedigree, the *Protocols* found a huge audience, especially in the turbulent times following World War I and then again during the Great Depression of the 1930s.[1] The work continues to appear and reappear throughout the world.

Why has the *Protocols of the Elders of Zion*, a shameless hoax, seized the imagination and informed the political judgment of men and women throughout the twentieth century? Answering this question is a daunting task because the patent absurdity of the scheme described in the *Protocols* has had little or no bearing on its credibility for a large and varied public. Indeed, almost as soon as the *Protocols* assumed political significance in the 1920s, many trenchant analyses debunked the lie and libel. Critics swiftly discovered the book's plagiarized sources, exposed its faulty logic, laid bare its political motives, and condemned its defiance of common sense.[2] Yet seventy-five years of devastating judgments have failed to put an end to the book. It still turns up in likely and unlikely places all over the world.

On first reading the *Protocols of the Elders of Zion* today, one may be inclined to think that he or she is dealing with a none-too-humorous satire. The depiction of a two-thousand-year-old, arcanely elaborated Jewish conspiracy, directed by a committee of nameless but blood-thirsty individuals immune to every decent human impulse, will strike most readers as cartoonish. That the fictitious "Elders of Zion" stage manage world events and stand on the cusp of final victory will alarm few people open to reason. But the *Protocols of the Elders of Zion* is not satire, and its durability has nothing to do with reasonableness. Some people have been willing and some are still willing to find the work credible, and others gladly exploit that willingness.

Readers of the *Protocols* may be tempted to shake their heads either in dismay or amusement at yet another proof of the gullibility of the great public. We live, after all, in the age of the tabloids, both print and television, where ordinary citizens take jaunts on alien spaceships and others go on the "all pizza diet," expecting immediate weight-loss. Such pandering to people's lack of good sense, however, seems relatively innocent when compared to the malign uses of the *Protocols of the Elders of Zion.* From its first publication in 1903, the myth was meant to serve a political function, to influence powerful individuals or mobilize large groups of people to think or act in particularly destructive and self-deluding ways. Over time, the political agendas of the publishers of the *Protocols* have changed, but the sowing of hatred and urge to "self-defense [i.e., violence] against the enemy of all mankind" have remained common to them all. This is not innocent literature.

Although one might expect the *Protocols* to raise the gravest doubts in readers, no matter the degree of their sophistication, it clearly does not always do so. In the 1920s and 1930s, a significant number of people in all social strata believed in the authenticity of the document and took its revelation of a worldwide Jewish conspiracy at face value. They found in its pages a credible explanation of world events and both a familiar and accurate representation of Jewry. Such is still the case in certain areas of the world in the 1990s. This being so, we would be mistaken to dismiss the *Protocols* as arrant nonsense. We ought, instead, to consider the reasons why the book has survived to the present day and examine the sources from which it draws strength.

1. THE *PROTOCALS,* CONSPIRACY THINKING, AND ANTISEMITISM

The *Protocols* combines two distinct motifs: the conspiratorial and the antisemitic. In the twentieth century both are familiar and both have peculiar appeal for particular, although not necessarily the same, audiences. Conspiracy thinking has never been the exclusive property of the weak-minded, the deranged, or the semi-educated. The dark doings of secret societies figured in the great nineteenth-century novels of Goethe, Scott, Balzac, Dickens, and Disraeli, in the grand operas of Mozart and Verdi, in the gothic romance, and in many other vehicles of popular and high culture. The fascination with conspiracy themes lives on in the modern thriller and the caper film, entertainments with their own broadly based appeal.

For most people conspiracy remains purely recreational or esthetic. But on occasion and for even the highly intelligent and well-educated, conspiracies acquire the power to explain the real world, sometimes to be seen as "the best explanation" of events. Jesuits and Jacobins, Wobblies and "eastern bankers," suffragettes and misogynists have all, at one time or another, been endowed with both the power and motive to control the unfolding of history from behind the scenes. In our own day, the number, depth, and breadth of conspiracy theories spun to explain the assassination of John Kennedy provide convincing proof of the continuing viability of this mode of thought. For many, the idea that sinister and invisible forces could control our lives did not destroy but rather enhanced the credibility of the "Elders of Zion."

When seen in this context, understanding how the *Protocols* gains access to literate circles becomes somewhat clearer. I would argue that this is the most important task for students of this particular work and those who would like to render it politically impotent. The *Protocols* never reaches a mass audience without the mediation of intellectuals; it is a work rarely read by the mob but often read to them, cited, interpreted, and waved in front of their faces. They are rarely expected to read it themselves.

One ought not exaggerate the intellectual gifts of these champions of the work. For many who succumb to it, the least likely explanation of great events seems the best, because it is also the most effortless. Painstaking study of the data is not the strength of these people. Examining structural shifts in the economy, demographic trends, sociological changes, and the making of fine distinctions among life's complexities demand serious work and rigorous thinking. By contrast, accepting the existence of a conspiracy provides the believer with a shortcut to "the cause" of the evil in question; he or she has but to fill in the details, make the obscure connections, expose the intricacies of the plot. This is the kind of ingenuity many possess and almost everyone enjoys exercising.

But the effectiveness of conspiracy thinking has not only to do with mental laziness or esthetic pleasure. An investigation of disturbing public happenings carried out with respect for the laws of evidence often means that no satisfactory conclusion can be reached. To many caught up in the numerous crises of modern times such a lack of certainty is psychologically unbearable. They seize upon a simple and dramatic version of political realities because they prefer even truly terrifying "truths" to gnawing uncertainties. The *Protocols of the Elders of Zion* exploit this all-too-human need in an unoriginal, yet powerful, manner.

Typical of the genre, the *Protocols* portrays a community unaware of the true laws of its existence.[3] Thinking itself autonomous and self-regulating, it is, in fact, being ruled by a secret society of evil men with access to a global network of operatives. Although the society has origins deep in the past, its aims have never wavered: the overthrow of the fundamental institutions, values, and traditions of the community. The cabal is infinitely flexible in the means it chooses and especially adept at recruiting unwitting agents from within the community itself to further the gradual process of destruction. Spreading discontent among the naive, sowing moral corruption in the young, turning class against class, the conspirators work their will on the hapless victims.

The *Protocols* goads the "victims" of conspiracy to rage, hoping perhaps that they will retaliate against their oppressors. But the book appeals to its audience in more subtle ways as well. The promoters of the forgery wrote long, appreciative commentaries on the *Protocols*, inviting at least the literate to join the elite of those "in the know." They are offered the veritable "Rosetta Stone of history," the single key which unlocks all the perplexing mysteries of the modern world, including "the hidden language of the Jews." [Gilman] After being enlightened by this document, readers will rise above the helpless ignorance that characterizes the majority of their unsuspecting countrymen. Although this delicious sense of superiority comes at a high price—the horrifying prospect of imminent Jewish triumph, the *Protocols* offers the antidote against this terror. Knowledge of the Jews' conspiracy, as Hitler promised in *Mein Kampf*, renders it conquerable.

The *Protocols of the Elders of Zion* also draws strength from another well-established tradition, which I can only allude to here.[4] The body of ideas about Jews and the ever-changing suggestions about what ought to be done with them were already enormous by the late 1890s, when the *Protocols* was fabricated. Its creators had at their disposal traditional representations of Jews disseminated ever more widely by antisemitic political movements in Europe and beyond. The strategies of the antisemites are also apparent in the text: guilt by association; outlandish and unprovable charges; appeal to fear, envy, and hatred; scapegoating; and demonization.

But the use of these established techniques and images does not wholly explain the phenomenal popularity of the *Protocols*. That success is at least in part attributable to the book's "literary qualities" and its innovations.

By the turn of the century, the diatribes typical of antisemitic polemics seemed to be preaching only to the converted. To reach the broader public, which was both hostile toward Jews and yet suspicious of the antisemites' motives, a new device was needed. The forgers of the *Protocols* inadvertently answered this need. By pretending the book was of Jewish authorship, an "authentic" document that luckily fell into the hands of the intended victims of Jewish plotting, the authors skirted the issue of their own motives and relieved themselves of the necessity of proving their horrific charges. The *Protocols* appeared to the public as the unguarded revelation of the secret leaders of Jewry, the terrifying blueprint for world conquest, and the uncanny fulfillment of ancient prophecies.

Unlike almost every other antisemitic work, the book has no national context or identity. It names few names, speaks to no specifically national problem, and is therefore able to serve a great variety of political purposes. Its many publishers, annotators, commentators, and translators added and subtracted from the text at will to make the work speak directly to the targeted audience. Thus, in Germany the Jewish world conspiracy was said to work hand in glove with the victorious Allies of World War I, while in Great Britain the Germans appeared as the accomplices of the Jews. In America, Jews, said to be in cahoots with the English, were declared the "real winners" of the world war. Over its long career, the *Protocols of the Elders of Zion* has proved infinitely adaptable.

2.   ORIGINS AND PURPOSES OF THE FORGERY TO 1917

Between its fabrication in Paris in 1897-98 and the revolutionary events in Russia of 1905, the manuscript version of the *Protocols*, which no credible person has ever seen, appears to have had no purpose beyond influencing the policies and rather minor personnel decisions of Tsar Nicholas II. Most scholars see the 1905 Russian publication of the *Protocols* in book form as a sinister escalation of the forgery's functions. To preempt forces working for change, a shadowy collection of secret policemen, reactionary aristocrats, extreme nationalists, and religious cranks sought to discredit liberal reformers by associating them with Jews and by representing the tsar's reform-minded ministers as the dupes or agents of Jews. "Read properly," the *Protocols* urged upon the tsar and the supporters of his autocracy the necessity for ruthless repression of its enemies. At least in part, they hoped to light a fire under the notoriously feckless Nicholas II.[5]

Without the Russian revolutions of 1917, the *Protocols of the Elders of Zion* might have remained the obsession of reactionary imaginations, unknown to the world at large. It certainly would never have achieved any serious political importance. However, the revolution, the civil war, and the international communist movement gave birth to a powerful new myth. "Judeo-Bolshevism" rescued the *Protocols* from obscurity and until recent times has proved the most unfailing "proof" of its genuineness. To the supporters of Russian autocracy who fled west with the *Protocols* in their baggage, the Bolshevik Revolution was the unmistakable work of a Jewish conspiracy. And they found in Europe, North and South America, and the Muslim world a large audience prepared to believe that this was so. Responsible lay and spiritual leaders, politicians, and respected newspaper publishers—people who should have known better—were too easily persuaded that the revolutionary events in Russia constituted a Jewish assault on western civilization itself.[6]

3. THE *PROTOCOLS* SINCE THE HOLOCAUST: THE USSR AND USA

The Holocaust of European Jewry ought to have been the suitable end to sixty-five years of political antisemitism and the public career of the *Protocols of the Elders of Zion*. But neither missed a beat. Counting "studies" of the *Protocols* and titles which disguised true contents, there were 8 fresh printings in the 1950s, 16 in the 1960s, 23 in the 1970s, 20 in the 1980s, and 5 thus far in the 1990s.

The forum of the *Protocols* has altered dramatically. In postwar Germany, antisemitic literature became unthinkable in the East and illegal in the West. Elsewhere in Europe, neo-Nazis, orthodox Christians, nationalist superpatriots, and their sympathizers have from time to time produced new versions. But these are clearly marginal phenomena, the politically unproductive efforts of die-hard fanatics.

The same cannot be said of several other situations where the *Protocols* continues to exercise its negative influence on political life and threatens the rights and lives of Jews. This was particularly apparent in Latin America during the 1960s and 1970s. And the forgery remains influential today in the Arab world, the countries of the former Eastern bloc, and in some quarters of the United States. I will close with a discussion of three of these cases because they illustrate the continuing viability of the *Protocols*.

The hiatus in governmental antisemitism in the Soviet Union lasted only a short while after the Revolution of 1917. With Joseph Stalin, and particularly after World War II, officially sanctioned literature revived the tradition of tsarist days. Great Russian patriotism, rehabilitated during the war, brought with it occasional campaigns against "internationalists" and "cosmopolitans." These popular buzz-words identified Jews as the cause of economic or foreign policy setbacks. Just as Stalin died in 1953, the so-called "Jewish doctors' plot" against the lives of prominent Soviet officials was assuming menacing dimensions. Stalin's successors dismantled this witch-hunt, but after the Arab-Israeli War of 1967, they launched a far more sustained effort of their own.

Because antisemitism carried the unmistakable taint of counter-revolution, a clumsy fiction was contrived. Zionists, not Jews, were the carriers of evil; it was they who engaged in a worldwide conspiracy to undermine the USSR from their headquarters in Jerusalem. To forward their world-conspiratorial ambitions, Zionists fomented and manipulated antisemitism, sowing disunion among otherwise fraternal peoples. In fact, Zionists bore most of the characteristics antisemites habitually ascribed to Jews, and, as one writer guessed, fully ninety per cent of Soviet Jews were open or secret Zionists. During the 1970s the familiar depiction of world Jewry as a tightly-knit, awesomely destructive force gained complete access to the state-controlled media. Between 1967 and the early 1980s, the government approved over 150 anti-Zionist works, many of them clearly inspired by or quoting from the *Protocols of the Elders of Zion*. In 1977, a television documentary, aired twice and commented upon extensively in the press, equated Jews with apartheid, fascism, and capitalism.

With the collapse of the Soviet Union, a more traditional and popularly based antisemitism, visible for many years in the dissident press, was suddenly free to express itself openly. Today, Jews in the former USSR once again find themselves accused of being wire-pullers, millionaires, pornographers, warmongers, and saboteurs—crimes historically assigned to them in the *Protocols*. The image of the Jew as Bolshevik gangster, which had no utility for the heirs of the Revolution, is now back in vogue. Elements of the army, press, and unions are virtually unrestrained in their antisemitic agitation. *Pamyat*, the most vocal of the many extremist nationalist groups, produced its own edition of the *Protocols of the Elders of Zion* in 1992.

Soviet government antisemitism helped create the climate in which the latest outbreak could take place by making use of existing representations of Jews and the literature of conspiracy for political purposes. But government directed antisemitism in the modern period served circumscribed ends. As a political tool it stopped well short of overt incitement to violence. Indeed, one of its paradoxical functions was to dissuade Jews, a highly educated and skilled part of the population, from leaving the Soviet Union. The fear of being branded a Zionist, it was hoped, would pressure Jews into conformity. The "new" antisemitism has no such purpose, and in the post-communist crisis, with the central government no longer able to maintain absolute control, Jews appear to be in jeopardy.[7]

Only in the United States has the *Protocols of the Elders of Zion* never gone wholly out of fashion; it has been uninterruptedly in print here since 1920. Since, and in spite of, the Holocaust, the book has continued to exercise fascination, primarily for Christian fundamentalists and the anti-communist right. Still wedded to the myth of Judeo-Bolshevism, they stubbornly cling to the forgery even though the threat of international communism has now lost whatever credibility it might once have enjoyed. As of 1992, thirty-three printings of the *Protocols*, or Henry Ford's version of it, *The International Jew*, or pseudo-scholarly studies of them have appeared here.[8] Nothing, however, suggests that they have been able to gain a wide audience for the *Protocols* or to exploit its political potential.

Still, two recent efforts along these lines are worth mentioning as examples of the adaptability of the *Protocols* to new purposes. In the 1980s the Californian Noontide Press, a purveyor of extremist literature to the radical right, offered the book on its list of publications. Among the press' close connections is the Institute for Historical Review, the foremost advocate of Holocaust denial. The self-styled revisionists claim that the Holocaust never happened, that it is, in fact, the "greatest" hoax of the twentieth century.[9] Their debt to the *Protocols of the Elders of Zion* is unacknowledged but scarcely mistakable. The group's own publications depict Jews as engaged in a gigantic conspiracy of evil, a destructive force in past and present, worthy of hatred and fear. Their *Journal of Historical Review*, once a quarterly, now a bimonthly, represents itself as interested only in historical truth, but, entirely in keeping with the mindset of the *Protocols*, it specializes in "unmasking" sensational conspiracies. The exact political agenda remains obscure. However, documented relations with European neo-Nazis and racists and financial support from long-time radical rightists in the United States point to the usual political orientation of those who take the *Protocols* as their inspiration.

In light of current developments, the Holocaust deniers cannot be consigned to the lunatic fringe without further ado. They have recently attempted to break out of the narrow confines of America's radical right subculture to reach a more mainstream audience. Spokesmen appear on college campuses and field questions on talk shows. They have succeeded in placing their advertisements in respectable newspapers and posing as champions of free speech. The Holocaust deniers have thus far steered clear of too close a connection to the *Protocols of the Elders of Zion*, for the forgery has a questionable reputation with all but the most gullible in the audience they are now targeting. Such tactical restraint may not last, however, and it is altogether possible that Holocaust denial will win a new lease on life for the *Protocols*, as it already has for the idea of an ongoing Jewish world conspiracy.

Holocaust denial can be seen as the latest instance of the antidemocratic and antisemitic purposes the *Protocols* has almost always served. The same cannot be said for its appearance in a small segment of the African-American community. Black nationalists close to Louis Farrakhan and several academics independent of him have accused Jews of engaging in a range of conspiracies directed against African-Americans.[10] Unnamed Jewish doctors, goes one such claim, knowingly infected blacks with the AIDS virus in order to further their plan of world domination. Another charge claims that Jews conducted the African slave trade, and that the enormous wealth they thus gained is still being used to keep blacks in powerless misery.[11]

Now, according to this fable, Jewish academics, backed by an all-powerful "Jewish" media, are busily engaged in covering up the truth. The *Protocols of the Elders of Zion*, offered at a nominal price by Farrakhan and readily obtainable in black nationalist bookstores, stands ready to integrate these separate fictions into an all-embracing historical perspective.

Familiarity with the history of the *Protocols of the Elders of Zion* can shed some light on why a few individuals in the African-American community have chosen to clothe their grievances in theories of Jewish conspiracy. Whether they are captives of the myth themselves or whether they cynically seek to use it to mobilize a following, they have noticed that an antisemitic interpretation of their problems wins the instant and emotionally charged attention of their audience and of onlookers in ways that more sober discussions of realities do not.

Although these individuals share few of the right's programmatic motives for propagating the *Protocols*, their readiness to engage in conspiracy thinking has undoubtedly worsened relations between American Jews and African-Americans, former allies in the struggle for civil equality. And, once again, overheated fantasies have obscured rather than clarified the underlying causes of conflict. The tragedy here is that legitimate grievances have been overwhelmed by escalating rhetoric, deepening suspicion, and anger; charges and countercharges have supplanted discussion.

While it is certain that antisemitism in general and the *Protocols of the Elders of Zion* in particular can solve no real problems, they have demonstrated the capacity to poison political life and human relations. Reasonable people have a right to be downhearted about ever conquering such a long-lived, adaptable, and serviceable lie. They have no cause to believe that the *Protocols* will soon vanish.

NOTES

1. The modern authority on the textual history of the *Protocols* is Norman Cohn, *Warrant for Genocide: the Myth of the Jewish World Conspiracy and the Protocols of the Elders of Zion* (London: Eyre & Spottiswoode, 1967; 2nd ed. 1970). I have treated the post-1970 history of the work in the introduction to Binjamin Segel, *A Lie and a Libel: the History of the Protocols of the Elders of Zion*. Edited and translated by Richard S. Levy (Lincoln, NE: University of Nebraska Press, 1995).

2. The literature on the *Protocols* is extensive. I list below only the most well-known, still usable treatments: Herman Bernstein, *The History of a Lie. "The Protocols of the Wise Men of Zion:" A Study* (New York: Ogilvie, 1921); and his *The Truth about "The Protocols of Zion:" A Complete Exposure* (New York: Covici, 1935; new edition, 1971); Vladimir Burtsev, *"Protokoly Sionskikh Mudretsov" Dokazanny Podlog* (The Protocols of the Elders of Zion a Proven Forgery) (Paris: O. Zeluk, 1938); Pierre Charles, S.J., *Les Protocoles des Sages de Sion* (Paris: no pub., 1938), translated as *The Learned Elders of Zion* (New York: Pantheon Books, 1955); John S. Curtiss, *An Appraisal of the Protocols of Zion* (New York: Columbia University Press, 1942); Otto Friedrich, *Die Weisen von Zion. Das Buch der Fälschungen* (Lübeck: no pub., 1920); Philip Graves, *The Truth about the Protocols: A Literary Forgery* (London: Times Publishing Co., 1921); John Gwyer, *Portraits of Mean Men. A Short History of the Protocols of the Elders of Zion* (London: Cobden-Sanderson, 1938); Emil Raas and Georges Brunschvig, *Vernichtung einer Fälschung: der Prozess um die erfundenen "Weisen von Zion"* (Zurich: Verlag "die Gestaltung," 1938); H. Rollin, *L'Apocalypse de notre temps: Les dessous de la propagande allemande d'après des documents inédits* (Paris: Editions Allia, 1939); Sergio Romano, *I falsi protocolli: il "complotto ebraico" dalla Russia di Nicola II a oggi* (2nd ed., Milan:

Corbaccio, 1992); John Spargo, *The Jew and American Ideals* (New York: Harper, 1921); Lucien Wolf, *The Jewish Bogey and the Forged Protocols of the Learned Elders of Zion* (London: Jewish Board of Deputies, 1920); and the scholarly study that provided the basis for the translation alluded to in note 1, above, Binjamin W. Segel, *Die Protokolle der Weisen von Zion, kritisch beleuchtet. Eine Erledigung* (Berlin: Philo Verlag, 1924).

3. On the general patterns of conspiracy thinking, see John M. Roberts, *The Mythology of the Secret Societies* (London: Secker & Warburg, 1972); Johannes Rogalla von Bieberstein, *Die These von der Verschwörung 1776-1945: Philosophen, Freimauerer, Juden, Liberale und Sozialisten als Verschwörer gegen die Sozialordnung* (Frankfurt am Main: Lang, 1976). For historical perspective on the representation of Jews as arch-conspirators, see Sander L. Gilman, *Jewish Self-Hatred: Anti-Semitism and the Hidden Language of the Jews* (Baltimore and London: John Hopkins University Press, 1986).

4. For a more thorough discussion and an attempt at an historically derived definition of the term, *antisemitism*, see Richard S. Levy, ed., *Antisemitism in the Modern World: an Anthology of Texts* (Lexington, MA: D.C. Heath, 1991), 1-27.

5. What role the *Protocols* played in official Russian government policy is a vexing issue. Claims that the central administration used the book to foment antisemitic violence as a means of deflecting attention from a failing autocracy are not well grounded in hard evidence. The *Protocols* never achieved significant political influence in pre-revolutionary Russia because police controlled censors denied it the designation that would have permitted mass circulation. Even Tsar Nicholas II was said to have rejected use of the book. For a reasoned discussion of government antisemitism, see Hans Rogger, *Jewish Policies and Right-Wing Politics in Imperial Russia* (London: Macmillan, 1986). However, a high-ranking participant in the tsar's regime, Sergiei Dmitrievich Urusov, held the central administration morally, if not materially, responsible for antisemitic violence. See James Cracraft, ed., *Major Problems in the History of Imperial Russia* (Lexington, MA: D.C. Heath, 1993), 420-24.

6. The flirtation with Judeo-Bolshevism and the *Protocols* was short but intense in England. Winston Churchill was one who subscribed wholeheartedly to the former. See Gisela Lebzelter, *Political Antisemitism in England 1918-1939* (London: Macmillan, 1978), 96-100. Both the *Times* of London and the *Morning Post* were strongly inclined to believe the *Protocols* were authentic; the *Times* quickly came to its senses and was instrumental in debunking the fraud. The *Post*, on the other hand, became the most zealous champion of the forgery, for the shabbiest of monetary reasons. See Colin Holmes, "New Light on the *Protocols of Zion*," in *Patterns of Prejudice* 11 (Nov.-Dec. 1977): 13-21.

On the worldwide dissemination of the *Protocols* and its years of greatest political prominence between the wars (a subject which cannot be treated adequately within the scope of the present essay), see my introduction to

Segel, *A Lie and a Libel: The History of the Protocols of the Elders of Zion*, 20-32, 40-45.

7. On antisemitism in the Soviet Union, see William Korey, *The Soviet "Protocols of the Elders of Zion": Anti-Semitic Propaganda in the U.S.S.R., August 1967-August 1977* (Washington, D.C.: Public Affairs Division of the B'nai B'rith, 1977). See also the useful anthology by Theodore Freedman, ed., *Anti-Semitism in the Soviet Union: Its Roots and Consequences* (New York: Freedom Library Press of the Anti-Defamation League, 1984).

8. Much has been written on the antisemitism of Henry Ford. The most balanced treatment of the subject is by an ex-employee and non-Jew. See Albert Lee, *Henry Ford and the Jews* (New York: Stein and Day, 1980). On the career of the *Protocols* in the United States during the 1920s and 1930s, including a lengthy excerpt from Ford's *Dearborn Independent*, see Levy, *Antisemitism in the Modern World*, 166-77.

9. Arthur R. Butz, *The Hoax of the Twentieth Century* (Newport Beach, CA: Institute of Historical Review, 1992).

10. Glenn C. Loury, an African-American professor at Boston University, makes an important point about the appeal of the *Protocols* among ordinary members of the community that may well apply to other groups as well. He says that he is much less worried about grass roots antisemitism among blacks—it always measures less than in comparable white groups—than the effect that the myth of Jewish world conspiracy may have on young black intellectuals. See his *One by One from the Inside Out: Essays and Reviews on Race and Responsibility in America* (New York: Free Press, 1995), 275. It is impossible to measure the effect the *Protocols* has on the beliefs or behavior of ordinary people, but I too suspect that the work has greater impact upon those in search of an integrating mechanism, a systematic justification for their real failures and fear of failure, and that these individuals are always more likely to be found among the educated than the masses. It is the educated of many communities who more often compete with Jews for scarce goods and positions; it is the educated who have historically and fervently embraced the *Protocols*. Some of these champions of the myth are no doubt cynical opportunists. But many, many others give every evidence of sincere, even desperate, belief.

11. See the definitive refutation of this myth by David Brion Davis, "The Slave Trade and the Jews," in *The New York Review of Books* 61 (December 22, 1994): 14-16.